Transformation in Christ

Transformation in Christ

Paul's Experience of the Divine Mystery

DAVID A. ACKERMAN

Foreword by Carl C. Campbell

WIPF & STOCK · Eugene, Oregon

TRANSFORMATION IN CHRIST
Paul's Experience of the Divine Mystery

Copyright © 2019 David A. Ackerman. All rights reserved. Except for brief quotations in critical publications or reviews, no part of this book may be reproduced in any manner without prior written permission from the publisher. Write: Permissions, Wipf and Stock Publishers, 199 W. 8th Ave., Suite 3, Eugene, OR 97401.

Wipf & Stock
An Imprint of Wipf and Stock Publishers
199 W. 8th Ave., Suite 3
Eugene, OR 97401

www.wipfandstock.com

PAPERBACK ISBN: 978-1-5326-7114-2
HARDCOVER ISBN: 978-1-5326-7115-9
EBOOK ISBN: 978-1-5326-7116-6

Manufactured in the U.S.A.   APRIL 22, 2019

Unless otherwise noted, all Scripture quotations are from the ESV® Bible (The Holy Bible, English Standard Version®), copyright © 2001 by Crossway, a publishing ministry of Good News Publishers. Used by permission. All rights reserved.

Other translations as noted include:
English Standard Version® (ESV), copyright © 2001 by Crossway, a publishing ministry of Good News Publishers. All rights reserved.

Good News Translation® (Today's English Version, Second Edition) (GNT), copyright © 1992 American Bible Society. All rights reserved.

New International Version® (NIV), copyright © 1973, 1978, 1984, 2011 by Biblica, Inc.TM Used by permission. All rights reserved worldwide.

New Living Translation (NLT), copyright © 1996, 2004, 2007, 2013 by Tyndale House Foundation. Used by permission of Tyndale House Publishers, Inc., Carol Stream, IL 60188. All rights reserved.

New Revised Standard Version (NRSV), copyright © 1989 by the Division of Christian Education of the National Council of the Churches of Christ in the USA. All rights reserved.

To
Rhonda Rae

My best friend
Partner in life and ministry
Who has modeled to me what it truly means to live *in Christ*

Contents

Foreword by Carl C. Campbell | ix
Preface | xi
Abbreviations | xiii
Introduction | xvii

1   **A Journey of Transformation** | 1
         The Worlds of Paul | 1
         A Journey of Transformation | 13
         Becoming a New Person "in Christ" | 17
         Conclusion | 21

2   **Paul, the "Mystic"** | 22
         The *Mystērion* of God | 23
         Experiencing the Divine in the Ancient World | 30
         Paul in His Early Christian, Jewish, and Hellenistic Context | 58
         Conclusion | 61

3   **The Divine Mystery "in Christ"** | 63
         Paul's Visionary Experiences | 63
         The New Life *in Christ* | 74
         Conclusion | 92

4   **Grace, Conscience, and the Law** | 93
         The Desperate Condition *in Adam* | 94
         Transformation through the Law | 98
         The Tool of the Conscience | 109
         Grace, Conscience, and Law | 116
         Conclusion | 119

| 5 | **Life in the Spirit** | 120 |

Christ and the Spirit | 120
Resolving the Fundamental Problem | 124
The Human Struggle against Sin | 130
Freedom through the Holy Spirit | 132
The Spirit-Filled New Life in Christ | 136
Conclusion | 140

| 6 | **The Missional Community in Christ** | 141 |

The Foundation *in Christ* | 141
The Mission of the Church | 150
Proclaiming the Good News | 157
Conclusion | 160

| 7 | **Victory in Christ over the Forces of Evil** | 161 |

The Relation of Sin to Satan and the Forces of Evil | 162
Victory in Christ | 178
Conclusion | 185

Conclusion | 187

Bibliography | 191

Foreword

THERE IS AN OLD saying that states, "One is your friend who brings you closer to God." And David Ackerman consciously and subconsciously has lived up to this adage throughout our friendship over the past twenty-five years.

I met David during an annual meeting of that august Wesleyan/Holiness/Methodist body, the Wesleyan Theological Society. We as strangers from different parts of the world and strands within the Wesleyan heritage sat together for supper on the last night of the meeting. Our brotherhood and journey in friendship has been one of feasting and sharing for the love of God and virtuous nurture in experiences ever since. The mission of the Wesleyan Theological Society is "to encourage exchange of information and perspectives among Wesleyan-Holiness theologians, stimulate scholarship among younger theologians, stimulate scholarship among younger theologians and pastors, convene an academically rich and inspiring annual meeting of members and publish a scholarly journal."

David has always impressed, challenged, and inspired me with the depth of his writings, which reflect his sharp academic acumen, research competence, pastoral experience, cross-cultural missionary work in theological education, and devotional life. David's work consistently combines passion, patience, and prayer for the fruitful productivity of his goals. His discipline of heart and mind to know and share the empowering truth of the gospel has crafted another book, *Transformation in Christ*.

"Transformation in Christ" is an appealing title from the many perspectives of the great prism of the Christian faith throughout the centuries. The ageless question for the believer, the honest thinker, the quiet observer, the faith seeker, or the critic is: "What does it mean to be 'in Christ,' a profound Pauline phrase? What does it look like to be a Christian?"

David in this timely book has sought to balance and demonstrate truth across cultures in a world of faith with biblical scholarship, an open heart for spiritual inspiration, a sensitive mind for students and preachers, and a shepherd's guide to those who believe and seek growth. There is a desired balance between antiquity and contemporary spirituality.

The author's research and analytical reflection offer clarity to endless query about a faith where God reveals himself, to seek, find, redeem, and transform. If one does find this book exhaustive, there is substantial material to help navigate the ethos of "visions," "glory of God," "mysticism," and "incarnational theology."

In *Transformation in Christ*, David draws on the Pauline corpus, highlighting the apostle's autobiographical journey where one reads of a new theology of the "indwelling God," a great, glorious, and mysterious transformation by being not under the law but by living in grace and "in Christ." It is Paul who startles David and encourages his research and writing. It is Paul's early life and conversion experience, preaching, teaching, and writing which reveal a new, strange, and transformative language, confirming a new relationship with God. Paul's zealous, adventurous, and unapologetic life is the fruit of transformation in Christ.

I proffer that no one can read this book untouched and close its pages without also acknowledging new spiritual insight, a sense of awe, and an appreciation for God's great grace. While Paul may have startled David, in essence the quality of life and faith is grounded and nurtured in Jesus, the captain of our faith, who said "abide in me and I in you."

Rev. Carl C. Campbell
Pastor, Nassau Methodist Church
Nassau, Bahamas

Preface

My journey with Paul took on new meaning after a Greek translation class on the Prison Epistles with Dr. Morris Weigelt at Nazarene Theological Seminary. We had just worked our way through the Greek text of Ephesians 1. I noticed for the first time how Paul (the assumed author) repeatedly used the phrase *en Christō* or a variation of it. I began to see this phrase in other letters attributed to him. In my doctoral studies, I discovered further how scholars over the past century have pondered and debated the significance of what he meant by the phrase "in Christ." Now after many years of thinking on this topic, I have organized my thoughts and research into this book. I have discovered that words are not adequate to describe the significance of what it means to be "in Christ." This phrase reveals the very mystery of God's being and what God has planned since the creation of the world.

The applications of this study are many. For me personally, it has helped me understand and apply the hope of the gospel to my own life. Various theological doctrines I once found confusing, such as what it means to be God's holy people, are now clearer in my thinking. I have encouraged my students and churches over the years to think deeply upon what it means to be in relationship to God in Christ through the Holy Spirit. This message is quite simple but its implications in real life are profound and transforming. My hope is that those who read this book will discover for themselves what this new life is about and how it can change them from the inside out.

This book cannot solve the many debates about numerous topics related to this theme. Nor can it trace the tremendous amount of scholarship and writing related to Paul's concept of union with Christ. I will take various positions in the study that I believe are faithful to the intent of the text. At times, I will refer to ancient sources and modern scholars in effort to clarify or compare to my own thoughts. I intend this book to be accessible yet challenging because we cannot take this topic lightly. What it means to be "in Christ" deserves the best attention and effort we can give it. Much is at stake in interpreting Paul's letters with accuracy and relevancy. My goal for those who read this book is that they will catch Paul's "spirit" and seek to experience the transforming power and presence available to those who faithfully and totally commit themselves to Christ's lordship. To that end I have written.

Abbreviations

Ancient Works

Apocrypha

Bar	Baruch
Sir	Sirach/Ecclesiasticus
Wis	Wisdom of Solomon

OT Pseudepigrapha

1 En.	1 Enoch
2 En.	2 Enoch
2 Bar.	2 Baruch
3 Bar.	3 Baruch
4 Ezra	4 Ezra
Apoc. Ab.	Apocalypse of Abraham
Apoc. Mos.	Apocalypse of Moses
Ascen. Isaiah	Ascension of Isaiah
L.A.E.	Life of Adam and Eve
Jub.	Jubilees
Pr. Jos.	Prayer of Joseph
T. Ab.	Testament of Abraham
T. Dan.	Testament of Dan
T. Levi	Testament of Levi

Dead Sea Scrolls

1Q14	
1QH	*Thanksgiving Hymns*
1QpHab	*Pesher Habakkuk*
1QM	*War Scroll*
1QS	*Rule of the Community*
4QShirShabb	*Songs of the Sabbath Sacrifice*
CD	*Damascus Document*
11QMelch	*Melchizedek*
11QT	*Temple Scroll*

Philo

Cher.	*De cherubim*
Conf.	*De confusion linguarum*
Decal.	*De decalogo*
Cherubim	*On the Cherubim*
Det.	*Quod deterius potiori insidari soleat*
Deus	*Quod Deus sit immutabilis*
Fug.	*De fuga et inventione*
Gig.	*De gigantibus*
Her.	*Quis rerum divinarum heres*
Leg.	*Legum allegoriae*
Migr.	*De migration Abrahami*
Mos.	*De vita Mosis*
Mut.	*De mutatione nominum*
Opif.	*De opificio mundi*
Plant.	*De plantation*
Post.	*De posteritate Caini*
QE	*Quaestiones et solutiones in Exodum*
QG	*Quaestiones et solutiones in Genesin*
Sacr.	*De sacrificiis Abelis et Caini*
Somn.	*De somniis*
Spec.	*De specialibus legibus*

Josephus

J.W.	*Jewish Wars*

Rabbinic Literature

Hek. Rab.   *Hekhalot Rabbati*
Pirke Aboth

Apostolic Fathers

1 Clem.   *1 Clement*
Ign. *Eph.*   Ignatius, *To the Ephesians*
Ign. *Rom.*   Ignatius, *To the Romans*
Ign. *Trall.*   Ignatius, *To the Trallians*

Other Church Fathers

Hippolytus, *Haer.*   *Refutatio omnium haeresium*
Origen, *Cels.*   *Contra Celsum*
Tertullian, *Praescr.*   *De praescriptione haereticorum*

Nag Hammadi Codices

Marsanes   *X Marsanes*

New Testament Apocrypha and Pseudepigrapha

Apoc. Paul   *Apocalypse of Paul*
Epiphanius, *Pan.*   *Panarion* (*Adversus haereses*)

Other Greek and Latin Works

Aeschylus, *Prom.*   *Prometheus vinctus*
Aeschylus, *Ag.*   *Agamemnon*
Apuleius, *Metam.*   *Metamorphoses*
Aristophanes, *Nub.*   *Nubes* (*Clouds*)
Dio Chrysostom, *Or.*   *Orationes*
Euripides, *Bacch.*   *Bacchae*
Herodotus, *Hist.*   *Historiae*
Lucian, *Men.*   *Menippus*
Pindar, *Pyth.*   *Pythionikai*

Poimandres	In the *Corpus hermeticum*
Plato, *Ep.*	*Epistulae*
Plato, *Phaedr.*	*Phaedrus*
Plato, *Resp.*	*Respublica*
Plato, *Symp.*	*Symposium*
Plato, *Thaet.*	*Theaetetus*
Plato, *Tim.*	*Timaeus*
Plotinus, *Enn.*	*Enneades*
Plutarch, *Mor.*	*Moralia* (*On Praising Oneself Inoffensively*)
Quintilian, *Inst.*	*Institutio oratoria*
Strabo, *Geogr.*	*Geographica*

Other Abbreviations

AD	anno Domini (precedes date)
BC	before Christ (follows date)
ca.	circa
ch.	chapter
BDAG	Bauer et al., *A Greek-English Lexicon of the New Testament and Other Early Christian Literature*
ESV	English Standard Version
GNT	Good News Translation
lit.	literally
NIV	New International Version (2011)
NLT	New Living Translation
NRSV	New Revised Standard Version
TDNT	Kittel, *Theological Dictionary of the New Testament*
v(v).	verse(s)

Introduction

A Personal Quest

PAUL WAS ON THE cutting edge of the beginning of the Christian church and one of the first theologians to explain the significance of Jesus Christ. He was a practical person, concerned with clear communication of the good news that would lead to change in the lives of those to whom he spoke or wrote. He used methods of persuasion from the Greco-Roman rhetoric of his day and the rabbinic methods of interpretation he had learned as a student. Central to his thought was a relationship with the God of the Jewish faith, whom he believed was most significantly revealed in the life, death, and resurrection of Jesus of Nazareth. He worked out his theology in the crucible of life. Whenever he mentions theological statements in his letters, he is always moving towards change in the lives of his readers.

Paul was a bold person, as a quick read of the Acts of the Apostles demonstrates. His boldness can be seen not only in his courage to share his faith in Christ with non-believers and even before antagonistic religious and political leaders, but also in his discourse with early Christian communities. His opponents said about him, "His letters are weighty and strong, but his bodily presence is weak, and his speech of no account" (2 Cor 10:10). This is likely a caricature by those who set themselves up as "super apostles" who tried to belittle him and his message (11:4–6). As his letters and mission show, he was highly skilled in the art of persuasion and was able to debate with the best speakers of his day and convince many people to accept Christ through his preaching (such as in Athens, Acts 17:16–34). He was a courageous and effective communicator.

At several significant points in his letters, he calls for his readers to imitate him. On his second missionary journey, he stayed in Thessalonica for only about three weeks before he was run out of town (Acts 17:1–9). Those who became believers through his testimony grew in their faith but soon began to face their own persecution. In 1 Thessalonians 1:6, he reminds them to become "imitators of us and of the Lord" by receiving "the word in much affliction, with the joy of the Holy Spirit" (see also 2:14). Likewise, he encourages the Philippians to follow his way of life in order that they might receive the heavenly prize with him (Phil 3:17). As the spiritual father of the Corinthian church, he urges them, "be imitators of me" (1 Cor 4:16). He could boldly set himself up as an example only because of the direction of his own life. Behind this call for imitation stands the person of Jesus Christ. Paul adds an important thought in 1 Corinthians 11:1: "Imitate me as I imitate Christ." Because Christ was working in Paul through the Holy Spirit, others could see the reflection of Christ in how he lived.

How could Paul make such bold statements? Only because he had personally experienced the change that Christ through the Holy Spirit makes in the lives of those captured by the power of God's grace (1 Tim 1:12–17). His goal for the readers of his letters was for them to experience and live out the transformationing grace of God in Christ like he had. His ministry was incarnational and transparent—by looking at him, the churches should see Christ's power at work. It was no longer Paul whom they saw but Christ working in him (Gal 2:20). He was but a jar of clay, an imperfect vessel yet useful to the Master because of the presence of the Holy Spirit (2 Cor 4:7). He committed himself in faith to reflect Christ and allow the power of God to work in him. This power ironically appeared in Jesus' death on a Roman cross (1 Cor 1:18–25). Paul learned in his moments of trial, weakness, fatigue, sickness, and persecution to trust in the power of God and receive God's grace in Christ (2 Cor 12:9). In imitating Christ, as John Schütz comments, "Paul does not *repeat* what Christ has done. He *reflects* what Christ has done."[1] Being "in Christ" for Paul involves relying on God's grace instead of human power (Phil 2:5–11; Gal 2:20).

The Influence of Paul

Outside of Jesus, arguably Paul has been the most significant person in the Christian faith and the most influential and original theologian of all time. His letters have had a significant impact on Western civilization and a growing influence upon the rest of the world through the growth of the modern church. One example has been Paul's letter to the Romans. This letter has been the spark that started major renewal movements in the church, including Augustine's conversion in the fourth century and the strengthening of the theology of the church, Martin Luther and the Protestant Reformation in the sixteenth century, John Wesley and the Methodist movement in the

---

1. Schütz, *Paul and the Anatomy of Apostolic Authority*, 206.

eighteenth century, and Karl Barth and Neo-orthodoxy in the twentieth century. Paul is a major voice in the New Testament. Half of Acts is about his missional ministry to the Gentile world, and thirteen of twenty-seven books are traditionally credited to his authorship.[2]

The church of the second century remembered Paul as a missionary (*1 Clem.* 5:5–6). He and his travel companions (Barnabas, Silas, Timothy, John Mark, Luke, and others) founded some of the first churches and were influential in taking the gospel message outside of the Eastern Mediterranean region and into Western Asia and Europe. Many of the first Christians became believers through the ministry of these early missionaries.

Paul was able to bridge the promises of the old covenant with their fulfillment in the new covenant. His letters have many quotations of the Old Testament, yet he looked to the fulfillment of the ages in Christ's return. It is commonly believed that his letters were the first Christian documents to have been written and preserved, possibly decades before the four Gospels and other Christian writings. By the end of the first century, many of his letters began to circulate as a group. This makes his letters the earliest extant written interpretations of the person and work of Jesus.

Emerging Christianity became quite diverse as the earliest churches began to multiply. With new believers coming from a mix of Jewish, Roman, Greek, and many other cultural and religious backgrounds, the ideas and practices within the new churches were diverse, sometimes resulting in conflict with one another. The Corinthian church, for example, was divisive, selfish, and too much like the culture around it (1 Cor 1:10–17; 3:1–4). Growth led to theological and ethical tensions within many early churches.

There was no one "orthodox" position accepted by all but a diversity of voices and experiences that were socially, regionally, and culturally influenced. There was no unified structure of authority outside of a few traveling apostles and missionaries. Walter Bauer noted the regional variations in early Christianity and argued that it is impossible to find any one orthodox position in early Christianity, and early "heresy" was only regional Christianity. These variations became heresy only at a later time when heresy was the loser in a power struggle.[3] Helmut Koester continued Bauer's thesis by arguing that the diversity in early Christianity was caused by two factors: "first, by the several different religious and cultural conditions and traditions of

---

2. This study assumes the Pauline authorship of the thirteen letters traditionally attributed to Paul. The purpose of this study is not to enter the debates on authorship but to understand Pauline theology as a whole.

3. Bauer, *Rechtgläubigkeit und Ketzerei im ältesten Christentum*.

the people who became Christians; and, second, by the bewildering though challenging impact of Jesus' own life, works, words, and death."[4]

Paul's letters (as well as the rest of the New Testament) had a profound affect upon defining "orthodox" Christianity. Paul used his authority as an apostle and founder of many of the churches to shape what people thought about Jesus Christ, ethics, and the church. Without his letters, the early church could have faced a significant rise of heresies since each church could have developed its own interpretation of the gospel influenced by a diversity of Jewish and pagan backgrounds.

Paul's Agenda

Studying Paul's letters has its challenges. A significant amount of Christian doctrine is built upon his letters to a few scattered churches over the course of a couple of decades. Although we know a lot of what he thought, we do not know everything. We only get glimpses of what he thought about a limited number of issues facing a handful of churches. It is appropriate to assume that what was most important to him would appear in his letters, either intentionally or unintentionally. Indeed, a close reading will indicate that of primary importance to him was what God had planned to do in and through Christ. Paul calls this a "mystery" once hidden but now disclosed (Rom 16:25). He devoted his life to proclaiming this as "good news" to all people. This message appears contextualized to the specific needs of the churches. He had to modify terms, images, and concepts from his context—Jewish and Greco-Roman—based on his own theological, ethical, and social agenda.[5]

Paul was a "driven," intense, and focused person, inspired from the deepest parts of his soul. He had strong convictions and held to them even to the point of facing persecution and martyrdom. He faithfully lived out the mission Jesus Christ gave him to take the gospel to the world of Gentiles (Acts 9:15). What could motivate a person to be so focused with his life?

Paul knew that he could not live victoriously based on his own abilities, what he calls in his letter to the Galatians "the works of the law" (Gal 2:16). What could bring him to the point of saying, "I count all things as loss because of the surpassing worth of knowing Christ Jesus my Lord" (Phil 3:8)? The response of the risen Christ to Paul's difficult life of persecution, shipwrecks, beatings, trials, and the unknown "thorn in the flesh" was, "My grace is sufficient for you, for my power is made perfect in weakness" (2

---

4. Koester, "Structure and Criteria of Early Christian Beliefs," 205.
5. Beker, *Paul the Apostle*, 37–38; Koester, "Paul and Hellenism," 193.

Cor 12:9). Something significant happened to Paul that changed him at the core of his being, summarized well when he writes, "I want to know Christ" (Phil 3:10). He believed this change was God's plan for all people, and so he devoted his life to proclaiming this message of transformation "in Christ."

This study explores how this change affected Paul's life and thinking and how he attempted to convince others to experience the power of God like he had experienced. After his vision on his way to Damascus to arrest followers of Jesus in Acts 9, he devoted his life to proclaiming the "good news" he once sought to destroy (Gal 1:23). His message was simple: "Jesus Christ and him crucified" (1 Cor 2:2). But this message was profound and full of divine power, wisdom, and grace because it could change the worst of sinners into a great missionary for Christ (1 Tim 1:14–16).

Paul uses the word *metamorphoō*, often translated as "transform," to describe this change (Rom 12:2; 2 Cor 3:18). This word can be defined as "to change inwardly in fundamental character or condition."[6] In the equation, there is a "change from" and a "change to." Paul optimistically believed that people can have a new way of living now that impacts relationships with others, values, behavior, and even our physical bodies. This change cannot happen by human effort but only through the grace of God brought through Christ, who "loved us and gave himself up for us" (Eph 5:2). The required human response is cooperation with the change agent, the Holy Spirit, evidenced by obedient faith. The significance of this message for understanding not only Paul's letters but the gospel itself cannot be overstated. This book attempts to unpack what Paul meant by being transformed into the likeness of Christ and how this changes our lives now and gives hope for eternity.

---

6. BDAG, 639.

1

A Journey of Transformation

I count everything as loss because of the surpassing worth of knowing Christ Jesus my Lord.
(Philippians 3:8)

The Worlds of Paul

Paul was a person of his time and culture, but it is difficult to determine how much this culture influenced his thought. Many different ideas competed in the Roman Empire of the first century AD. Some of these whisper in the background of Paul's letters. Paul's background was a mix of the Greco-Roman and the Jewish worlds, both of which shared many common ideas but conflicted with one another at critical points. Scholars have debated for the past two centuries whether Paul was influenced more by Judaism or Hellenism, whether he was a Jewish Hellenist or a Hellenistic Jew. That these cultures influenced his identity is certain, but to what degree is complex and problematic.

In many ways, he was forging a third world, one identified by the key confession, *Jesus Christ is Lord*. He was on a journey from this world to the new age *in Christ*. He expressed his flexibility to reach his goals in 1 Corinthians 9:19–23: "I have become all things to all people, that by all means I might save some. I do it all for the sake of the gospel, that I may share with them in its blessings" (vv. 22–23). Even though he consciously tried to be "all things to all people," he could not escape the religious, cultural, and political forces of his day. His letters are filled with words, concepts, and illustrations from both worlds.

Various sources help reconstruct the world of Paul, including his own letters, other parts of the New Testament, literature of the period, and the discoveries of archaeology. In the New Testament, we get two different—though not contradictory—perspectives about his life: his own autobiographical statements in his letters and Luke's biographical accounts in his second volume, the Acts of the Apostles. Though providing firsthand information, most of the places where Paul gives details of his life are reactions and defenses against opponents who threatened his "correct" interpretation of the gospel (Gal 1:6-7; Phil 3:2). This puts a limitation on what can be known about him because readers only see the Paul he wants them to see. It is like trying to interpret someone's life with only a few photographs.

Luke, on the other hand, adds many details in Acts not found in Paul's letters. Critical scholars have raised questions about using Acts to reconstruct the life and ministry of Paul. It is undeniable that Luke gives a selective history and a partial story, styled according to his narrative and theological purposes. Though Acts needs to be viewed as secondhand information *about* Paul, it can still be a useful source for reconstructing a basic history of his life and ministry. In his gospel, Luke made a concerted effort, after making a careful study and consulting eyewitnesses, to be accurate in his recounting of the story of Jesus (Luke 1:1-4). We can assume the same is true for Acts since the two documents are a set and written to the same Theophilus. In addition, in several places Luke was present with Paul during his missionary journeys, as is implied by the shift to the first-person plural pronoun "we" at several places (16:8-17; 20:5-15; 21:1-18; and 27:1—28:16).

The further out we go from Paul's letters as the direct source of information, the less we know about him. Literature and archaeology from the period help us know more about the world in which he lived than about him. As more discoveries are made, more insights are gained about the setting of his ministry. It is helpful to study about his "worlds" so that we can better understand the new "world" he was attempting to create.

The Hellenistic World

Paul as a Roman Citizen

Paul was born and raised in Tarsus in Cilicia (Acts 21:39), an ancient city with a rich culture. Tarsus was strategically located along the Cydnus river on a fertile plain, along one of the major trade routes of the ancient world. It was a center of education and in ancient times was known as a university city.¹ Paul may have spent his formative years in Tarsus, where he learned rhetoric, since his letters indicate a high degree of familiarity with the current styles of argumentation.

Quintillian, who lived a little after Paul, defined rhetoric as the means by which an audience is persuaded to accept a speaker's ideas.² This is what Paul does in his letters, which serve as written speeches and show many characteristics similar with ancient rhetorical communication.³ The New Testament was written during a period when rhetoric was one of the standard subjects of Greek education and provided the rules for public discourse. Not everyone was formally trained in the finer points of rhetorical theory, but most were exposed to rhetoric in the public arena in the Hellenistic culture.⁴ Burton Mack writes, "To be engulfed in the culture of Hellenism meant to have ears trained for the rhetoric of speech. Rhetoric provided the rules for making critical judgments in the course of all forms of social intercourse."⁵

In his defense before the Roman tribunal in Jerusalem, Paul said that he was born a Roman citizen (Acts 22:27), though he never mentions this in his letters. In order for him to have been born a citizen, his father had to have been a Roman citizen. How his family became citizens is uncertain, though it may have been by way of grant or service. Being a citizen of Tarsus (Acts 21:39) did not come easily either but at the great cost of two years of a laborer's wages.⁶ The Roman law known as *lex Julia de vi publica* gave citizens certain rights and privileges, including a fair and public trial, exemption from certain types of punishment like crucifixion, and protection against summary execution.⁷ Paul appealed to his citizenship three times to avoid death or serious harm (Acts 16:37; 22:25–29; 24:27).

The timing of the revelation of Jesus is significant, as Paul writes, "But when the fullness of time had come, God sent forth his Son" (Gal 4:4). The first century AD was a prime time for the planting and spreading of the gospel. Significant changes began to take place in the Mediterranean region after the conquests of Alexander the Great in the fourth century BC.

---

1. Strabo, *Geogr.* 14.5.12.
2. Quintilian, *Inst.* 2.15.10.
3. Raymond F. Collins, "Reflections on 1 Corinthians as a Hellenistic Letter," in Bieringer, *Corinthian* Correspondence, 57–58.
4. See Kennedy, *New Testament Criticism*.
5. Mack, *Rhetoric and the New Testament*, 31.
6. Dio Chrysostom, *Or.* 34.21–23.
7. Bruce, *Paul*, 39; Sherwin-White, *Roman Society and Roman Law*, 57–64.

After Alexander died around 323 BC, the world began to shrink, and the Hellenistic culture began to extend its influence through the growing links between East and West, the spread of Greek as the international language, the opening of trade routes, and the migration of people. This melting of ideas and cultures continued under the Romans.

After becoming emperor in 30 BC, Caesar Augustus built and refurbished roads, established fortifications, and founded a navy, thereby opening up new, unprecedented possibilities for travel by both land and sea for governmental, economic, religious, and personal reasons. Through Augustus' *Pax Romana* ("Roman Peace"), a secure and united empire emerged with a unified coinage, regular army patrols, paved highways to many major cities, cultural unity, and standard languages of Greek and Latin, making it possible for the average citizen to travel relatively unhindered.[8] But peace came at a price.

Imperialism

Although the Romans brought unity and safety to much of their empire, they also brought imperialism, domination, and oppression. When they conquered a particular territory, they often made their captives or those who resisted into slaves. The number of slaves in the empire is hard to determine, but more than 80 percent or more of the population in some areas were slaves.[9] A slave was considered a "thing," a piece of property that could be used according to the will of the master.[10] Roman society was structured according to social class, with the lower stratum often struggling for survival. To fund their military and expansion, the Romans taxed the inhabitants of their territories. The New Testament gives hints of the animosity people of Palestine felt towards the Roman collaborators who collected the taxes (Matt 9:10–11; 11:19; 18:17; 21:32). The cruelty of the Romans towards their captors, especially represented in death by crucifixion, is documented both in the New Testament and in other literature of the period.[11]

---

8. Stambaugh and Balch, *New Testament in Its Social Environment*, 37–38; Wengst, *Pax Romana*.

9. The exact percentage is difficult to determine, but see Patterson, *Slavery and Social Death*, 105–31.

10. Ferguson, *Backgrounds of Early Christianity*, 56–58.

11. For example, the thieves on the cross in Matt 27:38 and what Paul says in 1 Cor 1:23. It was considered taboo for people to talk about crucifixion because of its brutality. See Hengel, *Crucifixion in the Ancient World*, for other ancient references and descriptions.

When Paul and other early Christian evangelists preached the good news of Jesus Christ, people were eager for any sign of hope and liberation. Though they might not find immediate liberation from their physical bonds, spiritual freedom from the power of sin (Rom 8:1–11) placed hope in their hearts and lifted them above the misery of a world controlled by the rulers, authorities, cosmic powers of darkness, and the spiritual forces of evil (Eph 6:12). It was their new hope of salvation in Christ that sustained early believers through periods of political and economic hardship.

Religious Context

The inhabitants of the Mediterranean region were religious and lived in a pluralistic and polytheistic context.[12] Archeology has shown that the major cities of the Roman Empire were full of temples and shrines to a myriad of gods and goddesses. Typically present were the traditional Greek and Roman pantheons, mystery religions from the East, emperor worship, many different philosophies, including Neoplatonism, which was merging with Eastern religions to form Gnosticism, along with pockets of Judaism. As travel became easier, ideas and religions began to mix, leading to syncretism. Abraham Malherbe describes syncretism as "either the mixture of elements from several religions which influence each other mutually, or the acceptance of elements from one religion by another without any basic change occurring in the character of the receiving religion."[13] As the Romans conquered and resettled areas, they typically took over native religions and mixed them with their own national temper.[14] On different occasions independent city-states joined forces against common enemies like Rome. After these city-states were conquered, foreign elements merged with the native cultures and religions, resulting in the blending of thought and language into a complex *milieu*.[15]

The exclusive claims of Christianity's "one God and one Lord" came in conflict with the pluralism of "many gods" found in many cities (1 Cor 8:5–6). When Paul went to Athens on his second missionary journey and saw a city full of idols, he used the pluralism of the Athenians as an opportunity to share the gospel by pointing out that their "unknown god" was

---

12. See Burkert, *Greek Religion*, 216.

13. Abraham J. Malherbe, "Greco Roman Religion and Philosophy in the New Testament," in Epp and MacRae, *New Testament and Its Modern Interpreters*, 6.

14. Ferguson, *Backgrounds of Early Christianity*, 155.

15. On Greek religions, see Nilsson, *History of Greek Religion*. On Roman religions, see Lyttelton and Forman, *Romans*.

actually the creator God of the universe, and that this God had brought salvation through the person of Jesus (Acts 17:16–34). Some believed while others rejected Paul's message. The claim that salvation comes by no other name under heaven except Jesus (Acts 4:12) did not always go well with either Greeks or Jews.

Social and Cultural Context

Paul focused his evangelistic efforts on the cities, most of which were the major urban centers of the empire. His letters are full of urban images (1 Cor 3:12; 4:9; 9:24; 14:8). Located on major trade routes, the cities were the power centers of the empire and served as mixing pots for different ideas and religions. The many pagan temples were some of the largest structures in the cities. The remains of many of them, such as on the Acropolis in Athens, are still very evident today. The many different cults provided a focus to the social life of the populace. Urban life was densely packed with little privacy. People often lived in ethnic groups, such as the many Jews of the Diaspora who could be found in every major city of the empire, or near those involved in similar trades.

When Paul entered a city, he used the various social networks as avenues for evangelism. One of the first places he went was the local synagogue, where he found fellow Jews and God-fearers, those who believed in God but had not formerly become Jews by circumcision (Acts 13:5, 14; 14:1; 17:2). He felt it important to go to his own people first, since they should have been open to the good news of God's Messiah (Rom 1:16). However, he usually faced opposition from the Jews, so in Corinth he symbolically shook his clothes and said, "Your blood be on your own heads! I am innocent. From now on I will go to the Gentiles" (Acts 18:6).

Paul used other networks to make contacts. As a tentmaker, he could easily set up shop along one of the market streets so common in the cities. If we were to go looking for him, we could have found him industriously working in a small shop, supporting himself with the money he made, busily sharing the gospel with clients and training the people with whom he was staying.

His goal was to establish local churches, train local leadership, and then move on to new locations. He then kept in contact with the churches through letters and sending emissaries like Timothy (1 Cor 4:16) and Titus (2 Cor 8:23). The earliest churches, in many ways, functioned as extended families (called "fictive kinship"), with fellow believers being called "brothers and sisters" (Rom 1:13; 1 Cor 4:15). The churches were relatively small, possibly up to fifty people, what a good-sized home could host for a gathering. The new believers began to form a new identity focused upon Jesus Christ. With this identity came a set of behavioral standards resulting in tension with the surrounding pagan culture.

Another significant feature in the cities that Paul visited was the immorality influenced by pagan worship. For example, in Corinth there were a number of cults and temples that provided many opportunities for the inhabitants to participate in sensuality, such as the worship of Aphrodite, the goddess of love and sexuality; the worship of Hera Argaea, the goddess of marriage and sexuality for women and of sacred marriage; and the worship of Dionysus, the god of wine and ecstasy, which had a reputation for drunkenness and sexual immorality. Immorality was condemned not only by Christians but by other ethicists of the day.[16] Paul's ethical standards of holy living, influenced by his Jewish background and study of the Scripture and his faith in and relationship with Jesus Christ, collided with the common lifestyles of these urban centers. The relationship of Paul and the early church to their pagan environment is a critical point to keep in mind when reading his letters. His message urging believers to be sanctified and to flee sexual immorality in their cultures (1 Cor 6:18; 1 Thess 4:3) has a timeless ring to it.

Paul was immersed in the world of his day. He knew it well—both the good and the bad. What made him so effective in this setting? He confronted the wickedness of the cities with a message of love, hope, and freedom. His ethic was grounded in the grace of God in Christ Jesus (Titus 3:3–7). Holiness of life sprang from holiness of heart.

The Jewish World

Paul saw himself as part of the covenant people of God, a monotheist with "one God, the Father, from whom are all things and for whom we exist, and one Lord, Jesus Christ, through whom are all things and through whom we exist" (1 Cor 8:6; see also Rom 11:36). His autobiographical statements reveal a lot about what he thought of himself and the "world" in which he located his ideas. He usually writes about his Jewishness when defending himself or his interpretation of the gospel against the criticism of opponents (Gal 1; Phil 3). Other more implicit factors, like his upbringing and education, also contributed to his Jewishness. Acts fills in some of the details that he does not mention in his letters. For example, in Acts 21:39 he describes himself as a Jew from Tarsus. We would not know where he was born unless

---

16. See Malherbe, *Moral Exhortation*; Meeks, *Origin of Christian Morality*.

Luke recorded it. Paul saw himself and his message as part of the larger narrative of God's people stretching back to Abraham, the father of faith (Rom 4; Gal 3:7–9). Paul was not an innovator but was firmly planted in the traditions of his Jewish fathers. The gospel was the revelation of a mystery that was kept hidden for many years, of which the prophets had glimpses, but which now has been fully revealed in Jesus Christ (Rom 16:25–27).

Born a Hebrew

Very little can be known about Paul's early life. In the book of Acts, we meet him engaged in his career as a Pharisee after the Day of Pentecost and after the church had been growing for a while. His Jewish résumé is given in Philippians 3:4b–6: "If anyone else thinks he has reason for confidence in the flesh, I have more: circumcised on the eighth day, of the people of Israel, of the tribe of Benjamin, a Hebrew of Hebrews; as to the law, a Pharisee; as to zeal, a persecutor of the church; as to righteousness under the law, blameless."

Paul was born a Jew, "of the people of Israel," and his parents fulfilled the requirements of the law by circumcising him eight days after birth (Gen 17:12). When he was born is unknown but most likely within the first decade after Jesus' birth. Acts calls him a "young man" (*neanias*) in 7:58, a term used for young adults from twenty to forty years old.[17] He came from the Israelite tribe of Benjamin (Rom 11:1), a small tribe located around Jerusalem that became incorporated into the larger tribe of Judah and remained faithful to the house of David after the splitting of the kingdoms in 1 Kings 12. Paul was named after the hero from the tribe of Benjamin, Saul, the first king of Israel. In Acts, Paul is first called by his Hebrew name, Saul. According to John McRay, Paul may have had both names at birth and used them in different situations.[18] He begins to go by Paul, his Roman name (called *cognomen*), after Acts 13:9 when he appears before a Roman proconsul on Cyprus who shared his name, Sergius Paulus (13:7). He continued to use the name Paul throughout his journeys and ministry among the Gentiles and always in his letters.

He then calls himself a "Hebrew of Hebrews." The Hebrew Jews were part of the Aramaic-speaking dispersion and worshipped in Aramaic in local synagogues (see Acts 6:1). It is uncertain what his native language was. He knew Aramaic (Acts 21:40; 22:2; 26:14) but was obviously fluent in Greek as he evangelized in Asia Minor and Greece. At some point, possibly

17. BDAG, 534.
18. McRay, *Paul*, 25–28.

as early as age thirteen, when a Jewish boy became a "son of the law" (*bar mitzvah*), young Saul went to Jerusalem to study under the famous Gamaliel (Acts 22:3), the leading Pharisee of the time. Gamaliel took a moderate view towards the disciples in Acts 5:33–39 and urged the Sanhedrin to leave them alone. He was not completely successful in his appeals, and the disciples ended up with a scolding and flogging.

To some extent, Paul must have been raised in Jewish ways. He makes the claim in 2 Corinthians 11:22 against some opponents, "Are they Hebrews? So am I. Are they Israelites? So am I. Are they offspring of Abraham? So am I." Hellenistic Jews adapted to some degree to Greco-Roman culture and language. They worshipped in the synagogues scattered throughout the empire, often using Greek as their language and the Septuagint (Greek translation of the Old Testament) as their Bible. Paul's letters give evidence of someone schooled in Jewish ways, including the study of the law, rabbinic methods of argumentation, and learning a trade. Jewish rabbis were expected to learn a trade and be engaged in some form of work.[19] Paul's trade was "tentmaking," which likely included working with leather to make tents, awnings, and other products from animal skins (Acts 18:3). He also knew the Hebrew Scriptures and how to interpret them using standard rabbinic methods. Contemporary Pauline scholars are becoming more certain that Paul's Jewish upbringing had significant impact upon his later life as a Christian.

Paul, the Pharisee

One of the distinguishing marks of Paul's life was that he was a Pharisee. He calls himself a Pharisee three times: Philippians 3:5; Acts 23:6; and Acts 26:5. In Galatians 1:13–14 he describes his former life as a proud, loyal, and zealous Jew but does not use the term "Pharisee." Pharisees were one of three major sects in first-century Judaism (besides the Sadducees and Essenes) and considered themselves to be the most orthodox. They were known for their devotion to the Jewish Scriptures. The first-century Jewish historian Josephus called them "most accurate exegetes of the Law."[20] The word "Pharisee" is related to the Hebrew word meaning "separate" (*prs*), which has the connotation of purity. Pharisees were the "holiness movement" of the first century and sought to keep the Jewish people pure by strict observance of the law. For the Pharisees, holiness was maintained by strictly following the law. Jesus criticized them for overinterpreting the law,

19. *Pirke Aboth* 2:2, 12.
20. Josephus, *J.W.* 2.162.

with their reliance upon oral traditions handed down from their forefathers (called *halakah*) while missing out on the heart of the law as love to the neighbor (Matt 7:1–22, 9:9–13, 12:12–3; Mark 2:15–17). They believed in the resurrection of the body, against the Sadducees, who did not (see Acts 23:8). They were very zealous for their version of Judaism and were "missionary minded" in their effort to persuade Jewish proselytes who believed in God (called "God-fearers" in Acts 10:1–2, 22; 13:16, 26) and others to accept their views and become full Jews. This zeal also led to ruthlessly opposing their enemies.

Paul shared many of the same beliefs and qualities of his fellow Pharisees. Pharisaic ideals are implied in Acts 8 before Paul became a believer and in scattered places throughout his letters. Young Paul as a Pharisee distinguished himself above his peers by his strict observance of the law. His Pharisaic background and focus upon Scripture gave him a good foundation for the holy ethic he would later urge the churches to adopt. He never renounced Judaism nor left it but understood the church to be the new Israel, which includes all Jews and Gentiles who believe Jesus to be the Messiah (see Rom 9–11).

There has been a lot of discussion among Pauline scholars about how Paul the Pharisee, Judaism, and the law related to the early church. The traditional Protestant approach since Martin Luther has been to argue that Paul the Pharisee was trying to earn his way to heaven by obedience to the law. More recently, a so-called "new perspective" has emerged which argues that Paul and other Jews were not concerned about earning salvation by their obedience but that their obedience was the mark of their being the covenantal people of God.[21] In other words, obedience to the law (what Paul calls "works of the law" in Gal 2:16) does not get one in but is the mark of one who is already in. Holy living for both first-century Jews and Christians as the heirs of Judaism did not *qualify* one to be a child of God but *resulted* from grace in a person's life.

Messianic Expectations

Paul the Pharisee, like many Jews of the first century, expected God to intervene in history in a decisive way to bring about the restoration of his people, Israel, deliverance from their enemies, and final triumph over evil. The term

---

21. The primary proponents of the "New Perspective" are Sanders, *Paul and Palestinian Judaism*; Dunn, *Jesus, Paul, and the Law*, Dunn, *Paul and the Mosaic Law*; and Wright, *Paul*. There are also opponents to these ideas represented in Westerholm, *Perspectives Old and New on Paul*; Kim, *Paul and the New Perspective*.

"apocalyptic" describes these Jewish longings. The English word comes from the Greek word *apocalyptō*, meaning to reveal, disclose, or bring to light. In a religious sense, it is used for the revealing of divine revelation or certain supernatural secrets called "mysteries."[22] Jewish apocalyptic hopes emerged out of Old Testament prophecies like Daniel's vision of a new kingdom (Dan 7–12), the visions of Zechariah (Zech 1–6, 9–14), and the references to the coming day of the Lord in Joel and other prophets.

Apocalypticism arose in the third to fourth centuries BC in a context of uncertainty and despair and had gained momentum with the Roman occupation of Judea in 63 BC. The characteristic eschatology in apocalypticism included the belief in an early end to the world or this present age controlled by evil powers. There are two periods of time, called *aeons*: one controlled by evil that will come to an end when the second, the new age under the control of God and his Messiah, triumphs. Only those to whom God has revealed the secrets or mysteries know about the end, and this knowledge leads to salvation. The unrighteous are those who do not know or accept the revelation of God. The righteous are strangers in this age because they belong to the age to come. In apocalypticism, there is a void between God, who is far removed, and this present earthly existence. Intermediaries can transverse this distance by heavenly journeys or visions by which they receive secret wisdom and knowledge about the mystery of existence at the end of this age. A specific type of literature arose that embodied this apocalyptic, eschatological orientation.[23] For the Jews of the first century AD, there was no better time politically or religiously than at that moment for God to intervene and bring about his saving plan.

Because of his hopes for God's redemption of Israel, the pre-Damascus Saul prepared for the Day of the Lord by eliminating heretical followers of the false Messiah, Jesus of Nazareth. He wanted to preserve the traditions of his fathers (Gal 1:14), and like with other apocalyptic Jews, may have looked forward to a "new creation" (*Jub.* 11:29; 4:26; *1 En.* 72:1; *4 Ezra* 7:75; 1QS 4:25). Apocalyptic Jews expected God to do something great and to restore soon the people of Israel. There was a sense of anticipation in first-century Judaism. From time to time false Messiahs would rise up in hopes

22. BDAG, 92.

23. The book of Revelation fits into this genre, though it is uniquely Christian with its focus upon Jesus. The Society of Biblical Literature Genres Project has provided a broad definition of apocalyptic genre: "Apocalypse is a genre of revelatory literature with a narrative framework, in which a revelation is mediated by an otherworldly being to a human recipient disclosing a transcendent reality which is both temporal, insofar it envisages eschatological salvation, and spatial, insofar as it involves another, supernatural world" (Collins, *Apocalypse*, 9). See Marcus and Soards, *Apocalyptic and the New Testament*; Käsemann, *New Testament Questions of Today*, 134.

of ushering in the Day of the Lord. These all failed miserably as the Romans crushed any such apocalyptic hopes. Paul's zeal did not stop after his experience on the road to Damascus but only refocused on Jesus as the fulfillment of these hopes. Paul put his hope in Jesus Christ and believed that Jesus had begun a new way of life that would be ultimately fulfilled when he comes again. The focus of Paul's message became the newness that Christ brought through his death on the cross and the emergence of hope through his resurrection (Rom 6:4). All the promises of God found fulfillment in Christ (2 Cor 1:19–20). History was forever changed through Christ. The simple abbreviations BC ("before Christ") and AD (*Anno Domini*, Latin for "In the year of our Lord") have cosmic and spiritual significance for those "in Christ."

Paul, the Persecutor

Paul first appears in the New Testament as Saul, the persecutor of the church. After the coming of the Holy Spirit on the Day of Pentecost, the apostles and those gathered in the upper room boldly shared their faith in the risen Jesus. As a result of Peter's sermon, the number of believers grew to three thousand in one day (Acts 2). People from all over the Roman Empire had come to Jerusalem for the celebration of Pentecost. Many who believed in the message about Jesus undoubtedly returned to their homelands with their new faith. The Spirit-filled believers continued to share their faith in Jesus with others, and their numbers began to increase.

The Jewish authorities in the Sanhedrin, however, viewed the followers of Jesus as a threat. At first, their censure focused upon the message of Jesus' resurrection from the dead (Acts 4:2). As more and more miracles took place, the Jewish leaders felt their authority threatened by the message about Jesus and were afraid they would be blamed for his death, which would not go over well in a city excited with miracles being done in Jesus' name (Acts 5:28). The Jewish leaders debated about the status of the followers of Jesus: were they still within the boundary of Judaism? The conflict intensified and reached a critical point in the person of Stephen. Stephen was not afraid to lay the blame of Jesus' death at the feet of the Jewish leaders (Acts 7:51–53). This and the perceived threat to the temple (vv. 48–50) were too much for the Jewish authorities, who tore their clothes, drug Stephen out of the city, and stoned him to death. Standing there watching was a young man named Saul.

The death of Stephen gave the Jewish authorities more leverage, power, and inspiration to increase the intensity of their campaign against the church. Something in these events inspired Saul to begin also his own persecution campaign. What bothered him so much about Christians that he would go out of his way to persecute them? That is a difficult question to answer, but several possibilities can be suggested. For one, he wanted to preserve and purify Judaism. He saw the followers of Jesus as a heresy and threat to the Jewish identity centered around the law. He writes in Galatians 1:13–14, "For you have heard of my former life in Judaism, how I persecuted the church of God violently and tried to destroy it. And I was advancing in Judaism beyond many of my own age among my people, so extremely zealous was I for the traditions of my fathers."

Another possibility that may have bothered Saul was that he saw the idea of the Messiah dying on the cross to be a scandal. It was a shock to the Jewish mind. He later wrote to the Corinthians, "For Jews demand signs and Greeks seek wisdom, but we preach Christ crucified, a stumbling block to Jews and folly to Gentiles" (1 Cor 1:22–23). A person crucified in the first century was viewed by many as being under a curse because of a phrase found in Deuteronomy 21:23: "cursed is everyone who is hung on a *tree*" (see Gal 3:1, 13; 11QT 64:15). The Greek word for "tree" (*xylon*) can also be translated as "cross." Because Jesus died on a *cross*, he was cursed by God; how could the Messiah be cursed by God? The idea of the cross took on new meaning for Paul once he began to understand the depths of divine love that it represented. The death of Jesus, "who loved us and gave himself for us" (Eph 5:2), became the central theme of Paul's preaching (1 Cor 2:2). Only after he put his faith in Christ could he see that the message of the cross was no longer foolishness but the very power of God (1 Cor 1:18).

A Journey of Transformation

The Transforming Vision

Acts 9 begins with an aggressive Saul "breathing out threats and murder against the disciples of the Lord." For some unknown reason, he chose believers in Damascus as his target and asked for letters of authority to arrest and bring them to Jerusalem, evidently to put them on trial. As he and his companions were on their way, a voice spoke in Aramaic (the dialect similar to Hebrew spoken at that time, see Acts 26:14), "Saul, Saul, why are you persecuting me?" There are two critical points in this statement: 1) the identity of the "me," and 2) Saul's motivation suggested with the word "why." Saul is forced to think about both of these issues in this encounter. He asks back, "Who are you, Lord?" Saul, as a Jew and scholar of Scripture, knew the divine origin of the vision but had not connected Jesus of Nazareth with the plan of God. To make this very clear, the voice responds, "I am Jesus." And then Jesus makes an identification that has reverberated throughout history: "whom you are persecuting." By persecuting believers, Saul was actually persecuting Jesus. The identification of Jesus with the church became important to Saul throughout his later ministry. Saul is not given any chance to respond to the "why" question, but he must have thought about it and many other things over the next three days. The only answer he could give must have been one that he thought a lot about throughout the rest of his life and is given in one of the last letters he wrote, 1 Timothy 1:12–17:

> I thank him who has given me strength, Christ Jesus our Lord, because he judged me faithful, appointing me to his service, though formerly I was a blasphemer, persecutor, and insolent opponent. But I received mercy because I had acted ignorantly in unbelief, and the grace of our Lord overflowed for me with the faith and love that are in Christ Jesus. The saying is trustworthy and deserving of full acceptance, that Christ Jesus came into the world to save sinners, of whom I am the foremost. But I received mercy for this reason, that in me, as the foremost, Jesus Christ might display his perfect patience as an example to those who were to believe in him for eternal life. To the King of the ages, immortal, invisible, the only God, be honor and glory forever and ever. Amen.

Saul then went on into Damascus, not to arrest Christians but to become one of them. So overwhelmed was he with this encounter that he could neither see, eat, nor drink for three days. Meanwhile, the Lord had also been talking to the disciple Ananias in a vision, telling him to go find Saul and place his hands on Saul so his vision might be restored. The brave and obedient Ananias found Saul in the house of Judas on Straight Street as directed. Immediately after Ananias placed his hands on Saul, Saul's vision was restored and Ananias baptized him. Ananias said that he had come to help Saul "be filled with the Holy Spirit." This was a dramatic process that changed Saul's life forever, taking him from adamant persecutor to Spirit-filled "instrument to carry my name before the Gentiles and their kings" (Acts 9:15).

God had taken the initiative to *capture* Paul (Phil 3:12) and change the direction of his life. So important was this event not only in Paul's life but for the development of the church that Luke mentions it three times in Acts (9:1–19; 22:3–16; 26:1–20). In the last of these accounts, Paul quotes the voice of Jesus as saying, "It hurts you to kick against the goads" (Acts

26:14). This was a familiar proverb in classical literature that meant, "It is folly to resist what is inevitable."[24] Do not resist what God wants to do in your life. God's prevenient grace was at work in Paul before he ever set off for Damascus. He had been exposed to the gospel through the Christians he persecuted. What seeds could have been planted when he heard the dying Stephen say, "Lord Jesus, receive my spirit. Lord, do not hold this sin against them" (Acts 7:59–60)? The Damascus road was not an encounter between two strangers but two enemies. Nothing would be the same again for Paul. F. F. Bruce comments, "No single event, apart from the Christ-event itself, has proved so determinant for the course of Christian history as the conversion and commissioning of Paul."[25]

A New Perspective

What went through Paul's mind as he sat quietly in the house of Judas during the three days of physical blindness? Was it awe, wonder, conviction, questions, purpose, possibly guilt for what he had been doing, or other emotions and thoughts? As he sat in physical blindness, his spiritual eyes were opening to the grace of newness in Jesus Christ. There may be a hint of personal testimony in 2 Corinthians 5:16–17 when he writes, ". . . we once regarded Christ according to the flesh, we regard him thus no longer. Therefore, if anyone is in Christ, he is a new creation. The old has passed away; behold, the new has come."

His experience that day cannot be reduced to a few short statements or words. What this experience meant for him was not simply a date on the calendar of his spiritual journey but the beginning of an intimate relationship with his Lord that would be at the heart of all he would do for the rest of his life. In his own account of these events in Galatians 1, Paul describes how he went on to spend three years in Arabia and Damascus (Gal 1:17, 18), which, no doubt, was a time of introspection and contemplation of the person of Jesus Christ and his role in the redemption of humanity. We cannot assume that Paul had instantly worked out his theology based on this one experience. It took a lifetime to work out that Christ had taken hold of him (Phil 3:12). By the time he had written his first letters, he had been a believer for at least fifteen years. Subsequently, when he used his theology to guide the early church, he did not appeal to a past spiritual encounter but to a fresh and up-to-date relationship with God in Christ through the Spirit. He writes, "For me to live is Christ" (Phil 1:21).

24. Aeschylus, *Prom.* 323; v. 322; *Ag.* 1624; Pindar, *Pyth.* v. 95.
25. Bruce, *Paul*, 75.

If Paul became a new creation in Christ, what actually changed in his life? Most obviously, he was outwardly no longer a persecutor. Spiritually, his sins had been washed away (Acts 22:16). This was not a conversion to a new religion. He did not abandon his Jewish heritage and beliefs or cease to be a Jew or a Pharisee, nor did he forsake the law, but he continued to follow Jewish traditions and worshiped in Jewish ways (Acts 21:21, 24).[26] In spite of all the continuity with his past life, something profound had changed in his perspective.

Udo Schnelle suggests four ways God gave Paul new knowledge on the Damascus road, given here with additional comments.[27] The first is *theological knowledge*: God speaks, acts, and reveals his salvation in a new way at the end of the age. Paul's God was still the God of Abraham and Israel, but Paul's vision of God as loving was deepened in Christ (Rom 8:38–39).

The second is *Christological knowledge*: the crucified and risen Jesus of Nazareth now belongs forever at God's side as exalted Lord (Phil 2:9–11). He is the permanent mediator of God's power and revelation (Gal 1:12; 1 Tim 2:5). The Jewish longings were fulfilled in the person of Jesus. It took a physical encounter with the resurrected Jesus for Paul to change his mind. From that point on, he saw an inseparable identity of God and Jesus. What Paul once sought to destroy he now became a part. Out of his encounter with Christ and new relationship with him, Paul developed a strong doctrine of the church, with Christ as the head and the church as his body.

The third is *soteriological knowledge*: believers participate in Christ's reign now and are part of a transformation that began with Christ's resurrection, continues in the power of the Spirit, and will be completed with Christ's second coming. Christ replaced the law as the center of Paul's life. Paul had a new view of grace as a free gift that includes the offer of righteousness to those who accept it (Eph 2:8–9). This grace was so significant in his mind that he uses the word "grace" eighty-one times in his letters. His new knowledge was influenced to some extent by his new Christian community, but also, and primarily, by his own experience of God's grace and forgiveness (1 Tim 1:15–16).

And the fourth is *biographical knowledge*: God elected Paul and called him to take the good news to the nations. Paul believed he had a direct and real encounter with the resurrected Jesus that qualified him to be called an apostle (1 Cor 9:1; 15:3–8). His vision was a simultaneous call to apostleship (Gal 1:15). There are two ways to understand the word "apostle": 1) it can be

---

26. Stendahl, *Paul among Jews and Gentiles*, 7–9; Freed, *Apostle Paul*. For evidence of Paul's Jewishness in Acts, see the list in McRay, *Paul*, 50–52.

27. Schnelle, *Apostle Paul*, 98.

interpreted broadly as "one sent forth," or 2) it can refer more narrowly to one who has seen Jesus directly and been sent out specifically by him. Paul's vision of Jesus qualified him in the narrow sense. Paul's description of his calling in Galatians 1:13–16 sounds similar to the callings of the prophets Isaiah (Isa 49:1–6) and Jeremiah (Jer 1:1–11), suggesting that Paul had a keen sense of divine mission.[28] Furthermore, his apostleship was a specialized calling to take the gospel to the Gentiles (Acts 26:16–18). He had a new identity, determined not by ethnic lineage but by a faith relationship. His zeal shifted from a Torah-centered Judaism to a Christ-centered people of God that included both Jews and Gentiles—whoever put their trust in Jesus. Finally, his career shifted from a religio-political one that paralleled the Zealot party of the day to one that followed the way of the suffering of the cross (Acts 9:16; Phil 3:10; 2 Tim 1:11–12).

Becoming a New Person "in Christ"

The mission to which Paul was called took him from Damascus to Arabia, through Judea, on north to Syrian Antioch, then throughout Asia Minor and into southeastern Europe on what are known as his "missionary journeys," which are described in detail in the book of Acts. He even had his sights set for Spain at the western edge of the Roman Empire (Rom 15:24). The "good news" he proclaimed penetrated lives with a message of hope and purpose.

Paul's Message of Christ

Paul's message of newness *in Christ* was clothed in pastoral terms as he wrote to churches struggling with identity in hostile cultures. This practical approach to the challenges facing the church was built upon a theological foundation that emerged from a personal and intimate relationship with Christ. Paul's message was Trinitarian: fellowship with God by communion with Christ experienced through the presence of the Holy Spirit. At the focus of this was Jesus Christ who brings all things together (Col 3:17) and serves as the mediator between God and humanity (1 Tim 2:5). God had revealed himself to Israel through the Old Testament story, yet the problem of sin remained, resulting in a broken relationship between God and humanity (Rom 3:23). We were "enemies" of God, weak sinners going our own way (Rom 5:6, 8, 10), but God provided the answer for this universal

28. Sandnes, *Paul, One of the Prophets?*, 48–70.

problem through an immeasurable gift: "in Christ God was reconciling the world to himself" (1 Cor 5:19). For Paul, human life only makes sense as it relates to Jesus Christ.

Paul made claims about Jesus that shocked both Jews and Gentiles. One passage that especially reveals what he thought about Jesus is the opening of his letter to the Romans 1:1-6:

> Paul, a servant of Christ Jesus, called to be an apostle, set apart for the gospel of God, which he promised beforehand through his prophets in the holy Scriptures, concerning his Son, who was descended from David according to the flesh and was declared to be the Son of God in power according to the Spirit of holiness by his resurrection from the dead, Jesus Christ our Lord, through whom we have received grace and apostleship to bring about the obedience of faith for the sake of his name among all the nations, including you who are called to belong to Jesus Christ.

The message Paul preached was not something he made up but a fulfillment of prophecy (Rom 16:25-26). As a descendant of David, Jesus qualified to be King and Messiah and met every condition for Paul's devotion. As the Son, Jesus was the perfect representation of God. Jesus' sonship was confirmed by his resurrection; he was the only one ever to rise and never to die again. And then, Paul makes a significant claim that would speak loudly to both Jew and Gentile: "Jesus Christ our Lord." The name Jesus comes from the Greek word *Iēsous*, which is a translation of the Hebrew name *Yeshua* (Joshua), meaning "savior" (see Matt 1:21). *Christos* is the Greek word translated from the Hebrew *messiah*, meaning "anointed one." For many Jews, this person was expected to help usher in the "Day of the Lord" and re-establish the fortunes of Israel. Christ was both a description and title for Paul. Over time, it became more of a name to Paul. Its Jewish meaning would become lost as the church became more Gentile.

The next word was significant for both Jews and Gentiles. "Lord" is translated from the Greek *kyrios*, which is the Greek word translated in the Septuagint for the divine name, YHWH, the covenant name for God considered too sacred for a Jew to pronounce. Paul's concept of Jesus' lordship was grounded in the Old Testament but was easily understood in the Gentile world, where Caesar was also called "lord" or the various gods were "lords" (1 Cor 8:5-6). This title signifies power and position, and for Jesus, attributes divinity. Jesus was pre-existent, head over creation, and the one by whom all things came into existence (Col 1:15-17). Someday, all things will bow before him in worship (Phil 2:6-11). The title "Lord" also implies a master-slave relationship, and when Paul uses it, signifies the sovereignty of Jesus as "Master." For Paul, we are mastered by one of two things: sin (or the ways of the world) or Jesus.

Paul's message was the gospel *of Jesus Christ* (Rom 1:9; 15:29; 2 Cor 2:12; 9:13; 10:14; Gal 1:7; Phil 1:27; 1 Thess 3:2; 2 Thess 1:8). The good news of Jesus formed the primary core of his preaching. The message he received came *from* Jesus and was *about* Jesus.[29] The message is summarized in the form of a brief creed with four points in 1 Corinthians 15:3-5a: "For I delivered to you as of first importance what I also received: that Christ died for our sins in accordance with the Scriptures, that he was buried, that he was raised on the third day in accordance with the Scriptures, and that he appeared. . . ." This statement emphasizes the death of Christ by affirming his burial and emphasizes his resurrection by providing news of eyewitness reports of his post-resurrection appearances. This message was not something Paul or any other human made up (Gal 1:11), and what he "received" agreed with the teaching of the other apostles. Yet, there was a divine origin to this message that did not rely on any human-made tradition but came directly by revelation from God (Gal 1:12). This revealed message penetrated Paul's heart (Gal 1:16) and affected every aspect of his life, primarily because it was not simply a set of teachings or collection of words but was a person.

New Existence "in Christ"

Paul believed that the challenges faced by the early church were rooted in deep spiritual problems. He found answers to these problems in the person of Jesus Christ. Because of the disobedience of Adam and Eve in the garden of Eden (Gen 3), the shadow of sin swept over creation, leaving every human a slave to sin (Rom 5:12). All people join with the primordial couple in our own rebellion against God as we succumb to this power (Rom 3:23). This *disease* of sin affects every aspect of our lives, and without God's intervention, eventually leads to our destruction.

Paul's message of hope in Jesus Christ brings deliverance from the curse of the garden of Eden. Paul divided human history into two major periods: before and after Christ's death and resurrection. The age before Christ was controlled by the effects of Adam and Eve's disobedience, namely sin and death (1 Cor 15:21a, 22a). When our ancient parents disobeyed God, spiritual—and eventually physical—death entered the world. God had warned Adam, "In the day that you eat of the fruit, you shall surely die" (Gen 2:17).

---

29. In Gal 1:12, *Iēsou Christou* can be interpreted both as an objective genitive ("about Jesus Christ") and subjective genitive ("from Jesus Christ").

A separation between God and sinful humanity began that could only be healed by divine intervention. Life began to focus on self-preservation and gratification in created things rather than seeking worth in the one who created it (Rom 1:21-23). Finding worth in anything other than God (that is, *worshiping* anything other than God) leads to the breakdown of relationships with self, others, and the rest of creation. From the moment life begins, humans are on a journey to death, and sin, like a disease, accelerates this.

The good news, according to Paul, is that Jesus' death and resurrection decisively destroyed the power of sin and death. When Jesus died on the cross, he demonstrated God's love for us and redeemed us from the curse of sin (called justification). When he rose from the dead, he conquered the very power of sin, which is death (1 Cor 15:56; called sanctification). Death as the consequence of sin lost its power over humanity because Jesus the Messiah proved that he is superior to all other things, even death itself. The present evil age has lost its source of power and stands defeated before the cross. For the first time in history, with the Christ-event there is another alternative to existence *in Adam*. For the first time since Adam, sin no longer needs to be the dominant power (Rom 5:20-21) because Christ reverses the effects of Adam's fall. Christ restores what Adam lost in the fall, namely, the ability to have fellowship with the holy God. Those in fellowship with Christ can be restored to this holy fellowship and experience new freedom from the power and control of sin.

Paul believed that the death and resurrection of Christ inaugurated a new age of restored fellowship with the Holy One, but also that we still live in a time when sin and death are present, though they have already been defeated. There is a temporary overlap between this present evil age controlled by the way of Adam and the glorious age to come controlled by Christ. When Christ returns again, death will be finally defeated and the age of sin will come to an end (1 Cor 15:24-28). What brings freedom from the power of sin during this interim period is the Holy Spirit, who gives a new focus for life and transforms us into Christ's likeness by teaching us the mind of Christ and filling our lives with love. This happens only for those who have put their lives at the full disposal of Christ. The result of the presence of the Holy Spirit within believers is that they begin to model the holy character of God. They will live differently from those around them who remain controlled by the Adamic problem of *self*. Their relationships begin to heal, their outlook becomes optimistic, and their lifestyle follows a holy standard.

Conclusion

Paul's message cannot be reduced to just a few paragraphs. The message itself can be simply stated, but because it focuses upon the divine-human encounter, it invites readers of his letters to dig deeply and think broadly. There is more to this message than simply the ideas of forgiveness from the *past* and hope for eternal life in the *future*. For Paul, there is a profound relationship with God in Christ in the *present*. This message is not static or objective but significantly dynamic and penetrates to the very core of the human soul. This message changed Paul's life and he believed it could change those who openly received it into their own lives.

2

Paul, the "Mystic"

But we speak of the wisdom of God in mystery *which has been hidden, which God has destined before the ages for our glory.*

(1 CORINTHIANS 2:7)

AT THE HEART OF Paul's thought lies the *kerygma* (Greek for "proclamation") of Jesus Christ. This message involved more than knowing *about* Jesus the Messiah. Jesus was more than a person to be studied or admired; he was a power to be experienced. On the road to Damascus, Jesus captured Paul's attention and devotion, and from that point on Paul's attitude became, "I have been crucified with Christ. It is no longer I who live, but Christ who lives in me. And the life I now live in the flesh I live by faith in the Son of God, who loved me and gave himself for me" (Gal 2:20). The old Paul *in Adam* was gone and the new Paul *in Christ* had come (Rom 6:4–8). Paul was now part of a new creation *in Christ* (2 Cor 5:17). He presumed others could experience transformation through Christ like him, and so his mission was to proclaim this new life first to his own Jewish people and then, significantly in his mind, to the Gentiles.

His Christology is best described as experiential, as a personal encounter with the eternal God through Jesus Christ. Every key doctrine of Paul can find its roots in his experience of Christ, an experience not bound by a fading memory of the past but a present power through the abiding Holy Spirit. His most descriptive phrase for this relationship is being "in

Christ." In Colossians 1:26–27, he describes this relationship with God in Christ as a "mystery hidden for ages and generations but now revealed to his saints. To them God chose to make known how great among the Gentiles are the riches of the glory of this mystery, which is Christ in you, the hope of glory." This divine mystery should be the norm for all believers and is God's desire for all humanity.

Paul's communion with Christ has been interpreted as a form of mysticism. Mysticism is commonly understood to describe the experience, practice, or belief of a mystic, one who seeks experience or knowledge of that which is beyond the human realm of everyday existence, namely, an encounter with the divine. Albert Schweitzer, who interpreted Paul as a mystic, wrote, "The fundamental thought of Pauline mysticism runs thus: I am in Christ; in him I know myself as a being who is raised above this sensuous, sinful, and transient world and already belongs to the transcendent; in him I am assured of resurrection; in him I am a Child of God."[1] How Paul understood the experience of being in Christ has been a major topic of study. A first step in coming to some appreciation of the depth and dynamism represented in the Pauline letters is to consider Paul in his first-century context. By comparing his thought to other ancient sources, we can see his unique interpretation of mysticism.

The *Mystērion* of God

Interpreting Paul's Christology has been one of the most debated topics in the past century among Pauline scholars. Part of this debate focused on Paul's background; whether he was influenced more by Hellenism or Judaism, or some combination of the two. He used a number of words and concepts found in various religious movements of his time. One such word, "mystery," connects his experience of Christ with his theology. This word had a rich usage in the ancient world. Because many different religions used it for various purposes, careful consideration of the word in context will aid in interpreting what Paul meant by the divine mystery of Christ.

God's "Mysteries"

The English words "mysticism" and "mystery" share the same root ("myst") used in words describing something hidden or secret. A typical understanding of the word "mystery" in English is that it describes something

---

1. Schweitzer, *Mysticism of Paul*, 3.

enigmatic, secretive, or only partly understood. This English usage is similar but not quite the same as in ancient Greek and particularly by Paul.

These English words are derived from the Greek words *mystērion* ("mystery") and *mystikos* ("mysticism"). Both words come from the same Greek verb, *myein*, which means to close the mouth or lips, hence to keep something silent.[2] As with the modern English words, the Greek words were fluid in meaning, with different connotations depending on the context. This made it easy for Jews and early Christians to adopt them for a variety of situations. In a religious sense, *mystērion* refers to a divine, hidden secret humans are unable to understand unless it is revealed by God; unless God acts in grace or mercy, the secret will always remain a mystery. *Myeō* in the active voice denotes "to initiate" and in the passive "to be initiated." The uninitiated were unable to understand the secrets revealed to the initiated.

In Jewish literature, *mystērion* first appeared in the Hellenistic period. In the Wisdom Tradition, the word describes hidden secrets (Sir 11:4; 3:21) and is associated with wisdom (4:18; Wis 6:22). Wisdom is the means by which one is initiated into the mysteries of the knowledge of God (8:4). Elsewhere this word is used to describe cosmic secrets that God discloses to particular people (1 *En.* 41:3; 60:11; 3 *Bar.* 1:8).

In the Septuagint, *mystērion* often translates the Hebrew word *sod*, the secret "counsel" or "confidential speech" of God or of the heavenly assembly. God makes his *sod* known to those who walk in fear of him (Ps 25:14; Prov 3:32). The prophets had special access to God's *sod* (Jer 23:18; Amos 3:7). In Daniel, *mystērion* translates the Aramaic *raz*. In the Septuagint of Daniel 2:18–23, God's mysteries are revealed to Daniel in a dream as a result of prayer. Only God can reveal mysteries and make it possible for Daniel to reveal these mysteries to King Nebuchadnezzar (2:27–30, 47). Because the Spirit of the holy God was with him, Daniel could interpret the mysteries or meanings of the dreams of Nebuchadnezzar, which turned out to be about future events (4:6–27). Revelation is critical in the Septuagint for understanding God's mysteries.

The word *mystērion* is found in the New Testament outside of Paul in several places. The word occurs once in the Synoptic Gospels when Jesus speaks about the "mystery of the kingdom" having been given to the disciples (Mark 4:11; see Matt 13:11; Luke 8:10). In Mark, there is a steady disclosure of the person and authority of Jesus. The opposition to Jesus mounts as the battle lines are drawn regarding his authority. Jesus reveals himself by working miracles and speaking parables, but people do not understand his parables; a certain element remains a secret (John 10:24). People gain access

---

2. Bornkamm, "*Mystērion*," *TDNT*, 4:803.

to these mysteries by their openness to Jesus and his message. Mark 4:12, quoting Isaiah 6:9–10, mentions an intentional hardening of Israel; Jesus intentionally conceals some things so that the Jews will believe his word and not simply his works. Part of the concept of Mark's use of the singular *mystērion* for the kingdom is with reference to Jesus' ministry: the kingdom has come with the preaching and ministry of Jesus (1:15). In the Synoptic tradition, only the Father can reveal the significance of Jesus (Matt 11:27; 16:17), which is implied in the passive verb "has been given" (*dedotai*) in 4:11. Only the disciples and those of faith can understand the mysteries of Jesus' parables; those on the outside remain in the dark. Only special revelation available by faith in Jesus' words reveals the mysteries of the parables.

Mystērion occurs in the book of Revelation four times. Revelation as an apocalypse uses mystery to refer to supernatural communication. In 1:20 the hidden meaning of the seven stars and lamp stands is revealed to John. In 10:7 the long-hidden mystery of God will be accomplished, implying some action on God's part.[3] In 17:5 and 7 the mystery is something that must be told by an angel to be understood.

The Merging of *Mystērion* and *Mystikos*

The term *mystikos* was used in the mystery religions to describe the secret ceremonies of the mysteries. The word also appears in three types of literature in Jewish and early Christian traditions. The first was Jewish biblical interpretation most notably from Alexandria, Egypt, represented by Philo (ca. 20 BC – ca. AD 50). One of the first to merge the concepts of mysticism and mystery in the Christian context were the early church fathers from Alexandria, such as Clement of Alexandria (ca. 150 – ca. 215) and Origen (ca. 185 – ca. 254), who used the term *mystikos* like Philo for interpreting Scripture. They viewed Christ as the sole mystery of God revealed in Scripture. The word was used for all knowledge of divine things that came through Christ, and then by derivation, to those things themselves. Cyril of Alexandria (ca. 370–444) then used the term in a liturgical sense to describe the mystical experience illuminating Christ through the sacraments. Denis the Areopagite (mid-third century) finally used the term in a spiritual sense to describe the invisible spiritual world about which the Scriptures speak and which is revealed in Christ.[4]

---

3. Compare Amos 3:7, where the prophets are given a special revelation of God's plans.

4. Louis Bouyer, "Mysticism: An Essay on the History of the Word," in Woods, *Understanding Mysticism*, 42–55.

Although the two terms are related linguistically, "mystery" is more of a Pauline word than "mysticism." The closest use of the word *mystikos* by Paul would be the similar word *memyēmai* in Philippians 4:12, where he writes, "in all things I have learned the secret of." Since the term "mysticism" arrived later in the Christian tradition, it should not be used in reference to Paul without careful qualification.

"Mystery" is a more comprehensive word than "mysticism" to describe Paul's communion with Christ for several reasons. First, there is the simple fact that *mystērion* was part of Paul's vocabulary. Mysticism as communion with God through Christ arose out of the concept of the mystery of Christ. There is no exact equivalent in the Greek of Paul's letters for the term "mysticism" (*mystikos*), whereas there are many examples of "mystery" (*mystērion*). Paul's mysticism was intricately tied up in his understanding of the divine mystery. He describes this communion in terms of being *in Christ*, who, as the mystery of God, makes possible the relationship that could then be described as mystical.

Second, the word *mystērion* contains the eschatological connotations found in the Jewish apocalyptic tradition and expresses the longing for the end of the present evil world, which Paul believed had already begun with the death and resurrection of Jesus Christ. The concept of mystery in apocalyptic thought fits well with the new worldview and personal transformation that Christ brought in Paul's life. It also agrees with Paul's understanding of Jesus as the fulfillment of biblical prophecy. Paul maintained that the Scriptures spoke about Jesus, and because of Paul's experience of the mystery and commission to preach about it, he subsequently had the means to understand the prophecies spoken in the Jewish Bible. Like the community at Qumran who wrote the Dead Sea Scrolls, Paul held that he had the hermeneutical key (Aramaic *pesher*) to unlock the secrets of the Scriptures (see Rom 1:1–4).

Third, *mystērion* was a word Paul could define in his own way and fill with his own content. It was part of the common vocabulary of almost every major religion that he encountered in his travels. Like the modern word "mysticism," *mystērion* was so broad in its semantic range that he could use it in a context that fit his theology. He used the term much like others did during his time. In addition, by its very definition, *mystērion* had to be modified by some other word or concept to have meaning ("mystery of . . .").

Fourth, it was a word that Paul's converts knew and used in their former religious practices. By changing their concepts about the divine mystery, he could influence their beliefs. Both Jews and Gentiles may have been familiar with the concept of deity disclosing secrets to elect people. Paul may have perceived this and so used the term in reference to God's disclosure of the secret of Christ as a way to spread the gospel. He could contend that the mystery of Christ was the answer to the hopes of both Jews and Gentiles for a new revelation from God.

Mystērion in Paul's Letters

The word *mystērion* occurs only twenty-one times in Paul's letters.[5] Since the concept represented by the word was so important in his mind, one might wonder why he used the word so few times. The answer may be that the concept behind the word was more important than the word itself. The word described a much broader issue for him, namely, his communion with Christ and the implications of this relationship. It is only one of the many ways Paul describes his "mysticism." Context and usage are important when investigating his concept of *mystērion*. Just because he uses a word found also in the Greek mysteries or Hellenistic Judaism does not mean he is referring to the same ideas of these religions. He uses the term within the semantic range common in the Greek language of his day but fills it with his own content. He uses the term in at least six ways.

First, he uses the word without describing what the mystery is. For example, in 1 Corinthians 14:2 he uses it almost adverbially: "by the Spirit he speaks in mysteries." The one who speaks in a tongue speaks a spiritual language only God can understand and that does not edify the church. This type of language is inferior to prophecy because it is unintelligible and not useful for edifying the church or witnessing to unbelievers. In 1 Corinthians 13:2 Paul also uses the word in a generic way and with a negative connotation: even if one can "understand all mysteries," this is meaningless without love. Evidently, speaking in angelic tongues was one of the sought-after spiritual gifts for the Corinthians, yet Paul puts it below love. For the Corinthians, understanding secret matters of the Spirit came by means of prophetic powers. He debunks these attitudes in comparison to the superiority of love. The word occurs in a general sense in 2 Thessalonians 2:7 as the "mystery of lawlessness" that is already at work but will be revealed at the end of time through a "man of lawlessness."

Second, Paul uses the term in the plural for God's secret plans. In 1 Corinthians 4:1 Paul understands himself to be a steward of God's mysteries. He has access to the secrets of God and can make them known to others. Being a steward requires being trustworthy (4:2), which he tries to prove by his careful argumentation in this section of the letter. This stewardship gives

---

5. Rom 11:25; 16:25; 1 Cor 2:1 (a textual variant), 7; 4:1; 13:2; 14:2; 15:51; Eph 1:9; 3:3, 4, 9; 5:32; 6:19; Col 1:26, 27; 2:2; 4:3; 2 Thess 2:7; 1 Tim 3:9, 16.

him a special position of authority that he uses to convince the Corinthians to change their behavior. The content of these mysteries can be assumed from the context to be the ramifications of the gospel to which Paul as a spiritual person had access by the Holy Spirit.

Third, he uses the term in Romans 11:25 to refer to the final salvation of the Jews. He attempts to make sense of the difficult question of why the Jews had rejected Messiah Jesus. There is a certain, divine secret that troubles Paul as he writes this letter that he considers important for the believers in Rome to know. He had been granted knowledge of the divine plan for the Jews and wants the Romans to be aware of it. The basic content of this plan is that the gospel is to be preached to the Gentiles, an act that would eventually lead to the salvation of the Jews.

Fourth, Paul speaks of the mystery of the resurrection in 1 Corinthians 15:51. As in Romans 11:25, Paul acts as a steward of the divine mystery here dealing with eschatological promises. By revealing this mystery, he attempts to end the confusion or misunderstanding the Corinthians had about the resurrection of the dead. He wants to set them straight by making the divine plan understandable even though it still remains to a point mysterious to him.

Fifth, he refers to the cosmic mystery of Christ in 1 Corinthians 2:7. He speaks "in a mystery" of the wisdom of God, namely, Jesus' death on the cross. The ultimate wisdom of God long hidden has now been revealed in Jesus Christ. This wisdom is the ultimate divine mystery, the highest and most significant divine secret ever to be revealed. "The mystery of God" in 2:1 is amplified in verse 2: "Jesus Christ and him crucified."[6] Romans 16:26 also gives the content of the divine mystery as Jesus Christ. Paul uses two parallel phrases, "according to my gospel and the proclamation of Jesus Christ" and "according to the revelation of the mystery." He describes this "mystery" as something revealed, kept secret for a long time, disclosed in part through the prophets, for all nations, in line with God's command, and for the purpose of the obedience of faith. The divine mystery is Christ, and this revelation is not to be kept secret any longer but is for all who will respond in faith to the message. First Timothy 3:9 states that one of the essential qualities of deacons is that they must hold to "the mystery of the faith," likely referring to the confession given in verse 16. Verse 16 uses the phrase "mystery of godliness" for the following hymn reflecting the revelation of Christ from birth to glorification.

---

6. There is a textual variant in v. 1 with the reading *martyrion* ("witness") having strong manuscript support, but the earliest manuscripts have *mystērion*, which fits better the context and later usage of the term in v. 7.

The most developed use of *mystērion* in Paul's letters can be found in the Prison Epistles of Colossians and Ephesians. In these letters can be found the logical conclusion to what is implied in the other letters. As in 1 Corinthians 4:1, in Colossians 1:26 Paul has become a steward of the divine mystery (here in the singular), which is described as "the word of God" (1:25). The mystery is specifically made known to the Gentiles in 1:27. This verse also significantly equates the mystery as "Christ in you." Here, the goal in Paul's proclamation of the mystery is that every person will become perfect or mature in Christ (*teleion en Christō*, v. 28). This thought is reiterated in 2:2, where Paul desires that the Colossians and Laodiceans might understand the disclosure of God's mystery, which is Christ. The theme of Paul's preaching about the mystery of Christ is repeated in 4:3.

The Letter to the Ephesians develops these concepts the most and locates the mystery on the cosmic level. In 1:8–9 God reveals his mystery in wisdom and insight. Significant in the context is the repeated use of the phrase "in Christ" or its variations. Paul's visionary experiences of the mystery described in 2 Corinthians 12 and Galatians 1 are combined with the content of the mystery in Ephesians 3:1–11. Several other important themes are merged here. Once again Paul describes himself as a steward of the mystery (3:2) and is granted special insight into the meaning of the mystery (3:4). The mystery which had been hidden has now been revealed to the apostles and prophets by the agency of the Spirit (3:5), a theme consistent with 1 Corinthians 2:6–16. Part of the mystery is that the Gentiles can participate in Christ (Eph. 3:6, 8). Paul was chosen as minister of the mystery (the "gospel," v. 7) by grace. The mystery is also connected with the revelation of God's wisdom (v. 10). The mystery long hidden shows God's eternal purposes, which have been revealed in Christ Jesus (v. 11). This passage provides the highest logical conclusion of Paul's understanding of the divine mystery as Jesus Christ. In 5:32 the mystery referred to is the relationship between Christ and the church. Finally, 6:19 states that the mystery is the gospel.

In summary, Paul uses the term *mystērion* mostly in reference to God, Christ, and the gospel, but at the heart of the divine mystery is Christ. Paul was able to put the divine plan into one comprehensive term. The mystery shows several stages of being revealed. The first is that God has disclosed his divine plan most fully in Christ. The next stage of revelation is to apostles and prophets. The final stage is disclosure of the mystery to all people, both Jew and Gentile, by means of the apostles and prophets. Gunther Bornkamm comments, "Since the *mystērion* of God as such is disclosed in revelation, its concealment is always manifest with its proclamation."[7]

Experiencing the Divine in the Ancient World

Often in ancient literature, the divine mysteries are disclosed by means of mystical experiences. This raises two important questions: what precisely is a "mystical experience"? And, is there any justification in calling Paul a "mystic" or in investigating Paul's "mystical experiences"?

Part of the problem of whether Paul was a mystic has to do with the definition of "mysticism." Those who deny any mystical element in Paul generally view mysticism as the human becoming completely absorbed in the divine, a complete melting of human and divine until the human is lost. As Alfred Wikenhauser comments, "According to them, a mystic is one who indulges in religious feelings while remaining passive in matters of conduct, and who strives for an ecstatic vision of God in order to become divine."[8] Paul as a Jew kept a distance between himself and God, although an intimate communion with God is evident in many passages in his letters. Often the presuppositions of the interpreter determine the label of mystic. Samuel Brainard writes that "though we certainly ascribe to mystics the more knowledgeable judgment in matters of mystical phenomena, the judgment of an experience's veracity—of whether an experience is genuinely mystical or merely delusionary—is made by the one applying the label 'mystical.'"[9] Wayne Proudfoot also suggests that calling an experience "mystical" "is very likely an artifact of the past two centuries of European scholarship on the subject . . . [and] that we cannot accurately ascribe it to people in other cultures and other periods."[10]

Scholars of religion vary on their definition and description of what is called a "mystical experience." Most definitions share one essential quality evident in Paul's testimony: the dualistic experience of transcendent reality, or as Rudolph Otto describes it, the identification of the personal Self with the transcendent Reality.[11] Evelyn Underhill defines mysticism as "the art of establishing" a "conscious relation with the Absolute," or the "innate tendency of the human spirit towards complete harmony with transcendental

---

7. Bornkamm, "*Mystērion*," *TDNT*, 4:822.
8. Wikenhauser, *Pauline Mysticism*, 101.
9. Brainard, "Defining 'Mystical Experience,'" 379.
10. Proudfoot, *Religious Experience*, 124.
11. Otto, *Idea of the Holy*, 22.

order."¹² William James provides four defining traits or marks of experiences that might be called mystical: (1) ineffability, (2) noetic quality, (3) transiency, and (4) passivity on the part of the mystic.¹³ Andrew Louth writes that mysticism "can be characterized as a search for and experience of immediacy with God. The mystic is not content to know *about* God, he longs for union with God."¹⁴ Adolf Deissmann calls this union "direct intercourse with God."¹⁵ Gershom Scholem defines a mystic as one "who has been favored with an immediate, and to him real, experience of the divine, of ultimate reality, or who at least strives to attain such experience."¹⁶ Bernard McGinn opts for the terms, "an immediate consciousness of the presence of God."¹⁷ According to Brainard, "Scholarly usage of the phrase 'mystical experience' almost invariably intends a personal encounter with (or an enduring dwelling within) a domain of experience that is of principal metaphysical value and interest vis-à-vis other life experiences."¹⁸

With the rise of postmodern philosophy, scholars have recognized that taking mystical experiences out of their contexts makes them unintelligible.¹⁹ Brainard writes that the problem arises when one looks for universal traits across religious and cultural boundaries. Furthermore, the definition of mystical experience must be wed to its context to gain meaning.²⁰ Scholem asserts, "There is no mysticism as such, there is only the mysticism of a particular religious system, Christian, Islamic, Jewish mysticism and so on."²¹ Mystical experiences can be interpreted differently by different people.²² Paul More writes,

> There is thus a ground of psychological experience, potential in all men, actually realized in a few, common to all mystics of all lands and times and accountable for the similarity of their reports. But upon that common basis we need not be surprised to see them also erecting various superstructures in accordance with their particular tenets of philosophy or religion. At bottom,

---

12. Underhill, *Mysticism*, xiv.
13. James, *Varieties of Religious Experience*, 379–83.
14. Louth, *Origins of the Christian Mystical Tradition*, xv.
15. Deissmann, *Religion of Jesus*, 195.
16. Scholem, *On the Kabbalah*, 5.
17. McGinn, *Foundations of Mysticism*, xvii–xix.
18. Brainard, "Defining 'Mystical Experience,'" 375.
19. Katz, *Mysticism and Philosophical Analysis*, 47.
20. Brainard, "Defining 'Mystical Experience,'" 360, 368.
21. Scholem, *Major Trends in Jewish Mysticism*, 6.
22. Stace, *Teachings of the Mystics*, 10.

their actual experiences, at the highest point at least, will be amazingly alike, but their theories in regard to what has happened to them may be radically different.[23]

Furthermore, to call Paul's mystical experience "union with God" or "union with Christ" includes an assumption about Paul's belief about God. It is Paul's theological interpretation of an inward or spiritual experience based upon his faith in a divine Creator and Savior.[24] This is not to claim or deny the reality of this experience for Paul, but rather, to set his experience and thought within a specific context. This context was varied, with many possible overlaps and influences upon his thought and the world in which he ministered.

Platonism

The writings and philosophy of Plato (ca. 429–347 BC) permeated the ancient world and may have had some influence upon the thought of Paul through the *Zeitgeist* ("spirit of the age") of the Hellenic movement, which began with the conquests of Alexander the Great in 334 BC. Platonism was modified by various groups and used as the philosophical foundation for the thought of the Hellenistic culture. Platonism influenced Judaism through such Jews as Philo of Alexandria and the Jewish wisdom and apocalyptic traditions, which Paul may have known. Traces of Platonic mysticism can be seen centuries after Plato and may have played an implicit part in Paul's conflict with various opponents and movements affecting his churches.

Mystical experiences and thought penetrate Plato's philosophy. Plato held that God or the divine, what he sometimes calls the Demiurge, created the universe and gave the soul immortal reason. Lesser gods created the lesser parts of the universe and the human body (*Tim.* 40A, 41A–43A). The mystical core of Platonism is the idea that the soul is akin to the divine and makes it possible for humans to participate in divine existence.[25]

For Plato, the goal of the philosophical quest is vision of the divine, called the Beautiful, Good, eternal, incorruptible, or constant, and the ability to distinguish between real truth and its appearance (*Symp.* 210–11; *Resp.* 508–9). This is made possible by ascending to the divine and becoming like it (*Thaet.* 176B). By ascending from the world of sense perception to the realm of ideas or the real, the soul returns to where it properly belongs—with

---

23. More, *Christian Mysticism*, 93.
24. Stace, *Mysticism and Philosophy*, 37.
25. Louth, *Christian Mystical Tradition*, xiv.

God.²⁶ The soul is bound to this world by the senses. By detaching from the senses and the body, which hinders it from attaining truth and wisdom, the soul can once again join the divine (*Phaedr.* 65E–66A). Ultimate reality or the ultimate Good is unknowable except through contemplation and ecstasy (*Phaedr.* 64A; *Ep.* VII, 341). Death then is release and separation from the body (*Phaedr.* 75D).²⁷

The philosopher is the one who is able to break the hold of this world and transcend to ultimate reality. Only a limited number of people can become true philosophers (*Phaedr.* 69C). For Plato, the experience of the philosopher is also the experience of the mystic: "Both must undergo long and strenuous preparation in thought and life, both may hope at last to come to an illumination that is like the torches lighted at Eleusis or, as Plato puts it (*Ep.* VII, 341C-D), 'like a blaze kindled by a leaping spark.'"²⁸

The Platonic dialogue and contemplation are the processes by which one becomes enlightened. Andrew Louth comments, "In contemplation, then, we might say, the soul realizes its kinship with the divine; that in its flight from this world it becomes *divine*."²⁹ The purpose of the dialogue is to free the soul through contemplation and intellectual perfection from the ignorance that entraps it (*Phaedr.* 251A). The soul forgets its knowledge of eternal truths (forms and ideas) when it is confined to a body. Philosophy or education reawakens the soul by helping it see the bounds of the world of senses (*Resp.* 518B–D). In this way, philosophy is preparation for death (*Phaedr.* 66E–67A). Plato writes in the *Timaeus*,

> But he who has seriously devoted himself to learning and to true thoughts, and has exercised these qualities above all his others, must necessarily and inevitably think thoughts that are immortal and divine, if so be that he lays hold on truth, and in so for as it is possible for human nature to partake of immortality, he must fall short thereof in no degree; and inasmuch as he is for even tending his divine spirit and duly magnifying that daemon who dwells along with him, he must be supremely blessed.³⁰

Plato's philosophy had a lasting influence upon the mysticism of the ancient world. Many classical philosophers such as Plato visited Egypt and may have come in contact with the mystery religions. The procession of the

26. Louth, *Christian Mystical Tradition*, xiv.

27. The famous "Allegory of the Cave" in Plato, *Resp.* 7.527A–C, serves as a vivid example of this philosophical quest.

28. Finegan, *Myth and Mystery*, 178.

29. Louth, *Christian Mystical Tradition*, 14.

30. Plato, *Tim.* 90.

Eleusinian mysteries may have passed by Plato's academy in Athens on its way from Athens to Eleusis.[31] Walter Burkert suggests that Plato's *Phaedrus* later became the basic textbook for mysticism.[32] According to Louth, Christianity and Platonism met primarily on the level of mysticism.[33]

Platonism may have been a significant influence upon what Hans Jonas has called an "oriental wave" that swept through the Hellenistic culture at the turn of the era. He describes the general religion of the period as a "dualistic transcendent religion of salvation."[34] The religious atmosphere of the first century in respect to mystical experiences could be described with the following basic movements.[35] First, a new anthropological awareness arose of an inner, essential person viewed as immortal. Second, the goal became to transcend the earthly or bodily barriers that held the inner person captive, and then to ascend to the divine realm to which the soul belonged.[36] Third, there was a problem in reaching to the absolute transcendence of this realm. God was viewed as unknowable and indescribable. God could only be spoken of negatively—what God was not. Fourth, an intermediary or intermediaries reconciled these two problems and bridged the gulf between the soul and God. Fifth, this intermediary, seen as a *deuteros theos* or "second god," took different forms and titles: for example, *Logos* (word) for Christians and *Nous* (mind) for Middle Platonists and Gnostics. Giovanni Filoramo comments, "He has the dual function of manifesting and setting up the plan conceived by the Father within the divine world and realizing it in the external world."[37] Hence the mediator functioned as a savior figure. Sixth, liberation or salvation became an inward, spiritual struggle. Without divine intervention and grace, it was impossible to save oneself from the bondage of worldly existence.[38] Seventh, early on it was believed that

---

31. Finegan, *Myth and Mystery*, 177.

32. Burkert, *Ancient Mystery Cults*, 92.

33. Louth, *Christian Mystical Tradition*, xiii.

34. Jonas, *Gnostic Religion*, 31–32.

35. These points are based on Filoramo's discussion on new religious horizons leading to the emergence of Gnosticism in *A History of Gnosticism*, 22–37.

36. Grant, *Roman Hellenism*, 47–53, attributes the increasing emphasis upon transcendence, universal law, astrology, mysticism, and occultism to the new geocentric scientific view of the universe and its effects upon religious thinking: "for how else could men come in contact with these transcendent astral or super-astral deities ('the elemental spirits of the universe,' Gal 4:3) except by the inner pathway of renunciation, asceticism, the observance of rigid rule of life, and the cultivation of inner forces enabling one to lay hold upon the divine powers superior to external nature" (48–49).

37. Filoramo, *History of Gnosticism*, 26.

38. This period could be characterized by pessimism regarding earthly existence and the longing for a better, spiritual existence above. See Dodds, *Pagan and Christian*.

intermediary figures like priests, prophets, magicians, or interpreters were needed to find the divine will. But later a change occurred in that personal communication with the divine was sought. Finally, the rise of interest in ecstatic, revelatory visions through which mysteries of the divine realm were given, in other words, a communion with the divine, can be seen. Elements of this "oriental wave" and the Platonism that stands behind it appear with the same basic structure but in different terminology and content in the *Hermetica* and in the Jewish movements before and contemporary with Paul.[39]

The Old Testament

A more explicit influence upon Paul and the Judaism of his time was the Old Testament. Paul was immersed in the sacred scriptures of the Jews. The Hebrew Bible or the Septuagint, the Greek translation which Paul likely used in his travels, served as the primary source for his mysticism primarily because this literature was the dominant authority for him.[40] His writings show familiarity with the Septuagint through numerous quotations and allusions. His worldview was influenced by the Jewish Scriptures but significantly modified by his experience of the risen Christ Jesus.

Spirit-Possession

A significant motif for mystical experiences in the Jewish Scriptures can be seen in the Spirit of God dwelling within or possessing a person. One example of this is Paul's namesake, Saul, son of Kish. After Saul was anointed the first king of Israel by Samuel, he experienced possession by the Spirit of God described in 1 Samuel 10:9–11. Verse 10 gives an interesting sequence. First, the Spirit of God came upon Saul as an ecstatic empowerment. The result was transformation and the ability to prophesy, which was not a normal ability of Saul, as the question of a man implies in verse 12: "Is Saul also one the prophets?" The Spirit of God was the source of Saul's frenzy and subsequent transformation (10:6).

Possession of a person by the Spirit of God brought a change most often in the form of prophesying (Saul), added strength (the various judges such as Othniel, Gideon, Jephthah, and Samson), and speaking divine words (David in 2 Sam 23:2). The Spirit gave special insight as in the case

---

39. See Dodd, *Interpretation of the Fourth Gospel*, 14–17; Scott, *Hermetica*.
40. Ellis, *Paul's Use of the Old Testament*, 21; See Hays, *Echoes of Scripture*.

of Bezalel's construction of the tabernacle and ark (Exod 31:3; 35:31). Pharaoh recognized that some spirit was at work in Joseph, who was able to interpret Pharaoh's dream (Gen 41:38). The Spirit empowered Ezekiel to speak to twenty-five men (Ezek 11:5). Music could set the tone for Spirit-possession or for prophesying as in the case of Saul (1 Sam 10:5) and Elisha (2 Kgs 3:15). Spirit-possession also identified the true prophet (Mic 3:8). The prophets believed they were in direct contact with God and were God's mouthpieces (Isa 8:11; Jer 15:19; Amos 3:8). As a result of Spirit-possession, Ezekiel was unable to move after his prophecy (Ezek 4:4), and Jeremiah experienced pain and anguish (Jer 4:19). The prophets had a special relationship and experience with God by their knowledge of him and ability to speak his word (Hos 2:2).

In all of the above examples, communion with God through the indwelling Spirit was an occasional experience dependent upon the divine purpose (see Num 11:25). However, there was an eschatological hope in a universal outpouring of God's Spirit on all of Israel. Moses was unable to stop the seventy-two elders from prophesying, but said, "I wish that all the Lord's people were prophets and that the Lord would put his Spirit on them!" (Num 11:29, NIV). This longing is expressed again in Joel 2:28-32 (see Acts 2:14-21). In Ezekiel 36:27 this hope is found in an eschatological prophecy of the promise of a return of Israel to the promised land (see also Isa 44:3).

The people of Israel had a fear of God withdrawing his presence because of his judgment upon their disobedience (Exod 33:3). They believed that God's presence descended upon the tent of meeting (Exod 40:34-35) and the temple built by Solomon (2 Chron 7:16). This led to a false security against which some of the prophets spoke (Mic 3:1-4). Jeremiah and Ezekiel recognized that the only way to keep the terms of the covenant was for God to make an inward change marked by the indwelling presence of his Spirit (Jer 31:31-34; Ezek 11:19; 36:26). Isaiah, often called the prophet of the Spirit, had already foreseen that day in his hopes of the renewal of Israel (Isa 32:15; 44:3). For Paul, this longing for the indwelling Spirit was fulfilled and made possible through the death and resurrection of Jesus Christ. The indwelling Spirit of God was one of the confirmations of the divine mystery for Paul. The Spirit became for him the means by which one could have communion with God.

Visions of God

Another significant evidence of mystical experiences in the Old Testament can be seen in various visions of God. The use of the term "vision" here does not imply that the sight of God was either an inward psychological experience or an outward physical encounter, but was simply the experience of recognizing the divine presence. There are three basic types of visions of God given in the Old Testament. The first type is the vision of the radiant glory of God in a terrestrial setting. Moses serves as the prime example of such a vision of God.[41] During the exodus from Egypt, Moses had numerous encounters with Yahweh and functioned as the mediator between Yahweh and the Hebrew people. This can be illustrated with the incident in Exodus 33:12–23, where Moses interceded with the Lord so that the Lord would not withdraw his presence from among the people because of their sin with the golden calf. Moses had two personal goals in this intercession: to know God and to find favor with him (v. 13). God was willing to listen to Moses because God knew Moses by name (v. 17). The verb translated "to know" (*yada'*) denotes a close personal knowledge found in intimate relationships (see Deut 34:10; Ps 139:2). Moses believed the key for knowing God was to see God's glory (v. 18). God answered that no one could see his face and live (v. 23). The divine glory is associated here with God's face and is the very expression of God's person. God conceded and allowed Moses to see only reflections of this glory, which is described with the divine name Yahweh, compassion, grace, patience, love, faithfulness, and justice (Exod 34:6–7). God's holiness and transcendence stand out in this passage, as does the need for some type of mediation. Thus, Moses had a close and personal encounter with the divine, a mystical experience, yet was kept at a distance because of God's complete otherness.

After this encounter, Moses came down from the mountain with a radiant face that reflected the glory of God to which he had been exposed (34:29). Paul comments on Moses' experience in 2 Corinthians 3:7–18 in a comparison between the old and new covenants. The transformation of Moses and the glory he experienced pale in comparison to the glory and transformation brought with the new covenant in Christ (v. 10). In this passage, Paul uses the rare word *anakalyptō*, meaning "to hide" or "to bury" (3:14, 18). The mystery of the gospel remains veiled or hidden to unbelieving Jews. Only "in Christ" can the veil be removed (v. 14). In other words, Christ makes it possible for the glory of God to be unveiled and experienced in ever-increasing measures (v. 18). To see Christ is to see God in all his glory.

---

41. Moses, as well as Abraham and Jacob, served as a paradigm of the mystical experience for later Christian mystics. See McGinn, *Foundations of Mysticism*, 4.

Just as Moses' face was transformed by beholding God, so the believer's face or countenance is transformed by beholding Christ. Paul describes one of his experiences of seeing Christ later in the same letter in chapter 12.

The second type of vision is one of the heavenly throne scene. There are three illustrations of this in the Old Testament. The first occurrence is with Micaiah, son of Imlah, who received a message for King Zedekiah from God, whom Micaiah saw sitting on the throne in heaven surrounded by heavenly hosts (1 Kgs 22:19–23). Another example is when Isaiah saw a vision of God's throne when he received his commission (Isa 6:1–8). No information about the setting of Micaiah's vision is given, whereas with Isaiah the time, place, and full content of the vision is provided. Isaiah's vision occurs during the difficult and uncertain days following the death of the great King Uzziah of Judah. Evidently, Isaiah was in the temple when he had a vision of God's high and exalted throne in heaven. Flying around the throne were six-winged heavenly creatures called seraphs calling out, "Holy, holy, holy is the Lord Almighty; the whole earth is full of his glory." God's holiness is emphasized here with the seraphs' description of God and Isaiah's response of confession. Noteworthy is the fact that Isaiah did not give any other direct portrait of God besides the rather abstract description of God's holiness. Because of the great gulf between Isaiah the sinner and the holy God, God sent one of the seraphs to cleanse Isaiah's lips with a hot coal, making Isaiah ready to be God's holy mouthpiece to the rebellious people of Israel and Judah.

The next vision of the heavenly throne scene was experienced by Ezekiel. Ezekiel's vision is much more developed than the simple description of Micaiah's vision, and each major component of Isaiah's vision is elaborated upon in Ezekiel's vision but with different names and descriptions. For example, Isaiah's six-winged seraphs are similar to Ezekiel's four-winged living creatures with four faces, wheels, and spirits. The description of these creatures and their movement is given in much greater detail than the seraphs and takes up a majority of the verses (5–21) in chapter 1. Noteworthy in Ezekiel's vision is his obscure description of the throne and the figure who sits upon it, which is still more detailed than the one in Isaiah. This throne, situated above an awesome crystal expanse sparkling like ice (v. 22; compare Rev 4:6), shone like sapphire (v. 26). Ezekiel called the glittering figure sitting upon the throne "a man-like figure," who shone like glowing metal and fire with a brilliant rainbow surrounding him (vv. 26–28). Ezekiel like Isaiah fell face down before the scene of God's glory. Even in this description, Ezekiel says nothing about the face of this figure; he only heard a voice. He was able to respond to God's awesome glory only because the divine Spirit entered him and raised him up, after which he received his prophetic commission to go to rebellious and stubborn Israel in exile. He could have been sent to the Gentiles, who would have listened to him, but God sent him to the hard-hearted people of Israel (3:5–7). Ezekiel's vision ends with his transportation by the Spirit to the Jewish exiles, leaving him in a state of bewilderment (3:12–15).

Like Micaiah, Isaiah, and Ezekiel, Paul experienced rejection by his own people. According to Acts 18:6, he stopped preaching to the Jews in Corinth because of their opposition and lack of belief and thereafter focused on the Gentiles. On the one hand, he felt his special calling was as a messenger to the Gentiles, but on the other hand he never gave up on his own people and probably kept preaching to Jews whenever the opportunity arose (Rom 10:1–3). To him, all were in need of salvation through Jesus Christ (Rom 3:22–24, 29–30). Paul saw himself standing in the long line of prophetic messengers calling the Jewish people to return to God.

These visionary experiences of the heavenly throne stand in the background of many of the visions in Jewish apocalyptic literature. These visions highlight God's majesty and transcendence. There is no suggestion of the merging of the visionary and the throne figure. The visionaries realize their place as imperfect subjects before the mighty king. After each vision, a specific task is given to the visionary, a task that, without divine authority and empowerment, would be very difficult because of rejection. The vision provides the call and the authority to do the divine will. These are factors that inform Paul's visionary experiences as well. For him, mystical experience of the divine presence brings transformation and proclamation.

The third type of vision of God is mediated by angels. Ancient Israel had the belief that because of God's complete holiness, people could not see him face to face. Israel did not have a developed philosophy of God's transcendence in a Platonic sense in which God could not descend to the earth from heaven. In the Hellenistic age, the transcendence of God became an important issue, as demonstrated by Philo. One of the functions of angels in the Jewish Bible is mediation between the holy God and sinful humanity. Angelic messengers make an indirect vision of God possible. These angelic messengers are described with several different terms. The typical Hebrew term for the Greek *angelos* is *mal'ak*, which literally means "one who is sent to speak for another." Other terms include *qadoshim*, meaning "holy ones"; *bene 'elohim*, "sons of God"; *tseba'ot*, "hosts"; and *misharathim*, "ministers." Angels are always associated in the Bible with the mission of proclaiming the divine will and message (Job 33:23). They were the answer to God's holiness and transcendence. Their appearance is not described in detail but often they were human in form (Gen 18:2, 16; Ezek 9:2).

There are many angelic appearances in the Hebrew Bible. Genesis and Exodus, in particular, describe the angel of the theophany. When Hagar faced destruction in the desert after rejection by Abram and Sarai, an angel of Yahweh appeared to her. She understood the messenger in some sense as Yahweh himself, as her special name for God suggests: *'el ro'eh*, the God of seeing (Gen 16:7–14). In Genesis 18 Yahweh appears to Abraham in the form of three men. In Genesis 22:11, when Abraham was about to sacrifice Isaac, he heard a voice from heaven, later described as an angel of the Lord who spoke as Yahweh (vv. 15–18). The text in the Jacob narrative says that Jacob wrestled with a man (32:24), but Jacob believed he wrestled with God himself, as his new name, Israel ("struggles with God"), and the name of the place, Peniel ("the face of God"), indicate (vv. 28, 30). Another theophany occurs in Exodus 3:2 when God spoke to Moses in a burning bush. The voice was that of an angel (v. 2) but heard as the voice of God (v. 6). Even though it was only an angel speaking, the place was considered holy because of the presence of God. Later, the angel of the exodus carried the divine name and authority to forgive sins and should not be disobeyed (Exod 23:20–22). The Israelites understood that they were not to worship the angels but Yahweh alone (20:4–5). Other texts also speak of theophanic messengers (e.g., 2 Kgs 1:3). Angels were the answer to the need for God's immanence in the face of God's transcendence.

In apocalyptic texts, angels serve as human-like tour guides and interpreters of divine mysteries. In his tour of the new Jerusalem and temple, Ezekiel was guided by "a man whose appearance was like bronze" (Ezek 40:3). Zechariah was also guided in his vision by an angel who interpreted the various symbols given in the vision (Zech 1:7—6:8). The figure Ezekiel saw on the throne was in "the likeness of glory of the Lord" (Ezek 1:26-28). This figure latter guided Ezekiel on his visionary journey to Jerusalem (8:2-4). Daniel sought an angelic interpreter to help him understand his vision of the throne scene (Dan 7:16). The angel Gabriel, who had the "appearance as a man," helped Daniel interpret his vision of the end of time. Later the angel Gabriel again provided Daniel wisdom and understanding of his vision of seventy weeks (9:21-23). In apocalyptic texts outside Scripture, this theme is further developed. For example, Enoch is guided on his heavenly journey by an angel of the Lord (*1 En.* 17-36).

Paul's references to angels are a complex topic.[42] He may have known of the place of the mediation of angels in the apocalyptic tradition and surely knew of the angel of the theophany in Scripture.[43] What is particularly note-

---

42. See Carr, *Angels and Principalities*.

43. On the development of mediatory figures in Judaism, see Andrew Chester,

worthy is that Christ became for Paul the prime intermediary between God and humanity (Rom 8:34; 1 Tim 2:5). Paul did not see a vision of an angel of the Lord but saw the risen Jesus (Gal 1:12). He expressed his version of theophany in the concept of Jesus Christ being the image of God (2 Cor 4:4; Phil 2:6; Col 1:15). Angelic messengers were no longer necessary for him because of the presence in the life of believers of the Holy Spirit, who reveals the divine will (1 Cor 2:12, 16). He was immersed in Scripture and tradition but interpreted both through his own experience of the risen Christ Jesus.

Wisdom Traditions

A further basis for Paul's mystery and mystical experiences can also be seen in the Jewish wisdom traditions. These traditions had a long history, reaching back to oral legacies older than the patriarchs, and were developed through writing during the time of the rise of monarchy in Israel around the tenth century BC. Solomon has traditionally been attributed with the rise of classical biblical wisdom. The divine gift of wisdom did two things for Solomon: it gave him prestige and strength in the ancient world (1 Kgs 4:32; 10:1–13) and demanded that he be obedient to Torah (1 Kgs 3:14). The relationship of wisdom and commandment later became central to Jewish wisdom traditions.

Wisdom describes both a literary genre and a way of thinking. It tries to make sense of human life in this world in relation to God through knowledge and practical living. It shows that the way to obedient life and the way to please God is through the law. God is the source of all wisdom (1 Kgs 4:29–34; Job 28; 38:36). The way to gain wisdom is described in Proverbs 1:7—9:18. The point of departure for biblical wisdom comes at its beginning point: wisdom comes through fear or reverence of Yahweh (1:7). Exclusive worship of Yahweh is one of the central themes of the Torah and the faith of ancient Israel (Deut 6:4-6). One gains wisdom and understanding by obedience to the law through devotion to God. In contrast to the wise person, the fool is one who lives without God (Ps 14:1; Isa 32:6).

A noteworthy piece of tradition appears in Deuteronomy 29:29, which reads, "The hidden things [*nistharoth*] belong to Yahweh our God, but the revealed things [*nigaloth*] belong to us and our children forever, in order that we may do all the words of this law."[44] This statement echoes the pro-

---

"Jewish Messianic Expectations and Mediatorial Figures and Pauline Christology," in Hengel and Heckel, *Paulus und das antike Judentum*, 17–89.

44. In the Septuagint, the Hebrew words *nistharoth* and *nigaloth* are translated *krypta* and *phanera*. The emphasis in this verse is on keeping the law.

phetic, apocalyptic, and wisdom theme that God himself would reveal to Israel what was needed to follow adequately his commands. The answer to this longing in the wisdom tradition is that wisdom itself provides the answer to the human problem of keeping the law.

The intertestamental wisdom literature was built on themes found in the Hebrew Bible and began to incorporate mystical themes emerging in this period. One important theme is that wisdom is hidden; it is disclosed only through divine revelation. Wisdom is first and foremost a divine attribute, a reflection and emanation of God's power and an image of his goodness (Wis 7:25–26). Since one can gain knowledge of God through wisdom, one can understand all the hidden things of the universe by wisdom (Wis 7:15–21). The law is also central to this later wisdom literature. Wisdom is the key to understanding the interpretation of the law (Sir 39:8). A reciprocal relationship exists in that wisdom is contained in the law, but by studying the law one finds wisdom. The way to keep the commandments of God is to follow wisdom (Bar 3:9—4:1). Wisdom discloses the divine order given in the law (Sir 39:1–11). Keeping the commandments brings more wisdom (Sir 1:26; 51:35–36) for the simple reason that the heart of the law is the fear of the Lord, which is also the beginning of wisdom. In other words, the truly wise person heeds God's commands concerning the worship of God (Sir 19:20). Thus, the knowledge of wisdom and of the law leads to salvation and eternal life because one is following the God-given path to righteousness.

The central goal of wisdom is to know God, to be near him and reign with him forever, resulting in immortality (Wis 2:23; 3:4; 5:15; 6:17–19; 8:17). Wisdom is also the key to being initiated into the knowledge of God's mysteries (Wis 8:4). The mysteries of the divine will or, one could say, the mysteries of the law of God, are hidden from humanity but revealed to the wise (Sir 4:18; 11:4; Wis 6:22). Sirach 14:20–21 says, "Blessed are those who meditate on wisdom and who reason with insight. Those who reflect in their hearts on her ways will also consider her secrets."

There are two ways by which one attains the goal of wisdom. The first is through the inspiration of divine grace, the primary means of disclosure of the mysteries. The only way to find wisdom is through divine revelation (Sir 39:5). The mysteries of God are beyond human comprehension without the revelation of their meanings by God. However, human effort works with divine grace through a willing and open mind. There are three levels of people in regard to knowing wisdom. At the first level are those who have forsaken the law and, by this, forsaken wisdom; they are also called the ungodly and sinners, and are accursed at death (41:8–14). At the second level are others who have not forsaken the commandments and can see God's wisdom in nature, but they have not been given the secrets of the mysteries of God in nature (42:15—43:33). This is reserved for the third level, represented by the sage ("wise person"), who has direct access to God's wisdom (see the catalog of heroes in 44:1—50:23).

The ability of the sage to receive and interpret the mysteries of the law comes through divine inspiration (Sir 39:8-11). Wisdom reveals itself to those who are worthy, holy, and righteous (Wis 4:15-16; 6:16). The sage can achieve perfection in this life by pleasing God through seeking wisdom and obedience to the divine command (Wis 4:13; 9:6). The sage must actively seek wisdom and prepare for divine disclosure of its mysteries through preparation in prayer (Wis 9:9) and meditation (Sir 14:20-21). God then gives his Spirit to help in understanding these mysteries (Sir 39:6-11). The seeker after wisdom experiences intimacy with God, not through ascension, but through inner devotion to wisdom (Wis 6:17-20).[45]

One of the basic themes in this tradition is that wisdom is not accessible to those who reject it (Sir 1:20-32; 1 *En*. 42:1-3; 84:3) but is revealed to those who are prepared to receive the divine disclosure and actively seek it (Sir 24; Bar 3:9; 4:2; Wis 7:24-27). Wisdom literature seeks to reveal the mystery of the law. A variation of these themes can also be found in Paul's thought. Paul uses the same words about Christ as the wisdom tradition uses for wisdom and law, but he changes the focus of wisdom from the law to Christ. Human wisdom at its best comes from God through the Holy Spirit and results in proclamation of the gospel (1 Cor 2:2-5). For Paul, Christ is the revealed wisdom of God, the great mystery of God's wisdom (1:30). The requirement of righteousness on the part of the sage is replaced by the gift of divine righteousness in Christ (1:30). The wisdom of the world pales in comparison to this hidden wisdom of God that is available to those who seek it (1:18-25; 2:6-10). The seemingly foolishness of the cross-event actually is the means by which God reveals his wisdom to humanity. The cross-event then becomes the primary means of disclosure of the divine wisdom, Christ Jesus.

For Paul, there are levels of people in regard to the divine mystery of Christ. Unbelievers do not have access to the wisdom of God in Christ because they fail to see the significance of the cross. They are not called wise, although in their own eyes they are, but are called fools because they do not recognize Jesus Christ as the Lord in their search for wisdom (1 Cor 1:22-23; see Prov 1:7). Immature believers in the faith have only a partial knowledge of the mystery because they have only partially appropriated the mystery of Christ. Paul calls these people *sarkinos* ("fleshly"), or bound to this present evil existence, and puts some of the Corinthians in this class

---

45. McGinn, *Foundations of Mysticism*, 19.

(3:1). The *pneumatikos* ("spiritual") or mature are the equivalent to the sage in the wisdom tradition and have been given the secret of the divine mystery and are now "in Christ." They are no longer bound to this present age but live a new existence. The Corinthians misunderstood the full implications of the mystery of the divine wisdom, and so Paul seeks in 1 Corinthians to correct this fundamental error in their thinking.

Jewish Apocalypticism

Another and possibly more significant influence upon Paul was Jewish apocalypticism. Apocalypticism, both Jewish and Christian, relied on the Hebrew Scriptures as a source and motif-arsenal for apocalyptic statements.[46] Apocalyptic literature arose in a context of uncertainty when the present age led to despair and people longed for a new age in the future.[47] Both doom and hope are present in apocalypticism. Apocalypticism has been recognized as a distinctive literary genre distinguishable by its eschatological orientation.[48] In general, the word *apokalyptō* means to reveal, disclose, or bring to light. In a religious sense, it is used for the revealing of divine revelation or certain supernatural secrets.[49]

The characteristic eschatology in apocalypticism involves the belief in an early end to the world or this present age, which is governed by evil powers. Only the person to whom God has revealed the secrets or mysteries knows about the end, and this knowledge leads to salvation. The unrighteous are those who do not know the mysteries. The righteous are strangers in this age and belong to the age to come. In apocalypticism, there is a void between earthly existence and God, who is far removed. Intermediaries can transverse this distance by heavenly journeys or visions by which they receive secret wisdom and knowledge about the mystery of life at the end of this age.

---

46. Elisabeth Schüssler-Fiorenza, "The Phenomenon of Early Christian Apocalyptic: Some Reflections on Method," in Hellholm, *Apocalypticism*, 302.

47. von Rad, *Theologie des Alten Testaments*, 327, suggests that apocalyptic arose out of the wisdom traditions, thus the similar motifs.

48. The Society of Biblical Literature Genres Project has provided a broad definition of apocalyptic genre: "Apocalypse is a genre of revelatory literature with a narrative framework, in which a revelation is mediated by an otherworldly being to a human recipient disclosing a transcendent reality which is both temporal, insofar it envisages eschatological salvation, and spatial, insofar as it involves another, supernatural world" (Collins, *Apocalypse*, 9). Compare Richard E. Sturm, "Defining the Word 'Apocalyptic,'" in Marcus and Soards, *Apocalyptic and the New Testament*, 24, 36; Käsemann, *New Testament Questions of Today*, 134.

49. BDAG, 92.

The pseudonymous central characters in this literature were chosen from the Hebrew Bible as people who had special encounters with God (e.g., Enoch, Moses, Isaiah) or special access to God's prophetic work (e.g., the scribes Baruch and Ezra). These characters had visionary experiences, often at night, in which they saw certain events and symbols of the end that needed interpreting. These visions were mediated by an angel or some other heavenly figure (1 En. 60:11). For example, Baruch was grieving over the destruction of Jerusalem when an angel appeared to him to show him the mysteries of God, mysteries never seen before (3 Bar. 1:4, 6). The angel then led Baruch through various heavens revealing the mysteries to him (1:8).

During these visionary experiences, various mysteries were disclosed which focused on three key subjects. First, central to many visions is a character called by various names, including "Son of Man" (1 En. 46:2), "Chosen One" (40:5), "Lord of the Spirits," "Lord of Wisdom" (63:1-4), "Messiah" (48:10), the "Son of God" (4 Ezra 13:32), and others. He is identified with the "Lord of Glory" in 1 Enoch 63:2, 11. The "Son of Man" is the central figure of Enoch's vision (48:2-3), providing insight and understanding (49:3), revealing secrets to the worthy (46:3; 48:10; 49:3), but baffling the rulers of the world (46:4-6). He reveals the wisdom of God to the righteous and holy, and salvation is in his name (48:7). The "Elect One" has wisdom, gives thoughtfulness, knowledge, and strength (49:1-4).

Another subject disclosed through mystery is the wisdom of God, as seen in Enoch's second vision in 1 Enoch 37. Wisdom aids in the study and interpretation of Torah (2 Bar. 48:23-24). By wisdom one can also know the secrets of heaven (1 En. 60:11). The third revealed subject concerning future existence appears in an eschatological context where wisdom leads to knowledge and understanding of these future mysteries, which then give meaning to the present time. The idea of mystery is combined with eschatology (2 Bar. 81:4; 85:8; 4 Ezra 6:32-33; 10:38; 14:5), and the future events and plans of God are revealed in these visions (4 Ezra 4; 13:48).

There are several means by which these mysteries are disclosed. The explanation of the vision comes to a soul devoted to Torah, steadfast to God's wisdom (2 Bar. 38:3-4), and spotless before God (54:5). These visions come by the great mercy and grace of God (81:4). Because Ezra sought only God's ways, searched God's laws, and was devoted to wisdom, he was given the reward of interpretation (4 Ezra 13:53-56). He asked for the Holy Spirit so he could write down all the secrets revealed from the beginning. He then was given wisdom or the "lamp of understanding" as the key to interpretation (4 Ezra 14:15-48).

The effects of these visionary experiences are also noteworthy. Enoch was transformed at his ascent in anticipation of the transformation at the end of time (*1 En.* 14). Later his face was changed (39:14) and his spirit transformed (71:11). After this transformation Enoch cried "with a great voice by the spirit of the power, blessing, glorifying, and extolling" (71:12). Transformation in the eschaton can go two ways. Evil people become more wicked and suffer torment. The righteous become gloriously changed and are promised eternal life. They are changed into the splendor of angels, their faces into the light of their beauty (*2 Bar.* 51:1–6). The outcome of a visionary experience may not always be positive, as when Ezra awoke troubled and needed an angel to attend him (*4 Ezra* 5:14–15).

Paul's mystery is disclosed in apocalyptic understanding. He believed his kerygma was received as an apocalypse or revelation (Gal 1:2). Much of his thought is expressed in apocalyptic terms and images. Ernst Käsemann's statement is true also about Paul: "Apocalypticism is the mother of all Christian theology."[50] Apocalypticism was an ideology that could be used and modified by various groups for their own purposes. Paul consciously or unconsciously used apocalyptic concepts to express his understanding of the gospel. He, like many of the hero figures in Jewish apocalyptic, had visionary experiences, but the heavenly figure he believed he saw was the risen Christ Jesus. His perception of the dualism of the two ages—so common in apocalyptic thought—was significantly modified by his understanding of the cross-event. He held that the death and resurrection of Christ inaugurated a new age, but also that there is still a temporary overlap between this present evil age and the glorious age to come. The power of this present evil age, which is symbolized in sin and death, has been conquered by Christ's redemption and resurrection. Only those in Christ can live in victory over this evil age. The apocalyptic message of Christ impacts daily existence in the life of the community of believers. The heart of Paul's mystical experience of the divine mystery is cloaked in apocalyptic terminology and imagery.

Qumran

Another movement worthy of note in the Jewish milieu of Paul was the community of Essenes located near Kirbet Qumran in the Judean desert. It is unknown exactly when this community arose, possibly several centuries before Paul's time, but it was likely destroyed in the Jewish revolts against Rome in AD 66–70, which would put them roughly contemporary with Paul. It is generally assumed that when siege by the Romans was imminent in their eyes, these Essenes deposited their important documents

---

50. Käsemann, "Beginning of Christian Theology," 40.

in clay jars in nearby caves. Some documents are clearly sectarian and were authoritative to the community, and some of the biblical texts found in the caves show distinct sectarian interpretations. These ancient texts show that the Qumran sect shared in Paul's apocalyptic orientation, which has caused some scholars to consider whether Paul knew of this community or whether they both shared in a common Jewish heritage.[51] The latter is more likely, although it is not beyond possibility that Paul may have come in contact with the teachings of Qumran during his stay in Damascus after his visionary experience of Jesus.[52] The similar apocalyptic orientation makes a brief look of the mysticism found within the Dead Sea Scrolls helpful for a better understanding of general apocalyptic hopes during the time of Paul. According to Josephus, the Essenes were known for their interests in prophecy.[53] The community of Essenes at Qumran believed itself to be specially elected by God to restore the faith of Israel in terms of covenantal renewal in fellowship with God and with the angels (1QS 3:11; 4:22).

In this self-professed privileged position, the Qumran community considered itself to have access to divine mysteries that gave it special communion with God. The basic theology of Qumran centers around the concept that all things are dependent upon God and his sovereignty is over all (1QS 11:11; 1QH 10:1, 8–11; 15:8). Everything God does and allows ultimately reveals his glory (1QH 2:24). God has a secret plan for the outcome of history that is described with the term "mystery" (*raz*) or with the plural "mysteries." The mysteries are beyond human understanding and no one can access them except through divine grace in revelation (see 1QS 9:18; 11:19). In mercy God reveals knowledge of his truth and reveals his mysteries, which lead to salvation through cleansing from sin, resurrection from the dead, and joining the heavenly hosts in a new creation (1QH 11:8–14). The primary means by which God communicates the mysteries is through his Spirit (1QS 4:3; 1QH 12:11; 13:19).

There are two basic classes of mysteries: those given to all people (1QH 4:29) and those given only to the elect of the community (1QS 4:6; 9:17).[54] The one who has a spirit of flesh cannot comprehend the mystery of divine wisdom (1QH 13:12–14), nor can sinners see the truth of God (1QH 5:25). Part of God's mysteries is the grace of forgiveness of sins and the restoration of the remnant as the true Israel. The content of the mysteries varies but falls

---

51. Lapide, *Paulus—zwischen Damaskus und Qumran*, 104-26; Eisenman, *Maccabees, Zadokites, Christians*, 68–70.

52. Gal 1:17; William David Davies, "Paul and the Dead Sea Scrolls: Flesh and Spirit," in Stendahl, *Scrolls and the New Testament*, 158.

53. Josephus, *J.W.* 1.3.5.78–80; 2.7.3.111–13.

54. R. Brown, *Semitic Background*, 25.

under four basic categories. The first are cosmic mysteries, which are secrets of the created order hidden until revealed by wisdom (1QH 1:11-12). The second are the historical mysteries of divine election and salvation of the remnant of Israel, which is the community (1QM 7:14; 14:14). The third are future mysteries by which God has determined the end when the mysteries will be revealed (1QS 4:18-19) and the community vindicated (1QM 17:17). The theme of the *War Scroll* (1QM) is the eschatological battle at the end of time in the fashion of a holy war when the community will triumph over its enemies. God also will reveal his wisdom to those who are devout, which will lead to their salvation (1QS 11:3-5). The Teacher of Righteousness will be given the mysteries of God's salvation at the right time (CD 1:11; 1QH 5:11-12).

The fourth type is the mysteries contained in Scripture. The Scriptures are mysteries that need interpreting by the community. This can be seen in use of the term *pesher* ("interpretation"). *Pesher* is used in Daniel in the context of the mysterious handwriting on the wall of King Belshazzar's banquet hall (Dan 5:7, 12, 15). No one could interpret these words except Daniel because only he had the divine Spirit and the insight, understanding, and wisdom (v. 14). The Qumran elect may have had this context in mind when they used the word *pesher* to describe their own interpretations of the divine mysteries. In rabbinic literature, *pesher* was used to explain difficult passages in the Bible or Mishnah.[55] Behind *pesher* is the idea that the mysteries contained in Scripture must be interpreted or revealed in order to be understood. The sectarian community of Essenes believed it only had the key to the right interpretation (1QpHab 2:6-9; 7:4-5). The community thought it was given a higher revelation of the meaning of the Torah. The interpretations are always concerned with the eschatological outcome of the community. The community saw itself as the remnant that would restore the law for Israel (1QS 1:1-10).[56]

The official mediator of the divine mysteries to the community was the Teacher of Righteousness. The scrolls provide no name to this important person but assume he was a historical person. The Teacher of Righteousness held a significant place at Qumran (CD 1:11). His position was to instruct in the ways of God and prepare the people for salvation on the Day of Judgment (1Q14). The Teacher of Righteousness bears the mysteries that lead to the salvation of the community (1QH 4:27; 7:26; 11:4, 8, 9, 27, 28; 12:11) and that God has made known to him through inspired interpretation (1QpHab 7:3-4). The Qumran psalmist, possibly the Teacher of Righteousness (cf.

---

55. Ringgren, *Faith of Qumran*, 8.
56. See Horgan, *Pesharim*; Bruce, *Biblical Exegesis in the Qumran Texts*.

1QH 1:21 and 1QpHab 7:3-4), also was given the divine mysteries (1QH 7:26-33). In *Thanksgiving Hymns* he says, "But to the elect of righteousness thou hast made me a banner, and a discerning interpreter of wonderful mysteries, to try [those who practice] truth and to put to the test those who love correction" (1QH 2:13-14). He reveals God's hidden knowledge and glory to the community (1QS 11:5-6; 13:14-15). By the Holy Spirit the psalmist makes known the mystery of God's wisdom (1QH 12:11-13; 7:6; 17:26). The ultimate purpose of the divine mysteries is to show the community the way to salvation (1QH 1:21; 2:3). God opens the heart to saving knowledge of him (1QS 11:3) and provides insight into his truth (1QH 7:26-27). The mysteries of God's marvelous truth help the elect of the community to walk in the perfection that comes by obedience to God's laws and renewal in covenant (1QS 8:18, 21, 25; 9:5-9; 11:5-8).

The mystical tendencies of the community are suggested also by a lack of angelic intermediaries between God and humanity, a difference from the mediatory figures common in apocalyptic texts. This group believed it had a more direct access to God and that it was in a special position compared to those outside the community. Thus, angels were not seen as intermediaries but only as messengers in the line of the traditions of Scripture.[57] A passage in the *Melchizedek* scroll (11QMelch 24-25) suggests that Michael the archangel, here called Melchizedek, presides in the eschatological judgment and is the deliverer of the people. Yet, the community thought it would someday join in the fellowship with the angels (1QS 11:7; 1QH 3:21), and by this gain direct access to God (1QH 7:12). Mysticism also exists in the "Songs of the Sabbath Sacrifice" or *Shabbat Shirot*, also known as the Angelic Liturgy (4QShirShabb or 4Q400-407). These texts relate in detail the worship of angels and the movement of the heavenly throne-chariot and contain many elements common with early Jewish Merkabah mysticism, such as references to divine hierarchies, seven heavens, and the appearance and movements of God's throne-chariot.[58]

The Dead Sea Scrolls share many similar themes and vocabulary with apocalyptic literature, including dualism of light and darkness, the revelation of divine mysteries, salvation by divine grace, special position of elect people to know the mysteries, angelology, and eschatology. That the Qumran sect was interested in apocalypticism is evidenced by the presence of copies of some early apocalyptic literature in the collection of manuscripts

---

57. Ringgren, *Faith of Qumran*, 81-87.

58. See Segal, "Paul and Ecstasy," 560; Strugnell, "Angelic Liturgy at Qumran," 318-45; Newsom, *Songs of the Sabbath Sacrifice*; Gruenwald, *Apocalyptic and Merkavah Mysticism*, vii.

found.[59] Even though there are some shared elements, the community had its own interpretation of time and Torah. For example, the scrolls show no evidence of apocalyptic visions. Vision and knowledge of God comes directly to those chosen and ready to receive it.[60]

Some of the shared overlaps between Qumran and apocalypticism can also be seen between Paul and Qumran but significant differences also exist. Revelation of divine mysteries was central for both Paul and Qumran, but the subject of these mysteries differs significantly between the two. The revelation of Torah and renewal of covenant in the community were the focus of the mysteries for Qumran.[61] Paul connects the divine mystery to Christ and the gospel. For Qumran, the Teacher of Righteousness was the bearer of the mysteries but was not the mystery. For Paul, Christ is the mystery. Like the Teacher, Jesus was a historical person for Paul, but also the exalted Lord and Messiah. Walter Grundmann states, "Paul acknowledges in the crucified and risen Jesus the promised messiah, whom Qumran awaited but failed to recognize."[62] Divine revelation for Qumran was reserved for the elect community. Paul believed his message was to be given to all people. In other words, the exclusiveness of Qumran contrasts to the openness of Paul. Pierre Benoit has argued that the Qumran community lived in the world of the "Old Law" and its revelation never went beyond the prophets, while Paul saw himself standing at the dawn of a new age initiated by the revealed mystery of Christ.[63] The community claimed itself as the new covenant remnant of Israel (CD 6:19; 19:33), similar to Paul's claim of new covenant in Christ. The means of keeping covenant are significantly different. Obedience to Christ replaces obedience to Torah for Paul who saw Christ as the ultimate purpose of the law. Because Christ had come, time for Paul had been forever altered. Qumran still awaited restoration of the law and covenant. Simply stated, the most significant difference between Paul and Qumran is the content of the divine mystery and the implications of this revelation for humanity.

---

59. E.g., *1 En.*, *T. Levi*, and *Jub.*

60. See A. Brown, *Cross and Human Transformation*, 56.

61. Collins, *Apocalyptic Imagination*, 121.

62. Walter Grundmann, "The Teacher of Righteousness of Qumran and the Question of Justification by Faith in the Theology of the Apostle Paul," in Murphy-O'Connor, *Paul and Qumran*, 114.

63. Benoit, "Qumran and the New Testament," 24.

Philo of Alexandria

Philo of Alexandria provides a connection between the philosophical system of Plato and the Jewish apocalypticism familiar to Paul and illustrates how Hellenism had permeated Jewish thought by the first century. Philo, a contemporary of Paul, was a Jewish scholar from Alexandria who lived from about 20 BC to AD 50. He is best known for his attempts to Hellenize Judaism. According to Berger Pearson, Philo's thought is a fusing of "Hellenistic Jewish wisdom and Middle Platonic categories."[64] Philo was aware of classical Greek literature and rhetoric, which he used in his writing, but he tried to remain loyal to the basic tenets of Judaism. It is doubtful that Paul knew who Philo was, but not out of the question. More of a factor at this point is the Hellenistic Judaism Philo represents and how that Judaism shares common elements with Paul. Behind both Paul and Philo stands a common wisdom tradition as well as an interest in mystical experiences.[65]

The ultimate goal for Philo was to have knowledge or a vision of God.[66] The fundamental problem with this in Philo's theology is the Platonic concept that God is distant and unknowable. Knowledge of God is beyond human comprehension because of human fallibility and God's transcendence, and it comes only through divine grace (*Mut.* II.7, 10). According to Philo's interpretation, in reply to Moses' request to see God face to face, God replies, "But not only is the nature of mankind, but even the whole heaven and the whole world is unable to attain to an adequate comprehension of me" (*Spec.* I.44). The only way to know God is through the evidence of his works, which are knowable on the human level. In Platonic terms, humans can only see the shadow of God or the evidences of God in the world. Louth comments,

> We know him, it is because he has established a relationship with us. So, in that sense, God is unknowable in himself, and knowable only in so far as he relates himself to us. . . . God, then is unknowable in himself because of his simplicity and man's incapacity, but he can reveal himself according to man's capacity and does so, especially as Ruler and as the Bountiful.[67]

---

64. Pearson, *Gnosticism, Judaism, and Egyptian Christianity*, 176.

65. On the shared wisdom tradition between Paul and Philo, see J. Davis, *Wisdom and Spirit*.

66. Winston, *Logos and Mystical Theology*, 54. Sandmel calls Philo a "philosophical mystic" who goal was union with God (*Philo of Alexandria*, 124).

67. Louth, *Christian Mystical Tradition*, 21.

It is impossible in Philo's thinking for humanity to be in the exact image of God because God is perfect and beyond creation. To reconcile this, Philo believed that God created the mind, the highest part of the human, in the form of the Logos, which Philo called a "second god." The Logos is a mediator between the perfect God and the imperfect person. The Logos is the revelation of the essence of God and the image of what one can become (*QG* 2.62; *Spec.* 1.81; *Fug.* 101; *Somn.* 1.239). What one sees is the Logos (*Conf.* 97). James Dunn comments, "The Logos for Philo is 'God' not as a being independent of 'the God' but as 'the God' in his knowability—the Logos standing for that limited apprehension of the one God which is all that the rational man, even the mystic may attain to."[68]

A fundamental concept for Philo is that knowledge of God is given by God and not obtained by human contemplation. The soul can perceive God only because it has received part of God. Without any divine assistance, one cannot possibly cross the distance between God and humanity. Philo writes,

> The Creator made no soul in any body capable of seeing its Creator by its own intrinsic powers. But having considered that the knowledge of the Creator and the proper understanding of the work of Creation, would be of great advantage to the creature (for such knowledge is the boundary of happiness and blessedness), he breathed into him from above something of his own divine nature. And his divine nature stamped her own impression in an invisible manner on the invisible soul, in order that even the earth might not be destitute of the image of God. (*Det.* 86)

God has revealed himself on several levels, each of which must be mediated. On the simplest level, all people can see evidence of God in nature (*Leg.* III.97–99). Yet, nature alone gives only a partial glimpse of God. The next level of God's self-revelation is through Torah. Philo is similar to the wisdom traditions in that wisdom for him is the true path of philosophy by which one can know God through Torah. The highest level for Philo is direct communion with God without any mediation. Moses is the paradigm of this when God spoke to him directly in Exodus 33 (*Leg.* III.103). Louth comments,

> There is no guarantee of success on the quest: for God must reveal Himself, and the soul can do nothing to elicit this disclosure—it can only prepare. But even so, the quest by itself is sufficient satisfaction. One might say that the quest is the goal

---

68. Dunn, *Christology in the Making*, 241.

and the goal is the quest. In any case, to be engaged on the quest for God is what matters.[69]

Philo provides a number of steps in the migration of the mind or soul to God, or what could be called the quest for communion with God. The first thing one must do is to relinquish "genealogical science" or astrology, which makes the universe God and the stars causes of good and evil (*Migr.* 194). God grants knowledge of himself in response to beholding the world with the vision of the soul and longing for wisdom (*Spec.* I.49–50). One then continues by moving from outside oneself to within oneself by gaining self-knowledge, where the mind is able to overpower the body and its senses, which then enables one to know the nature of God (*Migr.* 195). For Philo, the *nous* or mind is the most important part of the soul. He says, "For the mind which exists in each individual has been created after the likeness of that one mind which is in the universe as its primitive model, being in some sort the God of that body which carries it about and bears its image within it" (*Opif.* 69). The *nous* comes to full realization of self and God. Eventually, it will be dazzled by the brilliance and greatness of God. The mind is considered perfect when it gives God proper tribute (*Migr.* 139). After putting off the world and the body, one can then comprehend God himself. The law plays a significant part in this quest. Obedience to the law is necessary in the path to perfection. The path of wisdom is the only way by which one can escape this world and find God (*Deus* 160). Central to the soul's quest for God is meditation upon the word of God, the "fountain" of divine wisdom (*Fug.* 97).

The sage who pursues wisdom is the one who attains knowledge or the vision of God. This person has freed him or herself from the bonds of the body and the world of senses and is drawn towards God. Philo writes,

> For while the mind is in a state of enthusiastic inspiration, and while it is no longer mistress of itself, but is agitated and drawn into frenzy by heavenly love, and drawn upwards to that object, truth removing all impediments out of its way, and making everything before it plain, that so it may advance by a level and easy road, its destiny is to become an inheritor of the things of God. (*Her.* 70)

This state of ecstasy is the result of viewing true reality that is in God, not the shadow of reality that appears in this world (*Her.* 71). As the soul returns to its creator, escorted by love, the guide of wisdom, it sees through its pure

---

69. Louth, *Christian Mystical Tradition*, 31.

intellect him whom it is alike. The soul becomes lost in its communion with the divine when it reaches this stage, as Philo writes elsewhere,

> It becomes seized with a sort of sober intoxication like the zealots engaged in the Corybantian festivals, and yields to enthusiasm, becoming filled with another desire, and a more excellent longing, by which it is conducted onwards to the very summit of such things as are perceptible only to the intellect, till it appears to be reaching the great King himself. (*Opif.* 71)

Philo describes four types of ecstasy in his work *Quis rerum divinarum heres sit*: madness or melancholy caused by infirmity of mind, consternation when something goes wrong, tranquility or stillness of mind through reducing the outward senses to a state of inactivity, and divine possession or frenzy. The last is the highest state for Philo and is the goal of prophets by which divine inspiration reveals hidden things (*Her.* 249-64). He says, "For the mind that is in us is removed from its place at the arrival of the divine Spirit, but is again restored to its previous habitation when that Spirit departs, for it is contrary to holy law for what is mortal to dwell with what is immortal" (265). God completely takes over the prophet so what is heard is actually the word of God. In *De Cherubim* Philo uses language reminiscent of apocalyptic and wisdom literature in describing those who have come to knowledge of God as "those initiated persons who are worthy of the knowledge of the most sacred mysteries, the whole nature of such divine and secret ordinances" (42). The special knowledge so desired by Philo is available only to those initiated or considered worthy to receive it. The mysteries are the secret interpretations of Scripture that tell the way to communion with God (48).

There are two noteworthy examples that illustrate mystical experience for Philo. The first is Moses, whom Philo holds in high esteem. Moses was initiated into the divine mysteries and instructs those with pure ears in these mysteries (*Gig.* 54). In other words, Moses knew God face to face, gave the law, which was supreme for Philo, and was able to instruct others how to know God through the law. Moses had a prophetic mind that became so filled with God that it was changed into the divine (*QE* 2.29; *Sacr.* 8-10; *Mos.* 1.158).[70]

The other significant example of mystical experience is Philo's own. Philo desired more than anything else to rise to the state of enthusiastic inspiration by which he could know God in heavenly love and inherit the things of God (*Her.* 70; cf. *Cherubim* 27). He considered himself also an initiate into the mysteries and took Moses, the chief visionary, and Jeremiah,

---

70. See Goodenough, *By Light, Light*, 215.

the paradigmatic prophet, as his teachers (*Cherubim* 49). He describes how he sometimes would go to study philosophy empty, but suddenly become full of ideas through divine inspiration. He would lose sense of time, place, and self as he became "conscious of a richness of interpretation, an enjoyment of light, a most penetrating sight, a most manifest energy in all that was to be done" (*Migr.* 35). In *De specialibus legibus* Philo describes this experience of studying the divine commands of Moses, "irradiated with the light of wisdom," transported in a sense beyond the physical world, and revealing "to those who wish to understand, the things concerning them which are not known to the multitude" (*Spec.* III.6).

A prime example of Philo's mystical tendencies can be seen in his allegorical interpretation of Scripture. In his allegorical method of interpretation, Philo sought the deeper, "spiritual" meaning of the Scripture. His goal in writing was to understand the depths of Torah and thereby experience knowledge and communion with God (*Post.* 18). Comprehending the deeper meaning of the law leads to relationship in covenant (*QE* 2.42). Allegory provides the means by which the soul may return to God.[71] In investigating Philo's allegorical method, one must remember his starting point that only God can illumine himself and enable one to see him. In this regard, God reveals the deeper meaning of the Scripture and the mysteries it contains by means of his Spirit (*Somn.* II.252). The Spirit provides inner illumination of the mysteries or deeper meanings of the Scripture (*Decal.* 1; *Spec.* 3.1–6; *Deus* 2–3). The Spirit does not possess the mind all the time because of the body of flesh (*QG* I.90). Therefore, the soul must migrate to God and leave the body through contemplation in order for it to receive the Spirit (*Gig.* 31). Thus, allegory is a tool that the Spirit uses within those who are in pursuit of wisdom in Torah with the ultimate goal of knowing God. Philo writes, "We must therefore have recourse to allegory, which is a favorite with men capable of seeing through it [or, 'men of vision,' *horatikos andrasin*]; for the sacred oracles most evidently conduct us towards and instigate us to the pursuit of it" (*Plant.* 36).

The most significant difference between the mysticism of Philo and Paul is that union with God for Philo comes through union with wisdom. For Paul, union with God comes through union with Christ. The means for mystical experience is also different. For Philo, mystical experience comes through meditation on Torah. The paradigm for mystical experiences is the ascent of the soul. Philo as a Platonist sought this ascent by disposing of the world of sense and freeing the soul from the bonds of matter. For Paul, mystical experience comes through the indwelling Spirit, who makes

---

71. Winston, *Logos and Mystical Theology*, 36; J. Davis, *Wisdom and Spirit*, 51.

communion with Christ possible. Paul was concerned with the practical matters of life and did not stress heavenly ascents in his letters. Communion with Christ was a daily experience for him. His contemplation led to the application of faith in the community. Likewise, he did not want to leave the world of the senses, but rather to find a freedom from the enticement and control of this world of sense, which he called *sarx*. He yearned for release from this world but knew it would happen only in death (Phil 1:21). Transformation in Christ makes purity possible. For Philo, however, one purifies oneself before transformation is possible. For Philo, the human is the agent in the search for the divine mind; but for Paul, God is the agent.[72] In assessing the differences between Paul and Philo, Michael Black concludes,

> If the Apostle was familiar with Philonic or pre-Philonic teaching, he is interpreting it in terms of his own mystical experience of the risen Christ. Or rather, he is making restrained and cautious use of current *theologumena* to give expression to his own Christology.[73]

Merkabah Mysticism

A distinctive motif runs through some Jewish apocalyptic literature dealing with the visions of the figure upon the heavenly throne-chariot. Vision of this throne figure forms the central theme in what has been called Merkabah mysticism. The word *merkabah* refers to the rabbinic term meaning "faces of the chariot," used for the throne-chariot of God described in Ezekiel 1. The key biblical texts for Merkabah mysticism are Ezekiel 1:26, Daniel 7, and Exodus 24, all of which tell of an angelic human-like figure seen sitting on the divine throne representing Yahweh.[74] This angel holds a special position of sharing the divine name or the glory (*kavod*) of God (Exod 33:18–23). God's glory became a technical term for God's human appearance in Jewish tradition. In the Hebrew Bible, this person is called an angel (Exod 23:20–21) or "the son of man" (Dan 7:13). Philo interpreted the figure on the throne as the ideal and immortal human. Various names are given to this figure in apocalyptic literature as noted above, including Melchizedek, Metatron, Adoil, Eremiel, and "the Son of Man." The *Apocalypse of Abraham* 10–11 gives the angel the name Yahoel, which is a combination of *YHWH* and a suffix denoting angelic stature. This figure is distinguished from other

---

72. See Hunt, *Inspired Body*, 39–40.
73. Black, "Pauline Doctrine of the Second Adam," 171.
74. Compare 1 Chr 28:18.

angelic creatures because he shares sometimes in God's own being or divine nature.

In some Jewish literature, certain heroes are transformed into angels or elevated to divinity (*T. Ab.* 11; *Pr. Jos.*). Enoch and Moses are two of the most important and prominent non-Christian figures who experienced transformation. Philo elevated Moses until he merged with divinity.[75] Enoch, like Moses, also experienced elevation in this literature. The Enochic literature attempts to explain what happened to Enoch since Genesis never says Enoch died but simply that "God took him" (Gen 5:24). In the *Parables of Enoch* 70–71 (in *1 En.*), Enoch is transformed into the throne figure of the "son of man" in his heavenly journey to see the *merkabah*. The goal of the mystic in Merkabah mysticism is to experience communion with God by gazing at the figure on the heavenly throne.[76] Only the one who is pure and has undergone preparation can achieve this vision.[77]

Certain techniques were developed to make heavenly journeys possible.[78] One could view the throne by ascent into paradise guided by angelic beings who aide the mystic through the various levels of heaven. To go through these levels, one must know the name of the angel.[79] Ascension to paradise, also known as *pardes*, a technical term for the Holy of Holies in the highest heaven where God appears in his glory upon the *merkabah*, could take place in four ways: in dreams, in waking visions, by the soul leaving the body, or by bodily ascents either in this life or in resurrection.[80] There is a well-known story told in Hekhalot, Talmudic and Midrashic literature, of four mystics who wanted to see the *merkabah*. Three of the four were stricken, but the fourth, Rabbi Aquiba, was able to go to *pardes* and return unscathed in peace.[81]

The emergence of Merkabah mysticism is difficult to date, but it most likely came out of a complex tradition that had its origins in Jewish apocalypticism.[82] Jewish Hekhalot literature, composed from AD 200 to 700, discusses Merkabah mysticism in detail. The term *hekhalot* refers to

---

75. Segal speculates that Philo may have been using earlier traditions that elevate the intermediary figure to the divine throne (*Paul the Convert*, 44–45).

76. Alexander, *Textual Sources for the Study of Judaism*, 29.

77. See *Hek. Rab.* 15.1–2.

78. See the account in *Hek. Rab.* 13–23. Also, the discussion in Dan, *Revelation of the Secret*; Himmelfarb, "Heavenly Ascent," 73–80.

79. Elior, "Mysticism, Magic, and Angelology," 3–53.

80. Smith, "Ascent to the Heavens," 405.

81. For the texts and a discussion, see Morray-Jones, "Paradise Revisited (2 Cor 12:1–12)."

82. Segal, *Paul the Convert*, 39.

the pilgrimage through "halls" or "palaces" on the way to the throne.[83] This literature claims to have been written by Rabbi Ishmael and Rabbi Akiba, who lived in the late first or early second century.[84] This would date the material later than Paul and most of the New Testament and make it irrelevant as a possible source for Paul's mysticism. What makes Merkabah mysticism relevant to Paul, as Alan Segal suggests, is that Paul is the earliest firsthand witness who describes his own ascent to paradise. Segal argues that scholars have without warrant distinguished between the literary genre of Jewish apocalypses and the realm of Jewish mystical experience. There is considerable overlap between the two, especially with accounts of mystical experiences in apocalypses.[85] Furthermore, other types of ancient Jewish literature discuss journeys to see the *merkabah*, which predate even Paul's own visionary accounts, such as the fragments from Qumran known as the "Songs of the Sabbath."[86] Paul is an excellent source for Merkabah mysticism, but caution should be used when utilizing sources dated after him. These sources are helpful to show the general trends in Jewish mysticism of the period of which he is a significant witness.

Paul in His Early Christian, Jewish, and Hellenistic Context

Paul's understanding of Christ as the mystery of God overlaps with other parts of the New Testament, suggesting that his experience was not unique and formed one of the central beliefs of the early church as it believed Jesus to be the fulfillment of its apocalyptic longing. In the Synoptic Gospels (Matthew, Mark, and Luke), the concept of mystery is related to Jesus and his proclamation of the kingdom of God. Jesus brought the eschatological kingdom into present reality, although not in terms that some expected. He used parables as the medium for revealing this kingdom. The mysteries of the kingdom were hidden to those who did not believe in Jesus. Those who did believe, however, understood the divine mysteries because they believed in the one about whom the mysteries spoke. Jesus was the supreme mediator between God and the world and was the true interpreter of the divine mysteries.

---

83. Gruenwald, *Apocalyptic and Merkavah Mysticism*, vii.

84. On the relation of the traditions about R. Ishmael and R. Akiba and Merkabah mysticism, see Scholem, *Major Trends*, 45; idem, *Jewish Gnosticism*, 6–8.

85. Segal, "Paul and Ecstasy," 558.

86. For a extensive discussion on the support for early dating of Merkabah mysticism, see Kanagaraj, *"Mysticism" in the Gospel of John*, 87–181.

Mystical union with God is more of an implicit understanding in the Synoptic Gospels. Union with Christ leads to union with God. The Synoptics approach Paul's emphasis that the mystery of God was disclosed in Christ, but lacking is the full implication of that disclosure in the crucifixion and resurrection of Jesus Christ that can be seen in Paul. Matthew 11:25-27 (Luke 10:21-22) reveals Jesus' self-understanding:

> At that time, Jesus said, "I praise you, Father, the Lord of heaven and earth, because you have hidden these thing from wise and learned people and have revealed them to children. Yes, Father, because this was good in your eyes. All things have been given to me by my father, and no one knows the son except the father, and no one knows the father except the son and the one to whom the son wishes to reveal him."

The mediation of Jesus in the union of the believer with God becomes more direct and explicit in the Gospel and Letters of John. These documents have many mystical elements, far too many to list here. The high Christology of the prologue of the gospel shows the significant link the author makes between Jesus and God (1:18). Jesus is the only one who reveals divine knowledge.[87] The believer can have union with God by loving Jesus and keeping his commands (10:38; 15:10; 17:21; 1 John 1:3, 6-7). Fellowship with God leads to transformation into the divine image at the appearance of God (1 John 3:2; compare 1 Cor 13:12). The ministries of Jesus and the Holy Spirit overlap so that the two are identified together. The Spirit is the present reality of union with Christ and, therefore, union with God (chs. 14-16). John uses the idea of union with Christ in a significant way with the allegory of the vine and branches (15:1-11). The allusion to the Eucharist provides one of the means to being united with Christ through participating in his death (6:62; 7:37).

The source of this mysticism is debatable. Jey Kanagaraj has argued that John shows some significant parallels with Merkabah mysticism. The motifs of ascent, glory, king, sending, indwelling, light, and the Logos show affinity with Hellenistic mysticism and Philo but stronger parallels with Merkabah mysticism.[88] If Kanagaraj is correct, one might wonder whether there was any link between Paul's and John's mysticism and if both relied in some way on Jewish apocalyptic mysticism. To address this issue would mean investigating the dates and provenances of the literature as well as a detailed comparison of the texts. Whatever the case, it does appear that

---

87. John 1:9; 3:11-12; 6:44-45; 7:16-18, 26-28; 9:1-41; 10:14-15; 12:46, 50; 13:31—17:26.

88. Kanagaraj, *"Mysticism" in the Gospel of John*, 184-317.

mysticism may have been a factor in the formation of early Pauline and Johannine communities.

The question could be asked, to what extent did Paul influence the early church with his mysticism or to what extent was he influenced by other early Christian traditions? Paul himself denied any outside influence in Galatians 1:12, yet in 1 Corinthians 15:1–11 he grounds the basis of his encounter with the resurrected Jesus in the primitive confession of the apostles and other early witnesses of this resurrection. Just as there may have been a common stream of apocalyptic hope in the Judaism of Paul's day, so also there was the common belief among early Christians that Jesus was the fulfillment of that hope. To this hope Paul added his own particular interpretation and experience.

Heavenly visions and the search for union with God were not isolated experiences found only within Judaism or early Christianity. The concepts of mystery and mystical experience permeated much of the world of Paul's time. For example, early forms of Gnosticism shared some affinities with Paul that caused some scholars such as Reitzenstein, Bultmann, Schmithals, and others to view Paul as a Gnostic. The Gnostic book *Poimandres*, with its description of heavenly ascent, could be compared to 2 *Enoch* and has the elements of a Jewish apocalypse. Likewise, the Nag Hammadi tractate *Marsanes* contains an account of visionary experiences and revelations. In this text, the goal of the soul is ascent to the heavenly world and reintegration into the divine (10, 12–23).[89]

The mystery religions also shared in the expectations of visionary experiences and union with deity. Although the mysteries had their biggest and greatest popularity from the first to third centuries AD, they were much older (seventh century BC). By the time of Paul's travels, the mysteries were well-grounded in many cities of the Roman Empire such as Ephesus and Corinth. Many of the mysteries contained the figure of a god who died and rose again (e.g., Osiris and the Serapis mysteries). The aim of these mysteries was to achieve union with this god through ritual acts and ceremonies that symbolized death and restoration to life. The result was salvation in the form of escape from the grips of fate. According to Jack Finegan, Origen quotes Celsus (*Cels.* 6.22) as saying that

---

89. Pearson, *Gnosticism, Judaism, and Egyptian Christianity*, 139. For heavenly ascent, see chs. 26 and 32. Pearson, however, dates this work later than Paul, likely as a result of the aftermath of the Jewish revolt in Egypt against Emperor Trajan in AD 115–17 (147). The similarities between Gnosticism and apocalypticism have prompted some scholars such as Rudolf to argue that Gnosticism came from the fringes of Judaism. He also points out similarities between Gnosticism, Qumran, and Wisdom traditions. Some of these overlaps might show direct genealogy, but likely the more indirect influence of the "Oriental Wave" discussed above. See Rudolf, *Gnosis*, 277–81.

in the mysteries of Mithras the ascent of the soul through the celestial spheres of the fixed stars and the seven planets is represented as on a ladder with lofty gates and, on top, an eighth gate. The first seven gates are characterized by the metals of which they are made and are named for the gods of the planets. . . . Salvation with Mithras eventuates in ultimate passage through the solar gate into the boundless beyond.[90]

Mystical experiences of transformation were also well known in antiquity. The account of Lucien's initiation into the Isis cult at Cenchrea in book 11 of Apuleius' *Metamorphosis* provides an example of such an experience. In this story, Isis appears to Lucius in a night vision with directions for initiation into her mysteries. A priest serves as an intermediary for Isis, leading Lucius through the required steps of initiation, and interpreting sacred books of unknown characters to him. Lucius then undergoes a ritual washing after which he is given secrets, followed by ten days of fasting. Then adorned in a new linen robe, he is brought to the most secret and sacred place of the temple and secretly initiated into the Isis mysteries. After this he says, "I approached near unto hell, even to the gates of Proserpine, and after that I was ravished throughout all the elements, I returned to my proper place: about midnight I saw the sun brightly shine, I saw likewise the gods celestial and the gods infernal, before whom I presented myself and worshiped them."[91]

Lucius then appears newly adorned before the crowd and offers a prayer of praise to Isis for her protection and affection as a mother in the daily problems he faced and also for her control of the stars (i.e., fate).

Conclusion

As Paul moved out into the Greco-Roman world of the Mediterranean, he came into contact with various forms of Hellenistic religions and mysteries but rejected them. His ideas about visionary experiences and communion with God show more similarity to other Jews of his time who shared in his apocalyptic hopes that God would reveal his eternal plans to them. Even with some of these other Jewish apocalypticists, Paul had some differences of outlook and experience, particularly concerning the interpretation of the person of the intermediary or throne figure and how one accesses the mysteries of God. He had his own brand of Jewish apocalyptic mysticism in that he believed the messianic age had already begun in the person of Jesus Christ. His experience of the risen Christ transformed his thinking, but not

90. Quoted in Finegan, *Myth and Mystery*, 211.
91. Apuleius, *Metam.* 11.17.

enough that he left his apocalyptic roots, which, for him, found fulfillment and modification in Christ.

Paul was not attempting to interpret his experience in the light of his Jewish tradition, his Hellenistic environment, or even the beliefs of the early church. What was at stake for him was the appropriation of his understanding of communion with Christ for his churches who were under his care and authority.

It is essential to consider how Paul altered and modified various terms and concepts from his environment—Jewish or Greco-Roman—based on his own theological, ethical, and social agenda.[92] The occasional nature of Paul's letters warns against quick claims of coherence outside of the basic contours of his thought.[93] His belief about the mystery of God in Christ begins with the recognition that the resurrected Jesus is Lord and Messiah. The history-of-religions school has shown that the questions about the origins of Paul's language and thought are complex and not easily answered. Although Paul shows affinity with many religious movements of his day, he parted ways with other Jewish apocalypticists and mystics in his insistence that Jesus is Lord and Messiah.

---

92. See Helmut H. Koester, "Paul and Hellenism," in Hyatt, *Bible in Modern Scholarship*, 193.

93. Beker, *Heirs of Paul*, 20.

3

The Divine Mystery "in Christ"

To them God chose to make known how great among the Gentiles are the riches of the glory of this mystery, which is Christ in you, the hope of glory.

(COLOSSIANS 1:27)

PAUL'S INTERPRETATION OF THE divine mystery can be seen in several key phrases in his letters, his broader theology, and his personal testimony of mystical experiences. He is not silent about his own experiences of the divine, although he appears reluctant to describe them in his letters. These experiences had a direct influence on his interpretation of the divine mystery of being in Christ. However, they do not stand by themselves in comprising this mystery but were interpreted by him through a complex mix of Jewish apocalyptic anticipation and early Christian traditions. He uses his mystical union with God *in Christ* to deal with the existential situations and problems of his churches.

Paul's Visionary Experiences

Paul claimed to have had visions in his ministry, but how these visions are interpreted is debated. On the one hand, scholars argue that he disparaged of visions. Representative of this view, Barrett writes, "To Paul, the spiritual world was unmistakably real, and from time to time he experienced it in an ecstatic way; but so far from cultivating this kind of experience he rather disparaged it, and laid no weight on it in his exposition and defense of the gospel."[1] On the other hand, although Paul may not have explicitly made reference to these experiences, he constantly referred to the ramifications of his visions and revelations in their power to transform his life. He may not have specifically mentioned heavenly journeys in the fashion of apocalyptic literature, but his visions influenced his worldview.

Two noteworthy passages that imply mystical experiences appear in the autobiographical sections in Galatians 1 and 2 Corinthians 12. In both passages, Paul is defending himself against opponents. In both experiences, he was granted visions and revelations of Jesus Christ. The vision in Galatians describes Paul's call to serve as Christ's apostle to the Gentiles. It is likely he is referring to his vision on the Road to Damascus recorded in Acts 9. He gives few details about this in Galatians and does not mention the location (compare Acts 9:3-6). Interpreters vary on whether or not the experience in 2 Corinthians also describes this same vision and experience, but most agree that it is a separate occasion. If this is the case, then two unique but possibly related mystical experiences in his life can be seen. Although he only writes of these experiences in these two places, he alludes to the outcomes of them in numerous passages in his letters.[2]

Galatians 1:11–17

In considering the context of Paul's account of his vision in Galatians 1:11–17, it is noteworthy that he replaces his typical thanksgiving with astonishment and denunciation (1:6–10). Instead of being thankful for the Galatians, he is amazed that they had so quickly departed from his teachings. The central issue for him when writing this letter is the perversion or distortion (*metastepsai*) of the gospel he preached to the Galatian churches (1:7). Some troublemakers had infiltrated the ranks of these churches and begun preaching a message different from his, which greatly disturbed him (4:17; 5:12). To him, these preachers were worthy of condemnation (1:9, 10)! Before he can condemn these false preachers, however, he must

---

1. Barrett, *Second Epistle to the Corinthians*, 34. For similar views, see W. Davies, *Paul and Rabbinic Judaism*, 87, 196–97, who argues that Paul's visions do not form the basis of any of Paul's teaching; Dunn, *Jesus and the Spirit*, 213–16, 339; Russell Spittler, "Limits of Ecstasy," in Hawthorne, *Current Issues*, 259–66; Lincoln, *Paradise Now and Not Yet*, 71–86.

2. Lyons has shown that the main theme of the autobiographical sections of Paul's letters is the contrast between his former and present life (*Pauline Autobiography*, 146–52).

establish his authority and remind the Galatians of his gospel which is succinctly summarized in 2:20.

Verses 11–12 function as the thesis statement for the autobiographical explanation in 1:13—2:14 and reveals the source of Paul's gospel.[3] He begins his *apologia* with *gnōrizō*, "I want you to know," a present active indicative showing intent; he wants them to know first and foremost the source of his gospel. The way he received this gospel was through a visionary experience. In verse 11 he bluntly and emphatically states that his gospel is not "by human means" (*kata anthrōpon*). This prepositional phrase shows both source and agency.[4] He completely discounts any human involvement in how he received this gospel.

This gospel came not by natural means but supernatural revelation. Verse 12 clarifies verse 11 and echoes the salutation in verse 1. Just as Paul became an apostle neither from human source nor through human agency but through Jesus Christ (v. 1), he also received his gospel neither from human agency nor was he taught it [by people] but received it through [divine] revelation of Jesus Christ (v. 12). His apostleship and gospel had the same origin. The content of his gospel is given in 3:1 and is simply Jesus Christ crucified, similar to words he used with the Corinthian church (1 Cor 2:2). He worked out this message in practical ways as he dealt with the various problems in the churches. The way he applied this in his own life is summarized in Galatians 2:20: "I have been crucified with Christ. It is no longer I who live, but Christ who lives in me. And the life I now live in the flesh I live by faith in the Son of God, who loved me and gave himself for me."

Paul was convinced that his gospel came by means of a revelation *of Jesus Christ* (1:12). This genitive phrase (*Iēsou Christou*) could be taken as an objective genitive showing Jesus as the content of the revelation ("revelation about Jesus Christ), which is suggested by 1:16a, or it could be taken as a subjective genitive with Jesus being the source of the revelation ("revelation from Jesus Christ"). Verse 1 adds support for the second option with the parallel "Jesus Christ" and "God the Father" both governed by the one preposition "through" (*dia*). Either case works well because the source and content are one and the same in Paul's thinking. The chronological sequence in 1:13–24 is significant. Here he describes his old life in Judaism as one of zealous persecution of the church and adherence to ancestral traditions. This testimony matches the description in Philippians 3:6. In verses 15–16 he describes this revelation of God's Son as happening "in" him. His experience of Christ led to a fundamental change in outlook implied by his

---

3. Longenecker, *Galatians*, 22.
4. Longenecker, *Galatians*, 23.

travels to Arabia, Damascus, Syria, and Cilicia. Word had spread that Saul the persecutor had become a messenger for Christ (vv. 17-24).

A closer look at his description of his experience is enlightening. The simple sentence is, "God was pleased to reveal his son in me." The subject of the participles in 1:15 (*aphrisas* and *kalesas*) is God (compare 1:6; 2:8; 3:5; 5:8).[5] Although Paul's message is timeless (compare Col 1:15-23), his calling and mission are unique. His call to preach the gospel echoes the call of Isaiah and Jeremiah (Isa 49:1, 6; Jer 1:5). He sees himself standing in a long line of prophets, but he now has the full message of God in Christ and the means through the Holy Spirit to carry out his mission. The infinitive "to reveal" (*apokalypsai*) completes the verb "pleased" (*eudokēsen*): what God was pleased to do was reveal to Paul the gospel of his Son. There is no mention of an outward vision as in 1 Corinthians 9:1 and 15:8, which both use the verb *horaō*. Hans Dieter Betz suggests that the difference between the words is not significant.[6] Here Paul is describing an inward experience "in me." He is not concerned about describing this visionary experience in detail, but rather intends to provide the source and authority of his gospel.

The sequence is notable: God provides revelation *of* Christ *to* Paul. The purpose of this description is different from those in Acts which are more miraculous and dramatic.[7] Paul may internalize his vision in this passage to make it clear that his message had no influence from outside sources. He emphasizes this by the statements that follow in verses 16b-17. No one needed to interpret this message for him, not flesh or blood or the Jerusalem apostles. The revealing of this "mystery" of God's plan in Christ was for the purpose of preaching this message to the Gentiles. The mystical encounters with God for Paul end with the clear purpose of the proclamation of the gospel.

Many scholars debate whether this was a conversion experience for Paul or more of a call to a specific task. The basic question in this debate is over the definition of conversion. Krister Stendahl proposes that problems result when modern psychological research or older theological understandings of guilt and conversion from Augustine or Luther are read back onto Paul.[8] Problems also result when attempts are made to describe

---

5. Several important manuscripts do not include *ho theos*, but the context clearly indicates the subject, especially the accusative *ton huion auton*, which could account for how the subject may have slipped into the sentence early on.

6. Betz, *Galatians*, 71.

7. See Howard Clark Kee, "The Conversion of Paul," in Gerger, *Other Side of God*, 55.

8. Stendahl, *Paul among Jews and Gentiles*, 7-23.

THE DIVINE MYSTERY "IN CHRIST" 67

conversion from sociological approaches.⁹ Each of these methods provides important insights into Paul's experience yet are unsatisfactory in themselves to explain the complete story of Paul—his past, present, future, call, attitudes, and ethics. His experience is too complex to be easily categorized by modern methods. One cannot say that he completely broke from his past. The statement in 1 Corinthians 9:19–21, that he became what he needed to become in order to win people to Christ, should be carefully considered. Paul the Jew remained a Jew, though a Jew no longer under the condemnation of the law but above it with freedom through Christ (Rom 8:1–2). His encounter with Christ changed him in significant ways, most notably in his attitude toward the church and the inclusion of the Gentiles in the divine plan. Both continuity and discontinuity can be seen in his story.

John Schütz attempts to solve the debate by taking a middle ground: "'Conversion' and commission collapse into a single whole for which we scarcely have the proper term, unless it be 'call.'" Paul collapses the two ideas into one.[10] Alan Segal offers a useful comment: "To understand what Paul means by conversion, Paul must be seen as one of the early mystical-apocalyptic adepts of divine transformation. In Jewish mysticism and pagan spirituality transformation is a term that suggests what may happen when a human encounters a gracious divinity."[11] He adds, "Outside of Jewish apocalypticism and mysticism the closest analogy to Paul's experience phenomenologically is also termed a metamorphosis by the ancient world."[12]

Rather than call Paul's experience a call or conversion, it might be better to call it a *transformation*. This term takes into consideration his mystical understanding of being in communion with Christ. The results of the revelation in Galatians 1:11–17 is seen in Philippians 3:7–11. His new perspective "in Christ" can be described as a dramatic transformation that included aspects of his call as well as his so-called conversion. Moreover, he uses the term *metamorphaomai*, which is most often translated "transformation," in 2 Corinthians 3:18 to describe this change that Christ brings in a believer's life, a change which is ongoing and affects every area of one's life. Paul's transforming experience described in Galatians provides important clues into his mystical experience in Christ. It was the starting point of an ongoing and dramatic change in the way he viewed himself, his world, and God.

---

9. See Kee, *Christian Origins*, 26, 101; Gaventa, *From Darkness to Light*, 17.

10. Schütz, *Paul and the Anatomy*, 134.

11. Segal, *Paul the Convert*, 22. In his book, Segal provides an appendix that examines the modern psychological discussion on conversion (285–300).

12. Segal, *Paul the Convert*, 23.

68 TRANSFORMATION IN CHRIST

2 Corinthians 12:1–10

Another of Paul's possible mystical experiences is described in 2 Corinthians 12:1–10. He begins this account of a vision in the context of self-defense, which is the focus of chapters 10–13.[13] To defend himself against his opponents,[14] the so-called super-apostles, he feels he must boast as a fool in human terms or in an earthly way (11:21–28).[15] By ironically boasting in his weaknesses, he hopes to prove himself their superior. He could be following ancient apologetic literary tradition that used ironic boasting as a weak fool to vindicate the speaker against sophistic opponents.[16] He boasts in this section not for himself but for God (10:17) who provides his approval (10:18; cf. Gal 1:10). His vision gives proof of God's approval, validates his ministry, and provides authority to "speak for the Lord."[17] The Corinthians wanted Paul as their founder and mentor to prove himself to be above the opponents (11:21–23).

The paradox of this section, however, is that his authority is one of weakness.[18] Genuine apostleship for him does not consist of ecstatic visions but the way of the cross, which meant for him suffering. He views his weakness as opportunity for God's grace to be made perfect or complete in him (12:9). His ultimate goal is to allow his weakness to be a vessel for the power of Christ (13:4). His weakness is a mark of his authority as an apostle and as a man in Christ. In chapter 12 he gives a vague description of his visionary experience in order to decrease its importance when compared to experiencing the power of Christ through the Holy Spirit in the present moment with the purpose of edifying the church. His opponents' boasting of

---

13. Tabor, *Things Unutterable*, 31, summarizes the scholarly consensus about chs. 10–13: (1) the battle lines are over who is a true apostle and that Paul is defending his authority as a true apostle; (2) there is a new situation developed from that of 1 Corinthians; (3) there is a new group of opponents likely from a Jewish background; and (4) both Paul and his opponents claimed pneumatic powers, ability to work miracles, various experiences of visions and revelations.

14. It is impossible to reconstruct or identify these opponents. Gunther, *St. Paul's Opponents*, 1, lists thirteen categories of identification of opponents and reflecting the positions of thirty-nine scholars.

15. The idea of boasting has already appeared in 10:8, 13, 15, 16, 17; 10:10, 12, 16, 17, 18, 30, and occurs a total of nineteen times in chs. 10–13.

16. Betz, *Apostel Paulus und die sokratische Tradition*, 89–100; Forbes, "Comparison, Self-Praise and Irony"; compare Lincoln, "Paul the Visionary," 206–7, who argues that Paul rejects the rhetorical apology and writes as a fool because that is what he is—weak in human ways (11:6, 23–33).

17. Tabor, *Things Unutterable*, 33–37.

18. For Paul, the apostolate sign is weakness (Barrett, *Second Corinthians*, 312); compare 12:5b.

visions does just the opposite and causes friction and division in the church precisely because it is humanly initiated.

A closer look at the account of this mystical experience provides more insight into Paul's mystery. Paul found it necessary to boast in order to challenge the authority of the false apostles. Ironically, he says he has nothing to gain by this, but he actually gains a rhetorical foothold for showing the ultimate source of strength—God's grace in Christ (12:1, 9). The last topic of boasting is Paul's last and most powerful weapon because it possibly got to the heart of his opponents' boasting.

This passage presents a number of interpretive challenges. Paul writes of visions and revelations that "a man in Christ" received. This passage is narrated in the third person, which raises the question, was this Paul's own experience or is he describing here the experience of someone else? The consensus among scholars is that Paul indeed is describing his own experience. At least five positions have been taken concerning why he uses the third person here. One is that he is simply reflecting his embarrassment or reluctance to boast of what he had done or in what he had been a part in order to avoid personal disaster.[19] A second is that he is making use of the Socratic tradition that forbids hubris or boasting about oneself but allows it to be done by someone else.[20] The third is similar and offers that he uses a rabbinic rule that forbids public discussion of mystic phenomena.[21] A fourth view suggests that he experienced the vision in an objective way and saw himself experiencing the vision.[22] The last view is that he speaks in the third person in the heritage of Jewish apocalypticism, which always uses pseudonymity in accounts of visionary ascents.[23]

In addition, Paul chooses to describe himself here as "a man in Christ." This implies more than a simply a designation for a "Christian." "In Christ" also carries with it the eschatological connotation of the communion with Christ made available through identification with his death and resurrection. Hence, Paul is describing a mystical experience in which mysteries of

---

19. Hans D. Betz, "The Problem of Rhetoric and Theology According to the Apostle Paul," in Vanhoye, *L'Apôtre Paul*, 28; R. Martin, *2 Corinthians*, 398–99; Furnish, *II Corinthians*, 542–44.

20. See Plutarch, *On Praising Oneself Inoffensively* 10. See also Baird, "Visions, Revelation, and Ministry," 651–62; Lincoln, "Paul the Visionary," 208–9.

21. Segal, *Paul the Convert*, 58.

22. M. E. Thrall, "Paul's Journey to Paradise: Some Exegetical Issues in 2 Cor 12, 2–4," in Bieringer, *Corinthian Correspondence*, 352–53, referring to Dunn, *Jesus and the Spirit*, 214–15, and Furnish, *II Corinthians*, 543.

23. McGinn, *Foundations of Mysticism*, 70.

God—stated here as "inexpressible things"—were disclosed to him because of his faith and communion with Christ.

In 12:1, both visions (*optasias*) and revelations (*apokalypseis*) are plurals, suggesting that Paul had numerous visionary experiences, which implies more about him as a mystic. Of these many experiences, he chooses to relate one that occurred fourteen years prior. These two words form a hendiadys and both are further modified by the genitive "Lord" (*kyriou*).[24] Is this genitive objective referring to visions of the Lord, or subjective as visions given by the Lord? Ralph Martin argues that most scholars view it as subjective, but he would rather call it a *genitive auctoris*, signifying that these visions were a gift of God: "The author of the visions could also be the object of them."[25] As Galatians 1:12 demonstrates, too sharp of a distinction between the two should not be made.[26]

Another challenge in this passage is the reference to this experience occurring fourteen years earlier (2 Cor 12:2). The date of fourteen years is difficult to pinpoint in Paul's life, but was probably about AD 44.[27] It could refer back to his transformation experience described in Galatians 1,[28] but most likely it is in reference to an experience not recorded anywhere in his writings. Andrew Lincoln comments, "That he could give a date indicates the outstanding nature of this particular vision, but that he could remain silent about it for so long is already an indicator of his assessment of such experiences as credentials for apostleship."[29] It was one of those moments too private to share but too powerful not to influence his thoughts and life in subtle but important ways.

The flow of thought in the passage is interrupted by the awkward syntax in verses 2–4 because of the twice-repeated phrase, "whether in the body or out of the body, I do not know, God knows." Bodily ascension to heaven or paradise is one of the central themes of apocalyptic and mystical texts.[30] For Paul, moreover, how this happened is not as important as what he ex-

---

24. Michaelis suggests that there is no difference between these words ("*Horaō*," *TDNT*, 5:352–53).

25. R. Martin, *2 Corinthians*, 396, 397.

26. Lincoln, "Paul the Visionary," 205–6.

27. R. Martin, *2 Corinthians*, 399; compare Jewett, *Chronology of Paul's Life*, 54–55; and Luedemann, *Paul Apostle to the Gentiles*.

28. Segal, "Paul and Ecstasy," 557.

29. Lincoln, *Paradise Now and Not Yet*, 77.

30. Many ancient texts mention bodily translation. Some Jewish examples include Elijah (2 Kgs 2:11), Enoch (Gen 5:24 and 2 *En.* 1:3–10), Abraham (*T. Ab.* 8:1–3; 12:12–14), Isaiah (*Ascen. Isaiah* 6:10; 7:5). A Greek example is Plato's story of Er in *Resp.* 614B–621B.

perienced, namely, hearing inexpressible words in paradise. William Ralph Inge comments, "It is true, no doubt, that what can be handed on to others is not the vision itself, but the inadequate symbols in which the seer tries to represent what he has seen and to preserve it in his memory."[31]

Paul states that he "was caught up to the third heaven" in verse 2 and "was caught up to paradise" in verse 4. The verb for "caught up" (*harpazō*) is used only one other time by Paul, in 1 Thessalonians 4:17, where all believers will experience on a permanent basis what he has been given a temporary foretaste through his vision. As Lincoln suggests, since this word is passive, Paul's experience may have been involuntary in which "God took the initiative rather than one brought about by preparation or special techniques."[32]

Another difficult issue with this text concerns what Paul means by the third heaven (v. 2) and paradise (v. 4). Is he referring to two different locations, since paradise was not always equated with the third heaven (e.g., the seventh heaven in *Ascension of Isaiah* 9:7)? Or, is he using two different descriptions of the same place and journey? Either choice may be possible. Many Jewish texts describe different "heavens" with various locations for paradise.[33] More important here than the descriptions of heaven is the connotation with these references. The word for "paradise" has its likely origins from Persia. The Hebrew Bible transliterates it as *pardēs* in reference to an enclosure and a nobleman's park (Eccl 2:5). In the Septuagint of Genesis 2:8, *paradeisos* translates the Hebrew *gan-be-'ē-den*. Only in apocalyptic literature does this word come to mean the abode of the blessed after death.[34] It is also connected with resurrection in some of this literature.[35] James D. Tabor writes, "Paradise is an image rooted in Genesis 2–3, and refers to either a preserved or restored garden of Eden, a place or state of pleasantness, removed from sin, suffering, and death. Whether it is located above or below, in the present or in the future (and we have examples of all of these variations), it seems to always symbolize God's intimate presence and access to the tree of life."[36]

---

31. Inge, *Mysticism in Religion*, 34.

32. Lincoln, "Paul the Visionary," 215.

33. Charlesworth, *Old Testament Pseudepigrapha*, 1:xxxiii, provides a list of the various levels of heaven given in Jewish texts. For example, *3 Bar.* gives five levels, *T. Levi* three or seven depending on version, *Apoc. Ab.* 7, Enoch sees paradise in the third heaven, and others.

34. *Apoc. Mos.* 37:5; *T. Ab.* 20; *1 En.* 60:7, 23; 61:12; 70:4; *2 En.* 9:1; *Apoc. Ab.* 21:6; *Jub.* 4:23; Luke 23:43; *T. Dan* 5:12; Rev. 2:7.

35. *T. Levi* 18:10f; *T. Dan* 5:12; *1 En.* 25:4ff; *2 En.* 65:9 (A); *4 Ezra* 7:36, 123; 8:52; *Apoc. Mos.* 13. See Jeremias, "*Paradeisos*," *TDNT* 5:765–73.

36. Tabor, *Things Unutterable*, 117.

Behind much of Paul's Christology stands Genesis 2-3 and the sin problem that resulted from Adam's disobedience. Christ as the Second Adam solved the problem of sin by his death on the cross (Rom 5:18-19) and restores within us the image of God lost by Adam in the garden (2 Cor 3:18). Paul is given a glimpse in his vision of this blessed setting of paradise which can only be seen in this life through a dim mirror (1 Cor 13:12).

Paul then says that this man in Christ "heard inexpressible things no one is permitted to speak" (v. 4). The word for "inexpressible" (*arrēta*) appears in the mystery religions meaning "unutterable." These are words that cannot be spoken because they are beyond expression, so great they cannot be shared, words that may only be disclosed in mystery.[37] One can only suggest what Paul actually heard. Thrall offers that the content of Paul's vision was Christ because when he uses *apokalypseis* with a genitive (here *kyriou*), the genitive appears to give the content of the revelation.[38] In apocalyptic, Tabor points out, "Rapture to Paradise meant that the visionary was taken before the throne of God, and that for the Christian this would have included a vision of the Christ who is seated at God's right hand."[39] Lincoln suggests that for Paul, it would be Christ as the Heavenly Adam who restores Paradise. "Paul's anticipation of it should be assumed to be also an anticipation of greater intimacy with his heavenly Lord."[40]

Ironically and possibly as a result of his vision of paradise, Paul received a thorn in the flesh that he never explains. This is similar to the afflictions suffered after visions of the throne scene in apocalyptic literature (*4 Ezra* 5:14-15). Robert M. Price notes that the term used for "thorn" (*skolops*) in classical Greek could also mean "stake" and be equivalent to "cross" (*stauros*). Price argues that the thorn may have literally been Satan or demons attacking Paul like the descriptions in Merkabah visions of the visionary being attacked by angels or demons on the way to the throne room.[41] The thorn may have reminded Paul of his own weakness in his fleshly existence and the power of the cross to overcome this weakness. He realized because

---

37. Apuleius, *Metam.* 11:23; Philo, *Leg.* II.56; *Somn.* I.191; *Det. Pot.* 175; Euripides, *Bacch.* 472; Aristophanes, *Nub.* 302; Herodotus, *Hist.* 6.135; Lucian, *Men.* 2; 11:23. Compare Isa 8:16; Dan 12:4. See BDAG, 109.

38. Thrall, "Paul's Journey to Paradise," 359. Compare Rom 2:5; 8:19; 1 Cor 1:7; Gal 1:12.

39. Tabor, *Things Unutterable*, 123-24.

40. Lincoln, "Paul the Visionary," 218. Later Gnostic groups claimed to have been given the words Paul received in Paradise and thereby they claimed authority for their own teachings. See Hippolytus, *Haer.* 5.8.25; 7.26.7; Epiphanius, *Pan.* 38.2.5; Tertullian, *Praescr.* 24; *Apoc. Paul.*

41. Price, "Punished in Paradise," 37, referring to Scholem, *Major Trends in Jewish Mysticism*, 51-53, and idem, *Jewish Gnosticism*.

of this vision that his fleshly existence along with the ongoing need to crucify the flesh (Gal 5:24) would end with Christ's return when he would be unhindered by the bonds of the present evil age. Meanwhile, he could live now by Christ's grace revealed most vividly through Christ's death and resurrection.

In this vision, Paul was allowed to peer into paradise where he heard "inexpressible words." He is silent concerning what he heard, but it is possible that what he heard came from the risen Jesus since he is describing "visions and revelations from the Lord." This vision was not the first nor probably the last he had. He chose not to place much merit in visions perhaps for several reasons: he did not want to give his opponents more fodder for their own boasting and thus create a game of "competition of the visionaries"; he thought that his elaborate descriptions of his visions had no edifying use for the church and could even lead to further problems (compare 1 Cor 12–14); his visions did not directly influence his communion with Christ, which came through the indwelling Spirit and not sporadic, ecstatic experiences; or what he saw belonged to a future reserved for believers in Christ, who already had a foretaste of this experience in the present age through the Spirit. Being "in Christ" was already participation in the eschatological age.

The vision described in Galatians 1 also falls within a polemical context. This vision led to a transformation in Paul's life and was how he received his message and direction for ministry. After this vision, he no longer persecuted the church with zeal but used his passion to preach the gospel to the Gentiles. He is not very descriptive about this vision here either but only writes that God revealed his Son in him and that he received his gospel from the Son. It is significant that he received the subject of his preaching through revelation since he places emphasis on proclamation in his letters. For him there is no difference between the spoken word and the vision because both are of the same substance: the resurrected Christ Jesus.

In the vision in 2 Corinthians 12, Paul received words that he was not to share, whereas in the Galatians 1 vision, he received words with the expressed purpose that he might preach to the Gentiles. He does not want to boast about someone who received visions that do not result in proclamation but are limited to eschatological experiences. In Galatians, however, he has the expressed intent of making known his vision and the source of his gospel. This difference between the two accounts is revealing about his understanding of the divine mystery. The divine mystery is first and foremost the revealing of Christ and the opportunity for relationship with God made possible by Christ's death and resurrection. Although Paul may have had visions of future experiences (1 Thess 4:13—5:11), these were not as important to him as preaching the clear message of Christ and the new creation promised in Christ to all people, including the Gentiles. In this sense, he is quicker to speak of the part of his mystical experiences that address pressing needs in his mission. These visions were only but moments in a life devoted to revealing the mystery given to him from God.

The New Life *in Christ*

The divine mystery for Paul is neither simply a subjective, inward mystical experience nor an objective fact that influences ethics or community formation. Rather, it is a way of existing in a new reality that profoundly influences every aspect of life. The mystery of God in Christ is the content of Paul's mysticism and makes communion with Christ possible for believers. Paul makes the claim that his ongoing communion with the risen Jesus Christ through the Spirit provided him further insights into the implications of the message he preached (1 Cor 2:6-16). James Stewart observes, "The heart of Paul's religion is union with Christ. This, more than any other conception—more than justification, more than sanctification, more even than reconciliation—is the key which unlocks the secrets of his soul."[42]

The Divine Mystery in Christ

The defining goal of the divine mystery for Paul is the possibility of fellowship with God through communion with Christ. This communion with Christ can be found particularly in the frequent phrase "in Christ" (*en Christō*) and its variations.[43] When Paul uses "in Christ," his primary meaning is a description of the new eschatological existence that the resurrection of Jesus Christ has inaugurated. As Albert Schweitzer writes, "This 'being-in-Christ' is the prime enigma of the Pauline teaching: once grasped it gives the clue to the whole."[44] Most students of Paul would agree in one degree or another with Schweitzer's statement. A problem surfaces, however, when

---

42. Stewart, *Man in Christ*, 147.

43. The exact phrase *en Christō* occurs in the Pauline corpus (disputed and undisputed letters) at least seventy-three times. See Campbell, *Paul and Union with Christ*, 67–199. It also occurs outside Paul: John 6:5, 6; 14:20, 30; 15:2–7; 16:33; 17:21; Acts 4:2, 9, 10, 12; 13:39; 1 Pet. 3:16; 5:10, 14; 1 John 2:5, 6, 8, 24, 27, 28; 3:6, 24; 5:11, 20; Rev. 1:9; 14:13. Also it appears in *1 Clem.* 32:4; 38:1; Ign. *Eph.* 1:1; *Trall.* 9:2; and *Rom.* 1:1; 2:2.

44. Schweitzer, *Mysticism*, 3. Schweitzer also notes, "Paul is the only Christian thinker who knows only Christ-mysticism, unaccompanied by God-mysticism" (5). See Wikenhauser, *Pauline Mysticism*, 183–242, for a comparison between Pauline and Hellenistic mysticism.

one attempts to define what Paul means by being "in Christ."[45] There are as many answers to this issue as there are interpreters, with no clear consensus concerning its interpretation.[46] "In Christ" is not so much a formula for Paul as it is a concept.[47] He begins with the concept and tries to express various aspects of this concept through different grammatical constructions.

Believers "in Christ"

As Ernest Best suggests, part of the problem with understanding the phrase "in Christ" is that Paul uses this phrase with more than one sense and in various contexts. Best gives the following possibilities:

1. "A is in Christ": Paul speaks of the saints "in Christ Jesus" (Phil 1:1), of "those who are in Christ Jesus" (Rom 8:1) and of himself as a man in Christ (2 Cor 12:2).

2. "A does something to B in Christ": the apostle urges the Thessalonians "in the Lord Jesus" (1 Thess 4:1; see Eph 4:17).

3. "A does something in the Lord": Paul exhorts the Philippians to "rejoice in the Lord" (Phil 3:1; 4:4-10; see 2 Cor 10:17).

4. "A is X in Christ": Appelles is tested and approved "in Christ" (Rom 16:10) and Paul's ultimate aim for his ministry is "to present everyone perfect in Christ" (Col 1:28; see 1 Cor 3:1).

5. "God gives (does to us) something in Christ"; e.g., he forgave us in Christ (Eph 4:32; see 1:6).

6. ". . . the gift of God . . . in Christ"; see Rom 3:24.

7. "A, B, C . . . are in Christ"; e.g., Gal 1:22.

8. The formula sometimes has cosmic significance, as it does in Col 1:16-17: "In him all things hold together" (see Eph 1:9-10; 3:10-11).

---

45. Barrett suggests that the reason why this phrase is so difficult to understand is that Paul himself does not always explain how "in Christ" describes union with Christ ("New Testament Eschatology," 149).

46. Ladd (*Theology of the New Testament*, 481-83), among others, gives a brief history of scholarship. Some of the significant work has been done by Deissmann, *Die Neutestamentliche formel "In Christo Jesu"*; Büchsel, "'In Christus' bei Paulus"; Oepke, "*En*," *TDNT*, 2:537-39; Best, *One Body in Christ*; Neugebauer, "Das paulinische 'in Christo'"; idem, *In Christus*; Bouttier, *En Christ*; Campbell gives a brief overview of the most significant voices in this discussion (*Paul and Union with Christ*, 31-64).

47. This was argued earlier by Büchsel, "'In Christus' bei Paulus."

9. The use of the phrase in Col 2:9 is unique: "For in Christ all the fullness of the deity lives."[48]

Great difficulty arises in determining the function of the preposition *en* followed by the dative case. This preposition is the most widely used in the New Testament, occurring about 2,698 times. According to Harris, the standard uses of *en* plus the dative express incorporative union, sphere of reference, agency or instrumentality, cause, mode, location, or authoritative basis.[49] In a survey of Greek grammars, Alexander Wedderburn gives the following uses: instrumental, temporal, local, sociative or modal, relational or respective, descriptive, and the sense of "in the power of."[50] Wedderburn warns against imposing one sense upon all the uses in Paul, something that Deissmann did in his classic study on "in Christ." Wedderburn argues that in saying that the phrase is used in one sense, "the decision is likely to have been reached on the basis of an overall interpretation of Paul's theology into which the interpretation of these *en* phrases is then fitted."[51] He argues further that since *en* is used with a person, namely Christ, "not a time or a place, an abstract noun or an instrument in the normal senses of these terms," then the "use of these phrases within these categories will be figurative, an extension of language, but still a quite intelligible one."[52] Ultimately, context determines the usage and meaning.[53]

Furthermore, Paul uses "Christ" with other Greek prepositions. John Nielson comments that these other prepositions are "spokes of the wheel of which *en Christō* is the hub."[54] Harris adds that over the course of time, the distinction between *en* and other prepositions was lost in Greek, until *en* is no longer a part of the spoken language. Furthermore, *en* "encroached on the territory" of *eis* with verbs of motion, *dia* with the genitive expressing instrumentality or agency, *dia* with the accusative expressing ground, *meta* or *dia* with the genitive denoting attendant circumstances, *syn* expressing accompaniment, and *kata* indicating a standard of judgment. "It is not that the distinction between *en* and any other prep. was obliterated, but the area

---

48. Best, *One Body*, 1–7.

49. Harris, "Appendix," *NIDNTT*, 3:1192. See also the twelve uses listed in BDAG, 326.

50. Wedderburn, "Some Observations," 84–86.

51. Wedderburn, "Some Observations," 87.

52. Wedderburn, "Some Observations," 88.

53. Campbell (*Paul and Union with Christ*) systematically goes through every occurrence in Paul's letters of the different prepositions used with "Christ" providing significant exegetical details for each.

54. Nielson, *In Christ*, 52.

and the frequency of overlap in usage became greater in Hel. and especially biblical Gk. than it had been earlier."[55] These distinctions of modern grammars may not have been present in the mind of ancient writers.[56] Any thorough investigation of "in Christ" should include other prepositions used in construction with "Christ." Likewise, Paul uses other constructions that have similar functions including "in the Lord," "in him," or "in whom." The various uses of "in Christ" and its variations can be analyzed into several general categories.

New Eschatological Life

The divine mystery for Paul is that Christ is the agent of a new existence and inaugurates the believer into a new life. It is by this agency of Christ that one can experience the eschatological promises of God. Benefits of the age to come can be appropriated in the present age because of Christ. In this new existence, Christ brings redemption from sin (Rom 3:24) and new life to the believer (6:11). Through his death and resurrection, he makes eternal life possible (6:23). Through him the Spirit sets one free from law, sin, and death (8:2). God's love has been given to humanity through Christ (8:39). God's grace comes through Christ Jesus (1 Cor 1:4). All those in Christ will be made alive (15:22) and will rise first (1 Thess 4:16). God's promises are fulfilled (are "yes") with Christ (2 Cor 1:19, 20).[57] In Galatians 2:4 Paul distinguishes his freedom in Christ from legalism and the law. In 2:17 he cautions against attempting to be justified in Christ through one's own efforts. Christ's redemption makes it possible for Gentiles to experience faith like Abraham's (3:14). God's riches come through Christ Jesus (Phil 4:19).

One significant benefit provided to the believers in Christ is the possibility of a new type of life. Paul writes in 2 Corinthians 5:17, "Therefore, if anyone is in Christ, this one is a new creation; the old existence has gone, behold the new has come."[58] The old existence under the bondage of sin and death is replaced by a new life of freedom and righteousness. Paul realizes that something fundamental must be done for people to find release from the bonds of the present evil age. His answer is in "transformation" (*metamorphosis*) into the image of Christ (2 Cor 3:18) through rejecting the

55. Harris, "Appendix," *NIDNTT*, 3:1190.
56. See Büchsel, "'In Christus' bei Paulus," 143.
57. Notice Paul's appeal with "Son of God" in v. 18.
58. Ladd comments, "The passing of the old does not mean the end of the old age; it continues until the parousia. But the old age does not remain intact; the new age has broken in" (*Theology of the New Testament*, 480).

old self and embracing the new life where Christ is Lord (Rom 6:6, 8). New creation in the image of Christ is Paul's most inclusive description of being "in Christ." New creation brings a complete change of devotion from the objects of the world to the person of Christ.

Paul also views Christ as the unifying force of this relationship. When people submit to the supremacy of Christ in their lives, the result is a deep and life changing relationship. This idea suggests a locative use of *en*. There is no condemnation for those who are in Christ Jesus because they live in a new sphere of existence (Rom 8:1). They have moved from the existence characterized by Adam to that controlled by Christ.

Paul also uses the phrase to show Christ as the object of hope. In 1 Corinthians 15:19 Paul writes that in Christ believers have hope in this life, but he urges the Corinthians to hope also for resurrection. Because Jesus has been raised so shall they someday. Since Paul puts no hope in the flesh but glories in Christ Jesus (Phil 3:3), he is assured that he will receive the prize for which God has called him heavenward in Christ Jesus (3:14).

Description of Believers

Paul uses "in Christ" as a form of label (periphrasis) to describe those in the realm of Christ as "Christian." Paul does not use the label "Christian" in his letters. Christ is the sphere of the believer's existence. Paul speaks from experience when he calls himself "in the Lord Jesus" in Romans 14:14. In 16:3, 7, 9, 11 he greets other Christians who, like himself, have experienced the resurrected Lord. Because of God, one can be in Christ (1 Cor 1:30). In 1 Corinthians 3:1 Paul says that he can only address the Corinthians as mere infants in Christ who still hold onto the earthly existence (3:2). In 7:22 Paul speaks of the call of a slave in the Lord, that is, when the slave became a Christian. A widow is free to marry anyone as long as he is a Christian (7:39). In 15:18 the Greek text suggests that the participle *koimēthentes* ("those who have fallen asleep") is modified by "in Christ," hence, those described are Christians. In 2 Corinthians 12:2 Paul says that he knows a man in Christ, i.e., a Christian. Paul describes the churches in Judea as being in Christ (Gal 1:22; 1 Thess 2:14). He writes to various churches who are in Christ (Phil 1:1, 1 Thess 1:1 [note 2 Thess 1:1]). He has brothers in the Lord (Phil 1:14). In Philippians 4:21 all the saints who are described as being in Christ Jesus are to be greeted. Epaphras is called Paul's fellow prisoner in Christ Jesus (Phlm 23). By using this designation for believers, Paul is implying the deeper, theological understanding of union with Christ.

Paul also speaks of those in Christ as the body of Christ. Christ is the instrument of bringing believers together into one unit. In Romans 12:5 Paul says, "in Christ we who are many form one body." The common bond of union with Christ unites those who have come under the lordship of Christ, although they each have different gifts. In Galatians 3:26—4:7 Paul describes the change of the believer's relationship with God from slave to son through "faith in Christ Jesus" (3:26). "Sons" in this verse is metaphorical for all believers and inclusive of both genders, male and female. It is describing the intimacy of family in which the traditional barriers of nationality, economic status, and gender are no longer valid because "you are all one in Christ Jesus" (v. 28). Baptism "into Christ" is the symbolic act by which one moves from the old sphere of division into the new sphere of unity. The Corinthians remained divided precisely because they had not fully moved into the new existence governed by Christ. They remained slaves, economically, socially, and spiritually stratified.

Christ is also the bond of fellowship that unites believers together. Paul directs the church in Rome to welcome Phoebe in Christ (Rom 16:2). Likewise, Epaphroditus is to be welcomed in the Lord by the Philippians (Phil 2:29). In Romans 16:22 Titius greets in the Lord as one with those to whom Paul writes. A married man and woman are bound together in the Lord (1 Cor 11:11). Euodia and Syntyche are to agree in the Lord (Phil 4:2). In Philemon 16 Onesimus the slave is referred to as a brother in the Lord to Paul and Philemon. Fellow believers show deep affection in Christ, such as when Paul admonishes the Romans to love Ampliatus in the Lord (Rom 16:8). William Barclay writes, "The fact that all individual Christians are in Christ is indeed precisely the source and origin of that unity which should characterize all members of the Church."[59] Or, as Bruce states, "There is little enough in Paul's writings that savors of 'the flight of the alone to the Alone.'"[60]

Furthermore, spiritual mentorship can develop between two parties who are in Christ. In 1 Corinthians 4:15 Paul says that the Corinthians do not have many spiritual mentors, but by means of Christ, that is, in service to him, Paul became their spiritual father. Christ is the common link between Paul and his churches, and conforming to Christ's image is Paul's primary goal for them. One of the jobs of leaders is to mentor other believers. In 1 Thessalonians 5:12 Paul speaks of those who have authority to admonish the Thessalonians "in the Lord." These people are to be given the utmost respect because of their representation of Christ.

59. Barclay, *Mind of St. Paul*, 123.
60. Bruce, *Paul*, 138, quoting Plotinus, *Enn*. 6.9.11.

Qualities of Being in Christ

Paul's mysticism is intensely practical and moral. Ethics is the natural by-product of experiencing new existence in Christ. Schweitzer comments, "The demands which Paul's view of ethics sets up presuppose not the natural man but the 'new creation' endowed with the Spirit, who has come into existence in the dying and rising again with Christ."[61] There is a new quality to new life in Christ. According to Furnish, Paul's ethic is grounded in his theological, eschatological, and Christological convictions.[62] All three of these convictions are integrally related in the concept of being in Christ. The relationship between Paul's ethics and his mystical union with Christ can be seen in Romans 13:14: "But put on the Lord Jesus Christ, and make no provision for the flesh, to gratify its desires." Being in Christ and being in the flesh are mutually exclusive alternatives. Identification with Christ's death through baptism symbolizes the death of the power of sin in the life of those in Christ (6:3-11). The power of sin controls the law making ethical living a matter of futile struggle (7:7-24). But in Christ there is victory over sin, which ensnares the law under its control (8:1-4). Being in Christ enables believers to live righteously (Rom 5:5; 8:15; 15:13; Gal 4:6; 5:5). Furnish writes,

> In Christ [the believer] has been engaged, renewed, and restored by the creative and redemptive power of God's love. Moreover, in Christ he knows that redemption is not just deliverance from the hostile powers to which he has formerly enslaved, but freedom *for* obedience to God. For Paul, obedience is neither preliminary to the new life (as its condition) nor secondary to it (as its result and eventual fulfillment). Obedience is *constitutive* of the new life.[63]

Being in Christ makes it possible not to gratify the desires of the flesh (Gal 5:16-17) and to keep the law, which is summed up in the command to love (5:14). The primary content of the Pauline ethic is love, which, when it is in the realm of Christ, replaces the sin-bound law of legalism. Paul's ethical emphasis can also be seen in the related concept of being "in the Spirit." Being "in the Spirit" provides the basis for how those who are in Christ can live in victory over sin and temptation. Wikenhauser comments that "the Spirit is the vital influence which gives the new life its quality."[64] In Galatians

---

61. Schweitzer, *Mysticism*, 296.
62. Furnish, *Theology and Ethics in Paul*, 213-24.
63. Furnish, *Theology and Ethics in Paul*, 226.
64. Wikenhauser, *Pauline Mysticism*, 55.

5:24–25 Paul equates those "of Christ," that is, those who live in the realm of Christ, with those living by the Spirit who will produce ethical fruit (22–23). Likewise, in Romans 8:9–13 Paul identifies those living in Christ with those who live according to the ways of the Spirit that are opposite from the ways of the flesh. Thus, to be "in Christ" leads to the ability to live out the law as God intended.

Furthermore, another quality of being in Christ is that a believer has a special standing in relation to others. In Romans 16:13 Paul describes Rufus as chosen in the Lord. He is a person of special standing before Christ, possibly for his service and obedience, though Paul does not say. Another example is Timothy who is faithful in the Lord to the gospel message. His life in relation to Christ allows Paul to recommend him to the Corinthians (1 Cor 4:17).

Another quality is that there are special benefits available to those in Christ. In 1 Corinthians 1:2 Paul writes to the church at Corinth, which is "sanctified in Christ Jesus." Christ here could function both as a means of sanctification and as the sphere in which those sanctified live. The Corinthians have been enriched in words and knowledge because of their relationship to Christ (1:5). But Paul uses sarcastic language in 4:10 by calling them "wise in Christ" when their actions betrayed their foolishness. Those in Christ have joy (Phil 1:26), encouragement (2:1), hope (2:19), confidence (2:24), and can rejoice (3:1; 4:4; 4:10). They can stand firm while being in the Lord (4:1; 1 Thess 3:8).

Certain characteristics of being in Christ set one apart from the way the world lives. Paul has a certain "way of life in Christ Jesus" consistent with the message he preached that he wants the Corinthians to imitate, implying that they must leave their old way of life (1 Cor 4:16–17). For those "in Christ Jesus," attempts at justification through works or ceremonial practices have no value, but only faith expressed through love (Gal 5:6). Those in Christ should also have the same mindset of humble service and self-sacrifice showed by Christ (Phil 2:5). Believers are called to give thanks even in difficulty times because it is God's will for them in Christ Jesus (1 Thess 5:18).

Means of Ministry

Being in Christ also provides the basis for ministry and authority. In Christ Paul can speak with confidence and authority because the Holy Spirit confirms his conscience (Rom 9:1). In 1 Corinthians 9:1–2 he tells the Corinthians that they are the result of his work in the Lord and validation of his apostleship. In 15:31 he boasts "in Christ Jesus our Lord" about the Corinthians because of their mutual connection because of hope in resurrection. Since he speaks with authority in the name of Christ, the Corinthians can be assured of his sincerity (2 Cor 2:17). In 2 Corinthians 12:19 Paul writes as one who is in Christ, in relationship with Christ, with the call of Christ (apostleship), and thus with the authority of Christ. His confidence is built on trust in the Lord (Phil 2:24). He can ask for proper conduct from a church since he is in the Lord Jesus (1 Thess 4:1). He could use his authority in Christ to persuade Philemon to accept Onesimus (Phlm 8) but instead pleads in a more congenial tone (20).

Being in Christ also provides motivation for service. In Romans 15:17–18, because he has been resourced by his fellowship with Christ, Paul is proud of his faithful service in preaching to the Gentiles. His motivation had always been to preach the gospel in unevangelized areas. In 16:12 he lists three women who have also worked hard in the Lord (i.e., for the sake of Christ). The Corinthians' work is not in vain because it is done in the Lord (1 Cor 15:58). Paul is confident in the Lord that the Galatians will agree with him about freedom in Christ and embrace fully the new existence in Christ (Gal 5:10). In Philippians 1:13 he describes his prison chains as being "in Christ," suggesting that he 1) is in prison because of his devotion to Christ, 2) is the only person of whom Paul is a prisoner is Christ, and 3) has voluntarily imprisoned himself under the authority of Christ. In 4:13 he says that he can do everything in Christ, including suffering, because Christ is the source of his strength. Because Paul lives in the new existence provided by fellowship with Christ, he is no longer bound by the circumstances of this temporary evil age but can find victory in any difficulty or suffering because he has experienced the life of the age to come (3:20—4:1).

Christ in Believers

For Paul, communion with Christ is a two-way relationship in which believers live a new existence under the lordship of Christ and in which Christ lives within believers. There are two ways to view Christ in believers. The first is the simple concept of the direct experience of Christ. Paul's own testimony in Galatians 2:20 reveals this relationship succinctly with, "I no longer live, but Christ lives in me." The intersection of human and divine in this statement reveals that the key for experiencing communion with Christ lies with sovereignty—who is in control. Paul realized the futility of living life to please his own desires (Phil 3:4–11). In verse 19 he says that he "died" in regard to the law held under the control of sin. Death symbolizes the cessation of relationship. He transferred from the realm of sin to the realm of Christ. Every thought, word, and deed came under the control of Christ.

The death of self is not a death of personhood, but a cessation of control. Bruce comments, "The risen Christ is the operative power in the new order, as sin was in the old."[65] There are two alternatives in Paul's mind: either sin is in control of the self or Christ is in control. Just as Christ gave himself on the cross and received resurrected life, so also believers give up themselves in order to receive new life (Rom 6:4–10). Morna Hooker writes, "It is not that Christ and the believer change places, but rather that Christ, by his involvement in the human situation, is able to transfer believers from one mode of existence to another."[66] Christ lives within the believer as the sovereign providing a new spiritual existence free from the condemnation and control of sin. Paul knew the Galatians had only partly experienced the sovereignty of Christ, as he writes in 4:19, "I am in labor with you until Christ is formed in you." This is his essential argument in 1 Corinthians as well. He writes to the Philippian church in the same manner: "For to me to live is Christ and to die is gain. But if I live in the flesh, this is fruitful work" (1:21–22a). Thus, Christ creates and is the new life for Paul. In Colossians 1:27 the mystery of God is described as "Christ in you, the hope of glory." Relationship with the risen Christ is at the heart of God's plan for the human race.

The second concept that builds upon the first is that Christ is present in the believer through the Holy Spirit. The indwelling Spirit of God is an ancient concept in Judaism and is frequently found in the New Testament. Paul builds upon these beliefs and identifies Christ with the Holy Spirit in several places. A revealing passage is Romans 8:9–11, where Paul has similar statements: "Spirit of God lives in you," "one has the Spirit of Christ," "Christ in you," "Spirit of him who raised Jesus from the dead is living in you," and "Spirit who lives in you." Similar is 2 Corinthians 3:17: "Now the Lord is the Spirit, and where the Spirit of the Lord is, there is freedom." In order to possess the Spirit, one must live in the sphere of Christ, fully accepting his sovereignty in spirit, soul, and body (1 Thess 5:23). Christ dwells within the believer through the Spirit. Being in the Spirit is dependent upon being in Christ, and the result of being in Christ being in the Spirit.[67]

---

65. Bruce, *Galatians*, 144.
66. Hooker, *From Adam to Christ*, 5.
67. For further discussion, see ch. 5 later.

Other Prepositions with "Christ"

Paul uses other prepositions with the person of Jesus Christ that also suggest mystical union. The genitive "of Christ" (*Christou*) implies relationship or intimacy with Christ. Romans 8:9 infers that to have the Spirit *of Christ* (*Christou*) means that one belongs to Christ (*autou*). Those who belong to Christ will experience resurrection (1 Cor 15:23). Those who are "in Christ" belong to Christ (Gal 3:28–29). Being the possession of Christ provides motivation for living (Rom 14:8). Over sixty-one different words occur in the genitive construction with the person of Jesus Christ. Paul specifies his motivation in 2 Corinthians 5:14, where he writes that the love *of Christ* is his control and motive for life. The genitive "of Christ" could be either a subjective or objective since both Christ's love for Paul and Paul's love for Christ motivated Paul's life. This new paradigm of love governs Paul by a present power derived from his union with Christ.[68]

Paul also uses the preposition *syn* ("with") plus the datives *Christō* or *autō* ("him") several times. To die means to be "with Christ," by far the better alternative for Paul. Although he believed Christ was with him in this life, to die would allow him to fully experience resurrection power and full knowledge of Christ (Phil 1:21–23; 3:10–11). This future promise of being with the resurrected Lord is a significant factor in Paul's eschatology (2 Cor 3:4; 1 Thess 4:14, 17; 5:10). Being "with Christ" could happen either at death or in life if one is fortunate to be alive when Christ returns (Col 3:4; 1 Thess 4:14). Yet, believers can experience a foretaste of this future promise now by rejecting sin and embracing new life in Christ (Col 2:13; 3:3). Wikenhauser notes that Paul "never uses the phrase 'in Christ' when speaking of his profound hope that he will be clothed in a spiritual body and will be forever with his heavenly Lord; in such cases his phrase is 'with Christ' (*syn Christō*)."[69] He adds, "'Being in Christ' comes to an end when it attains its purpose and we are 'with Christ.'"[70] Dwight Beck writes, "'With Christ' is Paul's eschatological expression and his assurance about the future is based on his present experience 'in Christ.'"[71]

Over forty compound words occur with the preposition *syn* that basically fall into two categories: life in the new eschatological community in Christ and communion with Christ as a present reality. These words (both nouns and verbs) designate a new existence begun with the death

---

68. Wikenhauser, *Pauline Mysticism*, 36.
69. Wikenhauser, *Pauline Mysticism*, 62.
70. Wikenhauser, *Pauline Mysticism*, 63. Compare Col 3:4; 1 Cor 13:12.
71. Beck, "Paul as Mystic," 441.

and resurrection of Christ in which believers share. In Romans 6:4–8, for example, Paul writes about imitating and appropriating Christ's death and resurrection by being buried with him (*synetaphēmen*, v. 4), united with him in death (*symphytoi*, v. 5), and united in resurrection life with him. The old self is crucified with him (*synestaurōthē*, v. 6), having died with him (*syn Christō*), resulting in new life with Christ (*syzēsomen*, v. 8).

Another important preposition used by Paul is *eis* followed by the accusative *Christon* ("into Christ") or *auton* ("him"). This preposition generally has a locative sense of moving towards a goal or new state. For example, one is baptized "into Christ" (Rom 6:3; 1 Cor 12:13; Gal 3:27), which carries the basic meaning that one has entered into the new life of Christ represented by the act of baptism. One is incorporated into the new community that belongs to Christ. Several different objects make existence in this new location possible: God as the ultimate source (2 Cor 1:21), the law as a temporary custodian (Gal 3:24), knowledge of what is good (Phlm 6), and faith (Rom 10:14).

Similarly, Paul writes about this new life coming *by means of* Christ by using the preposition *dia* followed by the genitive *Christou* ("through Christ"). Enlightening are the words Paul uses in the grammatical construction with *dia Christou* in the formula, "x" results through Christ: life (Rom 5:17), eternal life (5:21), victory (1 Cor 15:57), abundant comfort (2 Cor 1:5), reconciliation (5:18), fruits of righteousness (Phil 1:11), being "sons" of God (Eph 1:5), and salvation (1 Thess 5:6). Because of Christ, a person can die to the law as the way to salvation (Rom 7:4). Each of the above prepositional constructions points to the new existential union in Christ.

Two Spheres of Existence

For Paul, the opposite of being "in Christ" is being "in Adam." When he compares living in Christ with living in Adam, he is contrasting two realms of existence and two different ways of living. Both Adam and Christ function as corporate personalities who represent an individual or group who follow in the pattern of their progenitor. Swee-Hwa Quek writes, "Paul found that by juxtaposing Adam and Christ in a dialectical pattern he had a complete scheme for understanding the history of mankind."[72] According to Paul, human existence is bound up in the two persons of Adam and Christ. Paul may have broadly interpreted the Hebrew word *'adam* as not only the proper name Adam but also as humanity in general. Barrett writes,

---

72. Swee-Hwa Quek, "Adam and Christ According to Paul," in Hagner and Harris, *Pauline Studies*, 67.

"Everything that can be attributed to Adam can be said about humanity."[73] Dunn adds, "So if Paul was looking for language to describe the plight of sinful man, it was only natural that he should turn to the account of man as he was intended to be and as he became."[74]

The story of creation in Genesis 1–3 is foundational for Paul's thought. Important in the creation account is that Adam and Eve were spiritual and created in the image of God (*eikona theou*, 1:27; see 2 Cor 3:18), and earthly (*psychēn*, Gen 2:7) coming from existing substances (Adam from dust of the ground, 2:7, and Eve from the side of Adam, 2:21). The first humans had unlimited freedom, except they were not to eat from the Tree of the Knowledge of Good and Evil (2:16–17). The serpent's temptation focused on becoming like God by knowing good and evil (3:4–5). The forbidden fruit from the Tree of Knowledge provided three temptations to Eve: physical ("good for food"), emotional or psychological ("pleasing to the eye"), and spiritual ("desirable for gaining wisdom") (3:6). After Eve ate the fruit, Adam also became guilty through sharing in her disobedience. The sequence began with God's command; followed by deception, desire and temptation; then the act of disobedience; resulting in an awareness of good and evil and, more importantly, a broken relationship with God and each other. The consequence of broken communion with God was expulsion from paradise and eventual death.

The central theme of Romans 5–8 is the reversal of this condition through Jesus Christ. Paul's comparison of Christ with Adam in 5:12–21 highlights the qualities of living in the realm of Adam and the qualities of living in communion with Christ. In the first section of chapter 5, Paul describes the hope and assurance of justification and reconciliation because of the death and resurrection of Jesus Christ. He begins chapter 5 with *dia touto*, "on account of this," showing that what follows is related to and summarizes what has come before. He turns his thought from the example of Abraham in 4:1–22 to faith in the power of the death and resurrection of Jesus Christ in 4:23–25. Since believers have been justified through faith in Christ (*dikaiōthentes*, 5:1; an aorist passive participle used causally), they stand in a new relationship of peace with God (*eirēnēn*), which Paul describes as "this grace in which we stand" (5:2). Then, to show the surpassing greatness of the grace of God in Christ, he turns to a comparison of two spheres of existence, one headed by Adam as a type and the other by Christ as a type.

---

73. Barrett, *From First Adam to Last*, 6.
74. Dunn, *Christology in the Making*, 101.

Paul demonstrates the depravity of the old sphere of existence "in Adam" to highlight the greatness of the new life inaugurated by Christ. He is moving to his great statement in verse 21, "as sin reigned in death, grace also might reign through righteousness leading to eternal life through Jesus Christ our Lord." Adam only serves as an example to reach this rhetorical goal, since he is described as "a *type* of the one to come" (v. 14). The word *typos* in verse 14 occurs fifteen times in the New Testament and has the basic meaning of the imprint of a blow, with the further sense of model, mark, or mold.[75] According to Ellis, "In typological exegesis the 'type' is usually applied to the OT 'shadow' and the 'antitype' to the NT fulfillment. The NT writers see in certain OT persons, or institutions, and events prefigurations of New Covenant truths." The real significance of typological exegesis appears only in the "anti-type" or fulfillment.[76]

In verse 12, Paul describes the existential situation of all people: death came by Adam's sin, so also death comes to all who sin. Each individual is responsible for his or her own sins.[77] The power of sin is like a disease that has a pervasive power over humanity, causing people to fall short of the glory and image of God that Adam originally had (3:23). Christopher Davis points out that Genesis never identifies Adam and Eve as the direct cause of every human sin. However, Genesis does point to the sin of the first human pair as the cause for universal death, since their sin led God to deny access to the Tree of Life not only to Adam and Eve, but to their children as well.[78] Paul does not speculate how sin is inherited from Adam but the result is evident in every human being. The law is a catalyst for the power of sin and causes rebellion against God (5:20; 7:8-11). Ever since Adam, people have broken the law and, consequently, experienced spiritual and physical death (5:13-14; 1 Cor 15:20).

Beginning in verse 15, Paul contrasts this problem with the much greater life in Christ. The key words *pollō mallon*, "how much more," compare the trespass, death, and condemnation "in Adam" to the gift, grace, justification, and life "in Christ" (vv. 15-17). In verse 18 Paul has in mind

75. Goppelt, "*Typos*," TDNT, 8:246.

76. Ellis, *Paul's Use of the Old Testament*, 126-28. He says that Paul is not referring to some mythological *Urmensch*, but that "the historicity of Adam is quite as basic to Paul's thought here as the historicity of Christ" (129).

77. *4 Ezra* 3:21-23 states, "For the first Adam, burdened with an evil heart, transgressed and was overcome, as were also all who were descended from him. Thus, the disease became permanent; the Law was in the people's heart along with the evil root, but what was good departed, and the evil remained." Adam became the source of the evil inclination, but not responsible for the sins of all other humans (*4 Ezra* 4:30-31; 7:118).

78. C. Davis, "Trust which is the Gospel," 156.

two acts: Adam's disobedience in the garden (Gen 3) resulting *involuntarily* in death, and Christ's obedience on the cross resulting *voluntarily* in death. Hooker writes, "Christ became what we are—*'adam*—in order that we might share in what he is—namely the true image of God."[79] Christ identified with *'adam* (humanity) at the point of the curse in order to show the surpassing greatness of God's grace (5:8). Hooker adds, "It is necessary, not only for Christ to identify himself with us, but for us to identify ourselves with him. Our union with Adam is involuntary and automatic, but our union with Christ is the result of a deliberate action on our part, and therefore not completely analogous."[80] The comparison between the two realms of existence "in Christ" and "outside of Christ" or "in Adam" is not a comparison between two similar or equal entities. Although sin is powerful and increases its influence upon people (*epleonasen*, v. 20), the grace available in Christ can overcome (*hypereperisseusen*) this problem and bring eternal life (v. 21). Life in Christ is superior to life in Adam in all ways. One of the purposes in using Adam/Christ typology here is to show the results of Christ's death to those who believe (see 3:20–26), and one of those results is reconciliation (*katallassō*) or friendship with God (5:10).

This new life in Christ is eschatological; it is a foretaste of life eternal and a fulfillment of the primal life of Adam and Eve in the garden. James Dunn writes, "Christ as last Adam is *eschatological* man."[81] There exists in Paul a tension between the "already" and the "not yet." Those who are in Christ are being renewed into his image (2 Cor 3:18), yet are also stuck in this temporal world controlled by sin and death. When one is in communion with Christ, one is free from the power of the existence represented by Adam. The believer still lives in a world where sin appears to be the dominant force, but earthly life has no real bearing upon the believer's existence in Christ (Gal 2:20; Phil 1:21). The result is spiritual freedom and victory over temptation, sin, and the forces evil.

The real dialectic in the New Testament is between present and future,[82] which is particularly evident in Romans 8:1–11.[83] The person under the sovereignty of Christ walks with the Spirit (v. 5) and is indwelt by the Spirit (v. 9). In verse 9 the Spirit of God is also called the Spirit of Christ. When believers enter the sphere of Christ by placing themselves under his control, Christ relates to them through the Holy Spirit. The indwelling Spirit

79. Hooker, *From Adam to Christ*, 19.
80. Hooker, *From Adam to Christ*, 43.
81. Dunn, *Christology in the Making*, 126.
82. Cullmann, *Christ and Time*, 146.
83. See Hamilton, *Holy Spirit and Eschatology in Paul*, 26–36.

is the indication of being in Christ (8:11, 14–16; compare 1 Cor 15:45–49; 2 Cor 1:22; Phil 3:3; Gal 4:6). Schweitzer states, "The possession of the Spirit proves to believers that they are already removed out of the natural state of existence and transferred into the supernatural. They are 'in the Spirit,' which means that they are no longer in the flesh. For being in the Spirit is only a form of manifestation of the being-in-Christ. Both are descriptions of one and the same state."[84]

Fellowship with God through the Spirit of Christ reveals Paul's mysticism. This union with God in Christ does not mean that one is absorbed into the person of Christ, losing all sense of personhood, any more than one loses personhood in Adam. Rather, one lives in a new controlling sphere of influence where Christ becomes the paradigm for life and not Adam. It is more than cognitive or ethical but deeply personal and experiential. In Romans 6:12 Paul speaks of not letting "sin reign in your mortal bodies," but "to offer the members of your bodies as instruments of righteousness" (6:13). The way this is done is by rejecting the old life in Adam. Paul uses the word "crucify" to illustrate this denial. There is a greater power at work in believers that renders sin powerless (6:6). The body still suffers death and succumbs to the realm of Adam until the resurrection (8:10), but a person's inner spirit can experience the power of the new age in the present. But Paul is not happy with only that idea. He believes that by providing the Holy Spirit (8:11) God can even bring new life to the mortal body still stuck in the realm of Adam. This leads Paul to an eschatological ethic, that since believers have the indwelling Christ within them, they do not need to fulfill the lusts of the body because they are free from the power of sin and the pull of the flesh. They are God's children and heirs of God's promises. They have the Spirit of sonship, which is marked by freedom from adamic existence (8:14–16).

Christ made available the possibility of living in this new sphere of existence by his death and resurrection. Andrew Lincoln writes, "The eschatological prospect to which the first man failed to attain is realized and receives its character through the resurrection of the Second man who has become heavenly."[85] This is not merely a return to the bliss of the garden of Eden. Where Adam failed through disobedience and entrapped all humanity after him in the power of the sphere of sin, the believer can be assured of success and victory over sin because of the present communion with Christ through the power of the indwelling presence and guidance of the Holy Spirit. As Barrett comments, "The work of the new Adam is not simply

---

84. Schweitzer, *Mysticism*, 167.
85. Lincoln, *Paradise Now and Not Yet*, 190.

to produce a handful of new individual men, all bearing the image of the heavenly Man, but to produce a new unit of existence, which is truly one in Christ as the human race as a whole is one in Adam."[86]

God's Redemptive Plan in Christ

The following chart summarizes the concept of the two spheres of existence in Paul's mind. On the left are words or concepts Paul uses to describe the existence "in Adam," and on the right the new eschatological existence "in Christ."

Characteristics of being...

"In Adam"	"In Christ"
old person/*anthrōpos*	new person/*anthrōpos*
old	new creation
death	life and resurrection
flesh (*sarx*)	Spirit (*pneuma*)
guilt and condemnation	justification
disobedience	obedience
characterized by sin	characterized by grace
law bound	law free
slave to sin	slave to righteousness
marred image of God	restored image of God
present evil age	coming new age (*eschaton*)
wisdom of the world	mind of Christ
human/earthly (*psychikos*)	spiritual (*pneumatikos*)
not able to know (*ou dynatai gnonai*)	able to judge (*anakrinō*)
human wisdom	divine wisdom
human (*anthrōpos*)	spirit (*pneuma*)
spirit of the world	divine Spirit
childish (*nepios*)	mature (*teleios*)
foolish (*moria*)	wise (*sophia*)
the first Adam	the last Adam
living being	life-giving spirit
first	second
from dust of the earth	from heaven

---

86. Barrett, *From First Adam to Last*, 110.

earth bound	heaven bound
plan gone wrong	plan gone right
gave into temptation	overcame temptation
enmity with God	communion with God

The way to experience this new life is through submission to the sovereignty of Jesus Christ shown through refusing to worship anything or anyone other than him alone, including things that please the self. Only the one who has proven himself worthy of the title of "Lord" may hold this place of sovereignty (Phil 2:11). Faith is the open door to accepting Jesus' sovereignty. The gospel message promises this fellowship with God through the agency of Christ. This fellowship results in more than simply an impersonal or casual relationship but communion on an intimate and deep level. Believers have the mind of Christ (1 Cor 2:16) because Christ dwells within them through the Holy Spirit, not overpowering their personhood, but recreating it in the image it was meant to be. This is at the heart of the mystery of God for Paul. Another aspect of the "good news" is that because this fellowship is by faith and not obedience to any law code, Gentiles can experience it as well. The mystery planned long ago has been revealed to all humanity.

It would limit the depth of Paul's thought to say that this mystery impacts only individual existence. The divine mystery in Christ makes existence as church (community) possible (see ch. 6). In Paul's eschatological thinking coming out of his Jewish apocalyptic context, this mystery has changed the course of all history. J. Christiaan Beker writes, "The resurrection of Christ and the final resurrection of the dead are crucial events, not because they are the guarantee of eternal personal survival but because they express the inner connection of the salvation of the created order with the final triumph of God."[87] Schweitzer also stresses the significance of this when he writes,

> The conception of Redemption that stands behind this eschatological expectation is, to put it quite generally, that Jesus Christ has made an end of the natural world and is bringing in the Messianic Kingdom. It is thus cosmologically conceived. By it a man is transferred from the perishable world to the imperishable, because the whole world is transferred from the one state to the other, and he with it. The redemption which the believer experiences is therefore not a mere transaction arranged between himself, God, and Christ, but a world-event in which he has a share. It is impossible to form a right conception of the

---

87. Beker, *Paul the Apostle*, 155.

view of redemption held by the Early Christians without taking into count the fact that it was thus cosmically conditioned.[88]

Conclusion

There are many complex issues related to Paul's interpretation of the divine mystery. At the center of his thought, however, runs the distinct thread of communion with the resurrected Jesus Christ. His ideology of the mystery of God in Christ begins with the recognition of the resurrected Jesus as the Christ and Lord. Paul experienced this in a dramatic and personal way in his vision on the Road to Damascus and in at least one other known vision briefly described in 2 Corinthians 12. He parted ways with other Jewish apocalypticists and mystics in his insistence on Jesus as the Lord and Christ and object of his visions.

His primary way of referring to the resulting relationship between Jesus and believers is the concept of being "in Christ." This concept of union with Christ contained in this phrase is present in other grammatical constructions which serve as the raw data and starting point for his understanding of the divine mystery. This communion language is not simply theological or christological but also ethical and social. Being in Christ impacts every aspect of life for Paul. He believed that the answer to the needs of his followers came through the full appropriation of the divine mystery in their lives.

---

88. Schweitzer, *Mysticism*, 54.

4

Grace, Conscience, and the Law

*The aim of our charge is love that issues from
a pure heart and a good conscience and a sincere faith.*
(1 Timothy 1:5)

PAUL'S LETTERS WERE WRITTEN in response to pressing issues in the early church. One problem he devoted significant attention to was the relationship of Jews and Gentiles. Certain Jewish Christians were teaching that Gentiles had to be circumcised and follow Jewish regulations. These so-called Judiazers (Gal 2:14) were causing confusion, especially because they were distorting the place of the law and misunderstood freedom in Christ. They failed to comprehend that this new life in Christ is one of grace and not human effort. Acts 15 records a meeting of early church leaders in what is known as the Jerusalem Council. This group met to determine if Gentiles needed to become Jews or follow Jewish customs in order to be Christians. The conclusions of this council sent ripples throughout the early church as more and more Gentiles were becoming believers in Jesus Christ.

Against this backdrop, Paul clarifies in his letters to the Galatians and Romans the proper place of the law in the life of believers. Unfortunately, even readers of Paul today have a difficult time understanding how God's purpose for the law finds fulfillment in Christ. The key to appropriating the law in one's life is the inner work of the Holy Spirit upon one's inner self. The law can become a trap to spiritual development if it is not understood in the context of this new life in Christ. Even the law is affected by the sphere of Adam.

The Desperate Condition *in Adam*

Replacing Truth for a Lie

Paul begins the Letter to the Romans with an indictment of the human condition and the hopelessness that results: "For the wrath of God is revealed from heaven against all ungodliness and unrighteousness of people, who by their unrighteousness suppress the truth" (1:18). This verse begins with the effect and ends with the cause. God's wrath against godless and unrighteous people is the outcome of their suppression of the truth. Paul goes on to define this "truth" in verse 19 as the plain revelation of the existence of a creator. The human problem begins with rejecting God. There are consequences to rejecting the truth, but grace is available to offer a new way of life. Paul uses diatribe in the first three chapters of the letter to show that everyone to some degree has rejected God. It is a problem that began long ago when Adam and Eve accepted a lie about God's instruction. They essentially put their own desires before God's law. God's law was simple, symbolized in not eating the fruit of the Tree of the Knowledge of Good and Evil. If they kept this law in obedience, they would experience peace and love.

The truth is that love is shown through obedient love. The lie is that God's way of life (obedience to the single command) was suppressing Adam and Eve's freedom to be who they wanted to be. By failing to obey God's single command, Adam and Eve were also saying that God was not worthy enough to be loved above all else. Rather than seeking God, Adam and Eve sought wisdom to fulfill their curiosity. Sin began with misplaced love and worship. Those in rebellion against God likewise have "exchanged the truth about God for a lie and worshiped and served the creature rather than the Creator" (1:25).

Idolatry can be defined fundamentally as the usurpation of God's place with something created. The first act of sin led to the condition of sin that has affected every person since. Because of this condition, people have sought to find fulfillment in things of the created order. This has fueled pride which often results in self destruction. God's creative purpose for humanity has become distorted by selfish desires. What God created for our joy and benefit has ended up in our pain and misery. As a result of Adam and Eve's decision of self-assertion, humanity lapsed into a state of depravity and corruption. Each person follows the same deceitful course of sin, resulting in spiritual death and the disobedient lifestyle of pleasing the flesh (Eph 2:1–3). Disobedience has distorted love and brought death (Rom 5:12). Davies writes, "Rebellion against God has created a vacuum in human nature. That vacuum must be filled, if not by God, then by the devil of self. All lusts and excesses of human behavior are attempts to satisfy the 'aching void the world can never fill.' Man, as a result of his fall from Divine Grace, is cursed by an infinite craving."[1]

The Power and Pervasiveness of Sin

Humanity does not have the power to choose the way of obedience without God's intervention (Rom 6:23a). Harald Lindstrom adds, "From the point of view of salvation natural man has no resources of his own whatsoever. He is sinful through and through, has no knowledge of God and no power to turn to Him of his own free will."[2] The power of idolatry and self-love blinds us. God in His divine *agape* has not left us in this state of condemnation but has provided the way of escape (John 3:16). The heights of divine love reach down to the depths of human depravity.

The New Testament does not deal explicitly with the origin of evil or "original" sin. The results of our first parents' act of disobedience were enough evidence of a deep, human problem. Paul does not speculate about the original of sin but only that it "came into the world through one man" (Rom 5:12). He does not say that the serpent caused Adam and Eve to sin but that sin and death are the reality humans face now. Beginning in Romans 5:12, he uses the definite article *he* with the noun *harmartia*, essentially making sin an inanimate power. He personifies sin in chapter 6 by making it something that has mastery over us. In these chapters, he uses "the sin" to describe the whole matter of life opposed to God. Sin is an unseen force that compels humans to rebel against God and is the chief characteristic of life "in Adam." Dunn comments, "It is that power which turns humankind in upon itself in preoccupation with satisfying and compensating for its own weakness as flesh."[3]

The consequences of Adam and Eve's sin can be seen in at least three primary ways. More broadly, sin has affected creation when it "entered into the *world*" (Rom 5:12). In some way, all of creation suffered a setback because of human decision. Paul puts this later in 8:19–22 as creation being subjected unwillingly to futility, groaning, and in bondage to decay until the

---

1. D. Davies, *Down Peacock's Feathers*, 70.
2. Lindstrom, *Wesley and Sanctification*, 45.
3. Dunn, *Theology of Paul*, 112.

"revealing of God's sons," referring to the second coming of Jesus. Second, sin has affected humanity on a corporate level. Because of "Adam," death became a power and condition that affects all people. Death is a direct consequence of sin (5:12) and has reigned since Adam (5:17). Third, sinful acts often leave terrible scars, but the sin of Adam has left a deeper mark on the soul of every human. There is a reciprocal relationship between sin and death. Impending death brings a weakened state to the physical body, including the psyche, which then makes us vulnerable to temptation and tendency to sin. Furnish writes, "Death, like sin, is a demonic power which 'reigns' in this age (*basileuein*, Rom 5:14, 17) and is in fact the manifestation of sin's reign (Rom 5:21), the 'enemy' power which still holds out when all others have been conquered (1 Cor 15:26)."[4] Sin exemplifies the spiritual death and darkness that overcomes those who do not respond to the light of the gospel. Karl Barth writes, "When God has been deprived of His glory, men are also deprived of theirs. Desecrated within their souls, they are also desecrated in their bodies, for men are one."[5]

The way Paul begins the body of Romans is with a systematic treatment of the human problem. He shows the universal sickness of sin before he offers the universal solution in Christ. Seeing our need helps us appreciate even more the gift offered to us. Although Paul does not use the word "sin" until 2:12 (*hēmarton*), much of what he says before this defines what sin is, its causes, and how it affects our relationship to ourselves, others, and God.

The decisive issue is "knowing" God. Paul speaks of two kinds of knowledge in chapter 1. First, there is the basic knowledge or recognition of a creator (v. 19). Evidence of a creator is abundant and self-evident. God has not left creation without a witness to himself, but this evidence is not significant enough to some people who reject the idea of a creator as absurd and scientifically unverifiable. The more surprising issue, however, is that some people *do* realize there is a creator but fail to honor the creator as God (v. 21). Paul refers to another type of knowledge in verse 28 with the intensive word *epignōsei*, which can be translated as "acknowledgment" or a deeper awareness of something. Even though people might believe in a mighty Mover of the universe, they fail to act upon this awareness by acknowledging God in their own lives. This failure to "know" God only leads into deeper futility and foolishness.

Failing to know God in a personal, more intimate way only leads to further futility and distance from God. Paul graphically puts it as "God gave

---

4. Furnish, *Theology and Ethics in Paul*, 117.
5. Barth, *Romans*, 51.

them up" (vv. 24, 26, 28). God let them go the way of their hearts' desire. The proper response to God as creator is worship. Failing to worship God consequently ends up in worshiping something else. The most fundamental human temptation is to become one's own god using one's own conditions, essentially replacing the worship of God with something else. It is a matter of sovereignty: who will be in control? The core of all temptation is replacing God's perfect desire of obedient love with selfish desires that put God in a secondary or lesser position because of a distorted interpretation of love.

When the temptation to eat of the fruit gave way to the action of disobedience, something fundamental changed in the human condition. God's love and grace could not be perfectly experienced because of hearts turned away from him. God will not force relationship upon hearts that are not in love with him, for that would violate the essence of love, which must be a free choice. Rather, God decreed before time began that he would come in the form of his beloved creatures, both to demonstrate the depths of his love and to make this love the means of transforming the human heart, resulting in the ability to love God as God intended (Rom 5:8; 16:25).

The Human Struggle with the Power of Sin

For Paul, sin is a power and condition to be reckoned with. It leads to the total breakdown of human existence. He spends the first three chapters of Romans demonstrating that no one is without sin and that "all have sinned and fallen short of the glory of God" (Rom 3:23). Sin is a universal problem that affects every descendent of Adam, both Jews and Gentiles. Just as Adam and Eve were accountable to the simple law against eating the forbidden fruit, both Jews and Gentiles are accountable to the laws God has given them. The Jews had the written law and thus more revelation, and so would be judged more strictly. Gentiles only had the law of the conscience, an innate awareness of good and evil (2:14–16). Both would experience the "wrath of God" because of hardened and unrepentant hearts (1:18; 2:5).

It is not difficult to point fingers at the Gentiles and condemn them for their idolatry. No doubt Paul was very familiar with the many idols and religions of his day (Acts 17:22–23), and he knew the crisis of faith that resulted in giving these idols any authority in one's life (1 Cor 10:14). Many of the unrighteous deeds listed in 1:26–32 are evident in our world today. People never tire of their creative ways to rebel against God. Jews are held accountable to the written law (the Torah). Israel's story in the Old Testament shows the inability to meet the demands of this standard. In chapter 2 Paul demolishes any confidence of the Jews as the privileged people of God because they were doing the very same thing as the Gentiles: replacing God with something created (Rom 2:1), in this case, their futile efforts to obey the law without the "circumcision of the heart" (2:29). Bruce comments, "Paul's aim is to show that the whole of humanity is morally bankrupt, unable to claim a favourable verdict at the judgment bar of God, desperately in need of His mercy and pardon."[6] The problem of both Jew and Gentile was deeper than their *ability* to be right before God; the issue was their effort to *be* God.

Obedience to the law—even if it were possible to obey all the law—is not enough for salvation because salvation comes through faith (3:20, 24). Paul will deal more with the futility of obedience to the law in chapter 7, where he shows the power of sin to be greater than the power of the fallen human will. If God had not intervened into this crisis, no one would be able to stand in the presence of the Holy One. So, the Holy One comes in grace to instill within each person a ray of light that moves that person closer to himself.

Transformation through the Law

God through the law and the human conscience brings the fallen human race to the acknowledgment of sin and the realization of the need for salvation. The ultimate purpose of both the law and the conscience is to lead to faith in Christ Jesus. As a person comes to faith in Christ, the Holy Spirit continues to work, guiding, cleansing, and transforming through this same grace now experienced with sanctifying power. The standard that the Holy Spirit uses as the guide in this saving process is the law. The law serves as the tool of grace, to lead a person to holiness. For Paul, the law has an indispensable function in the transformation of the sinner into a saint.

The law was important to Paul both before his Damascus road experience (Acts 9:3–19; 22:6–16; 26:9–23) and after. Saul the Pharisee was deeply committed to the Jewish law, claiming to be blameless as to the righteousness under the law (Phil 3:6). Later as an apostle, Paul remained rooted in Torah and never completely broke from it. A radical transformation took place, however, in his life when he encountered the risen Jesus of Nazareth in his vision on the road to Damascus. So extreme was the change that he could later write that he counted his rich heritage as loss compared to knowing Jesus Christ as Lord (Phil 3:7–8). Bruce comments, "He had found a new way of righteousness, based on faith in Christ. Allegiance to a person had displaced devotion to a code—which was, indeed, not merely a code but

---

6. Bruce, *Romans*, 81–82.

more a way of life."[7] This experience totally changed his understanding of the law. Jesus Christ became the answer for Paul.

Law Defined

Paul uses the key word *nomos*, "law," 119 times in his writings, with 107 of those in Romans and Galatians. The Greek word *nomos* first meant "what is proper" in reference to any norm, custom, usage, or tradition in the political, cosmic, natural, or moral realm. In the religious realm, it referred to the will of a deity.[8] In the Septuagint, *nomos* is used over 200 times for the Hebrew word *torah*. *Torah* meant more than just "law" for the ancient Israelites, but ranged in meaning from "teaching" to the entire revealed will of God.[9] The law was closely related to the idea of covenant. God gave the law as a requirement by which Israel could live up to their part of the covenantal agreement.

Paul uses *nomos* in similar ways as it is used in the Septuagint and as *torah* is used in the Hebrew Bible. There has been no real consensus but much discussion on the meaning of this word in his letters, perhaps because he uses it with different nuances. Cranfield identifies five uses of *nomos* by Paul: (1) Old Testament law (especially the Pentateuch), (2) as the Old Testament as a whole, (3) as a principle, (4) as "compulsion," "restraint," or "necessity," and (5) as the commandment of Christ.[10] At its most basic, usual definition, the word "law" suggests some norm that governs the way things ought or ought not to be done. As with all words, the final interpretation rests with the specific context of usage.

Paul's Uses of the Law

Reveals the Will of God

For Paul, the law is a vital instrument in the process of salvation. Because he was a faithful Jew devoted to the Hebrew Scriptures, he understood the law as the revealed will of God and never rejected his Jewish heritage in the *Torah*. Parry comments, "Law was for him the expression of the will of God in application to the conduct of man, as revealed to Moses and embodied in

---

7. Bruce, *Paul*, 189.
8. Kleinknecht, "*Nomos*," *TDNT*, 4:1023–24.
9. W. Davies, *Jewish and Pauline Studies*, 3.
10. Cranfield, "St. Paul and the Law," 44.

the written law and its authorized interpretations."[11] As Paul progresses in his reasoning in Romans 7, he asks the rhetorical question (v. 7), "Is the law sin?"[12] He possibly feared that some of his readers might have concluded from what he had said in 5:20 and 6:14 that the law is negative or unimportant.[13] To this question he answers with the strong negative, *mē genoito*, meaning "Never," "Let it not be," or "Certainly not!" In Galatians 3:21, Paul asks another rhetorical question, "Is the law then against the promises of God?" He answers this question with the same strong, emphatic *mē genoito*. The law is neither sinful nor against the promises of God.

Furthermore, the law was given to impart life (Rom 7:10). Paul calls the law "holy, righteous, and good" (7:12). Since the law comes from God, it shares the same holy qualities as God. As John Wesley wrote, "The law of God . . . is a copy of the eternal mind, a transcript of the divine nature: Yea, it is the fairest offspring of the everlasting Father, the brightest efflux of his essential wisdom, the visible beauty of the Most High."[14] William Greathouse comments, "Since the law comes from God, who created us, it sets forth the only conditions under which life can be truly fulfilled. It is thus an index to the very structure of reality."[15] The law has our well-being in mind, not our harm.[16] Because the law comes from God and is a reflection of God, Paul can say that it is spiritual (7:14). Paul delights in God's law in his innermost being (7:22) and obeys it as a transformed person (7:25).

Defines Sin

The law also has a negative side because it defines sin (Rom 7:7; 5:20). In Romans 4:15 and 5:13, Paul argues that where there is no law, there is no transgression. The word for transgression (*parabasi*) has the idea of committing a sin by overstepping or violating a law of God.[17] A boundary must be fixed in order for one to step over it. Greathouse adds, "A sinful tendency may indeed be present in the absence of law, but it takes a specific commandment to crystallize that tendency into a positive transgression or breach of

---

11. Parry, *Epistle of Paul to the Romans*, 211.
12. From the context, Paul is using *nomos* to refer to God's commandments in general and in particular as seen in the Mosaic law.
13. Morris, *Epistle to the Romans*, 278.
14. Wesley, *Works*, 5:438–439.
15. Greathouse, *Romans*, 152.
16. Morris, *Romans*, 283. See also Ps 19:7–13.
17. Schneider, "*Parabasi*," *TDNT*, 5:739–40.

law. . . ."[18] Paul argues that the tendency to sin has been around since Adam, but when God gave the Mosaic law, the tendency to sin found a foothold (5:13). "Sin manifests itself in commandments to be transgressed."[19] This is not to say that sin had no effect until the time of Moses. Sin has always produced death (5:12), but since Moses it has had a catalyst in the law.[20] Brice Martin comments, "The real purpose in the giving of the law is thus a negative one as opposed to the positive purpose of the original commandment which was given to Adam. It is given not to bring life (Gal 3:21) but to make sin exceedingly sinful, to show man that he cannot save himself by means of the law, and to show man his need for a savior."[21]

Paul asks in Galatians 3:19, "Why then the law?" He answers, "Because of transgressions." Sanders points out that the phrase *tōn parabaseōn charin* can mean "on account of transgressions," "to produce transgressions," or "to deal with transgressions."[22] He goes on to argue that the law as a custodian (3:24) acts more like an enslaver than a protector. It is true that, according to Romans, the law provides fertile ground for sin and becomes enslaved by the power of sin. In Galatians 3:23-25, however, Paul seems to paint a different picture of the law. He claims that the law keeps us under restraint until faith is revealed. The law acts as a pedagogue (*paidagōgon*, 3:24) until we put our faith in Christ in order that we may be justified by faith.[23] But once faith in God is allowed to reign in Christ (just as faith reigned with Abraham, 3:14), the law no longer acts like a pedagogue.

---

18. Greathouse, *Romans*, 104.

19. Bruce, *Romans*, 123.

20. The question remains with Rom 5:14, why did people die before Moses if the law had not yet been given? The answer may lie in the context of Rom 1-3, where Paul demonstrates that both Jews and Gentiles have died because of breaking the law. For the Jews, the law is the Torah (2:12). For Gentiles, the law is written on the conscience (2:14-15). Before Moses, the only law people really had was written on the conscience, and since no one could keep this law, everyone sinned, and therefore everyone died.

21. B. Martin, *Christ and the Law in Paul*, 38.

22. Sanders, *Paul, the Law*, 66.

23. A pedagogue was a household slave whose responsibility was to prevent a child from making moral and economic mistakes. The pedagogue accompanied a child from ages six to sixteen away from home, often carrying the child's book boxes to school. The safety of the child depended upon this person, who, as a consequence, would protect the child from moral and physical dangers. The pedagogue was responsible for the child's behavioral development, and sometimes even the actual behavior of the child. See Lull, "Law Was Our Pedagogue." Like a pedagogue, the law protects, but life under a pedagogue is no better than being a slave. When Jesus Christ came, however, the slavery and alienation were destroyed. One is now able to say, "Abba, Father" with intimacy and trust (4:4-7).

The law has not only given sin a foothold, but it has even gone so far as to make sin increase. The reason for this is so that grace may increase even more and have the ultimate victory. Romans 5:20 begins, "But law came in" (*nomos de pareisēlthen*). *Pareisēlthen* carries with it the idea of sneaking in; the law does not have a primary place in the divine plan,[24] but is only secondary in creating the needed situation in which grace can work. The commandment is neutral (7:8), but sin, as personified in chapter 7, needs some agent with which to work, a role the law fulfills. "Apart from the law sin is dead." The tendency to sin because of the fallen human condition is still present although the law has not yet given an occasion for the act of sin. The law allows sin as a power to bring spiritual death (7:9, 11).

Leads to Christ

The law shows that the net result of sin is death (Rom 3:23), and in this capacity it shows the need for Jesus Christ. In Galatians 3:22 Paul argues that sin must be shown to be sin so that we can put our faith in Christ. We must be shown that we cannot earn our salvation by obedience to the law in order that we can recognize that justification is by faith in Christ alone (Gal 2:16).[25] Ernest Kevan writes, "It is the sharp needle of the law that makes way for the scarlet thread of the gospel."[26] Commenting on Romans 10:4, Wesley says, "It is the very design of the law, to bring men to believe in Christ for justification and salvation. He alone gives that pardon and life which the law shows the want of, but cannot give."[27] In Romans 5:21, the *hina* ("in order that") suggests that the law came to increase sin *so that* grace may reign.[28] Morris comments,

> ... God's way has always been the way of grace, and we misunderstand the law if we see it as the way of earning salvation. It

---

24. BDAG, 624.

25. Sanders comments, "Paul's logic seems to run like this: in Christ God has acted to save the world; therefore, the world is in need of salvation; but God also gave the law; if Christ is given for salvation, it must follow that the law could not have been; is the law then against the purpose of God which has been revealed in Christ? No, it has the function of consigning everyone to sin *so that* everyone could be saved by God's grace in Christ" (*Paul and Palestinian Judaism*, 475).

26. Kevan, *Evangelical Doctrine of Law*, 11.

27. Wesley, *Explanatory Notes*, 561.

28. Dunn states, ". . . if the agency of Adam's trespass gave free reign to sin and death, it is precisely the force which continues to come through the one man who defeated sin and death, which sustains the believer against their claims upon him and which will prove finally triumphant" (*Romans 1–8*, 300).

is rather God's way of showing us our shortcomings so that we turn to Christ for our salvation. This does not mean an abolishing of the law; on the contrary, faith establishes the law (3:31). It is only when we experience the love of God in Christ, that love which we see so vividly on the cross, that we come to see the place of the law and find that love is the fulfillment of the law (13:8, 10).[29]

God provides the law (revealed specifically in the Old Testament for the Jews and revealed generally through the conscience for the Gentiles) as a form of grace that leads to Christ. God's laws have always been a form of grace whereby God's will for holiness in relationship is revealed, yet consequently also revealing the inadequacy of humanity in its own power to secure this relationship outside of reliance upon God's mercy.

The Law in Adam

There is a problem with the law, however, because it falls prey to the power of sin. The law in the sphere of sin only serves to enhance the power of sin. Paul devotes much effort in Romans 1–3 in showing that the law itself can never repair the broken relationship between God and humanity begun in the garden of Eden with Adam and Eve. He demonstrates that both Jews and Gentiles are guilty of breaking the law of God. In Romans 1:18–32 he insists that when people are allowed to do as they wish by gratifying their sinful desires, described as "godlessness and wickedness,"[30] they become so hopelessly trapped and lost in their own passions that God gives them up to do as they please (1:24, 26, 28). In 2:9 all who do evil, both Jew and Gentile, will have trouble and distress. On the one hand, the Gentiles are guilty because they have a law unto themselves (2:14–15); they are morally responsible because of their natural reason.[31] In 1:19–32 "the Gentile without benefit of *special* revelation is guilty of a responsible act of rebellion against the Creator in view of God's *general* revelation in nature."[32] Jews, however, are also guilty because they have not lived up to God's revealed laws (2:17–19). Both Jew and Gentile are on the same level of guilt under

---

29. Morris, *Romans*, 145.

30. Greek: *asebeian* and *adikian*. *Adikian* is one who violates a divine law and who does not do *dikaiosynē*, righteousness and justice. The antithetical root of *asebeian* is *sebomai*, which means worshiping God in reverence. These people neither worship God nor follow God's laws.

31. Greathouse, *Romans*, 67.

32. Greathouse, *Romans*, 66.

the law (3:9). No one can boast in being justified by the law because the law calls all to accountability to God. This accountability spells condemnation (3:19-20) because all have sinned, both Jew and Gentile alike (3:23).

Sin and law work hand in hand. The law gives the opportunity for the descendants of Adam to assert themselves against God like Adam by disobeying God's commandments. The power and control of sin increases under the law in the lives of those *in Adam* (5:20). As long as sin is allowed to reign, it holds the law under its power. Paul urges the Romans to consider themselves dead in regard to the sphere and control of sin. In chapter 6 he consistently refers to sin as a power that controls people unless they die to their old life by submitting themselves totally to Christ as their new master. He begins the chapter using the noun "sin" as dative locative of sphere with the article (lit. "in the sin," *tē harmartia*; vv. 1, 2, 10, 11, 13) in reference back to the fallen condition Adam introduced through disobedience. Those outside of Christ are enslaved and bound in this fallen condition, which results in their inability to keep God's commands.

Paul urges the Romans to die to the law trapped in this Adamic sphere of influence (7:4). The law is not sin because it comes from God (7:7). The problem is that the commandment brings death because it allows sin to reign (7:9-10, 13). The person who is set on fulfilling the desires of the flesh (*sarx*) is unable to submit to God's law (8:7). Law in the sphere of sin condemns and enslaves because it is unable to do anything to overcome the power of sin. The law was never meant to be the solution to the sin problem. The law represents human effort to please God by attempting to be righteous outside of God's grace.

Sin also causes the law to be misunderstood and misused. This is especially seen in Galatians with the phrase "works of law" (*erga nomou*). Paul's basic position is summarized in 2:16: no one can be justified by works of the law but by faith in Jesus Christ. The problem for Paul is not moral obedience to the law, but using this obedience as the religious means for justification. Paul would agree wholeheartedly with the psalmist who says, "Blessed is the one . . . whose delight is in the law of the Lord, and on his law he meditates day and night" (Ps 1:1-2). Sanders states that Paul uses *nomos* in two contexts: "one in discussing how one gets 'in' (not by works of law), the other in discussing how one who is 'in' behaves (he keeps the law)."[33] There is nothing wrong with circumcision itself (Gal 6:15) but only when it is used as the requirement for membership.[34] "Works of law" for

---

33. Sanders, *Paul, the Law*, 10.
34. Sanders, *Paul, the Law*, 20.

Paul, then, are different than godly obedience.[35] Paul's answer to those who would try to gain righteousness through "works of law" might be, "We are so bound by what is antagonistic to God that we are unable to do his will" (see Gal 5:17). So-called legalism results from not realizing that Christ is the innermost meaning and goal of the law.[36] Paul radically rejects using the law in a legalistic way.

The law works with the conscience to stop anyone from boasting in self-righteousness and causes all to recognize that salvation comes by God alone through grace (Rom 3:19–20). If we could obey God's will perfectly (revealed by the law of the conscience or the written law found in Scripture), we could avoid the curse of the law that brings guilt, condemnation, and separation from God. The sequence of clauses in Romans 3:23–24 shows that it is because of sin that we have fallen from God's image and, thus, why we need restoration. Paul knew that complete obedience to the law is impossible. Both Jews (2:17–29) and Gentiles (2:12–16) have been a failure at it (1:18–32). In 7:14–24 Paul describes his own inability to meet the demands of the law.[37] He recognized that being under the power of sin and being set against God makes it impossible to fulfill the law of God. Parry adds, "The law, in fact, was essentially an external standard, embodying declarations, apprehensible by man, of what was right; but not an internal power providing or imparting the ability to do what was right."[38]

Law in the sphere of sin puts us under the wrath of God, resulting in condemnation. The law is unable to justify because justification has always been through faith in God and not in one's own ability (see Paul's discussion about Abraham in Rom 4). Finally, complete obedience to the law is proven by history and experience to be impossible because sin is too powerful for humans to overcome by their own ability. Something radical must happen to the law and sin for humanity to be restored to a relationship with God.

The Law in Christ

Paul argues that Jesus Christ is the answer to the problem of the law's enslavement to sin, so much so that he transforms the law from the sphere of

---

35. Sondgrass, "Spheres of Influence," 96.

36. Longenecker, *Galatians*, 114.

37. The use of the first person has created great debate as to whether Paul is using a historical present tense describing his past experience (autobiographical), or whether he is speaking of his present experience as a believer. At the simplest, he means someone trying to be righteous without submission to Christ's lordship.

38. Parry, *Romans*, 211.

sin into the sphere of grace, which is God's intention for the law. In Romans 10:4 Paul writes, "For Christ is the *telos* of the law in regard to righteousness for all who believe." There are two important considerations with this verse. First, Paul uses the connective *gar* ("for") to link this verse to the previous verses. He has argued that Israel has not been justified by their obedience to the law because they lacked faith (9:31–32). He wants to change that (10:1) by enlightening their zeal (10:2) concerning the true meaning of righteousness from God (10:3). Paul is against zeal that separates Jews and Gentiles and puts works over faith. This zeal leads to Israel's feeling of superiority, that only they can find justification because the law has been given to them exclusively.[39] In 10:5–13 Paul stresses that salvation is for all people through faith in Jesus as Lord, whom God has raised from the dead (10:9–10).

The second issue is how to understand *telos* in 10:4. *Telos* could be understood as "goal"[40] or as "terminus."[41] *Telos* carries the idea of completion of a task, the fulfillment of that for which something was intended. In a sense Christ completes the law, which beforehand had acted only as a teacher until he arrived. Christ met the obligation of the law because he had no sin, something that no one else can claim. The purpose of the law was to reveal the will of God for how people can keep in covenantal relationship, but the law was unable to do this because of the power of sin. Christ perfectly revealed God's will and sealed a new covenant through his blood. He also ends people's struggle to obey the law and shows that salvation is a free gift to all who believe (Gal 3:13, 24; 4:4–5).[42] Paul shows in Romans 9–11 that Christ breaks down all barriers between Jew and Gentile, especially the dividing wall of the law (see Gal 3:28; Eph. 2:11–18). Christ is the qualified "terminus" of the law. In its contractual aspect, Jewish nomism has come to its full completion and end in Christ.[43]

This raises the question: is the law still valid for believers? Martin argues that the enslaving, condemning, and death-dealing effects have ended, but not the law as an expression of God's will.[44] Being under grace does not give the believer freedom to sin. In Romans 6:15 Paul asks, "Are we to

---

39. Dunn, *Romans 9–16*, 530.

40. Cranfield, "St. Paul and the Law."

41. Hamerton-Kelly states, ". . . giving up the boundary markers is tantamount to giving up the Jewish way of life and that cannot be interpreted in any other way than as an abandonment of the whole law" ("Sacred Violence and 'Works of Law,'" 62).

42. Scholars can be found on both sides of the debate. For a brief description of both sides, see B. Martin, *Christ and the Law in Paul*, 130–41; and Moo, "Paul and the Law," 302–7.

43. Longenecker, *Paul, Apostle of Liberty*, 128.

44. B. Martin, *Christ and the Law in Paul*, 144.

sin because we are not under law but under grace?" He answers with the strong *mē genoito*, "Never," "By no means." Rather, the law was originally meant as a guide for those who are in a covenant of grace. The law (Exod 20) came *after* relationship (Exod 19). The law was given for instruction so that people might find hope in God (Rom 15:4). Paul is not willing to do away with the obligation of believers to love those around them. He insists that the transformed believer can now fulfill the law by loving one's neighbor as oneself (Gal 5:14). In the sphere of Christ, love as the purpose of the law becomes the characteristic of Christians. For those who remain trapped in the sphere of Adam and are controlled by the power of sin, the law remains a trap and at best, only a tool to seek to be self-righteous before God.

In this respect, Paul suppresses the cultic aspects of the law and uplifts the moral aspects. He speaks against rituals that separate Jews and Gentiles, such as circumcision (Gal 2:3; 5:2; 6:15; Rom 2:25–29; 4:9–12), food laws (Gal 2:11–14; Rom 14–15), and observing certain days (Gal 4:10; Rom 14:5–6). Although these laws have their place historically for the people of God, in Christ, a new people of God have been created who are characterized by love. All barriers, such as race, social standing, and gender, have been broken down in Christ and all people can be children of Abraham through faith (Gal 3:28–29). Those appropriations of the law that keep others from coming to God through faith are a distortion of the promise made to Abraham that all nations would be blessed through him (Rom 4:11–12).

Paul is not willing to depart from the entire law. He is very devoted to those parts of the law that fulfill "the law of Christ" (Gal 6:2). In Romans 13:8–10 Paul lists several commandments of the Decalogue that are summed up in the great command, "Love your neighbor as yourself."[45] In Romans 12:9–21 he gives specific, practical, and moral examples of how one ought to live as a transformed person. Likewise, in Galatians 5:22–23 he lists the "fruit of the Spirit." These and similar lists are moral to the core. Commenting on Romans 2:25, Schreiner says, "Clearly, he [Paul] means that Jews who are circumcised but fail to observe the *moral norms* of the law are condemned (2:25–29). Gentiles, on the other hand, who do not possess the ritual law, but who obey the moral law are justified."[46] Paul wants no stumbling block put in the path of anyone seeking Christ (Rom 14:13). He radically breaks from many Jews of his day and says that nothing is unclean in itself but only if it keeps someone from Christ (14:14–15).

45. Schreiner says, "The commandments cited here refer to matters which would be acknowledged universally as norms. It is not the case that Paul thinks these demands are normative only because they are loving; rather, there is a mutual and dialectical relationship between love and the demands cited here" ("Abolition and Fulfillment," 59).

46. Schreiner, "Abolition and Fulfillment," 65.

Paul says this because he had himself experienced transformation. The same transforming power that changed him can change all who put their faith in Christ, and as a direct result of this, the law will be transformed from the realm of sin into the realm of Christ. A key passage for understanding this transformation is Paul's testimony in Galatians 2:20. He put to death trying to be justified by his own efforts (2:15–19). Likewise, those who want to belong to Christ must do the same (5:24). This is a major theme in Romans 6, where Paul urges believers not to let sin reign (v. 12)[47] or to be under its control, but rather to live in the realm of righteousness (v. 18), which leads to sanctification and eternal life (v. 22).

Crucial to this transformation is the Holy Spirit whom Paul mentions twenty times in Romans 8. The law of the Spirit sets one free from the law of sin and death (8:2). Law controlled by sin and death leads to condemnation, but law in the sphere of the Holy Spirit provides freedom from condemnation. The law weakened by the power of sin falls prey to sin; it is unable to free a person from sin's grip (8:3a). To remedy this, God sent his Son as a human to show that sin could be conquered (8:3b). The power of sin is death (6:23), but Christ conquered death and, therefore, the power of sin by his resurrection from the dead (1 Cor 15:56–57). This same power can be made effective in believers through the power and presence of the Holy Spirit.

The result of this transformation is freedom from the curse of the law (Gal 3:13, 24) and the spiritual impotency from which the law cannot rescue (Gal 3:21).[48] It is the same law at work but it is changed from the sphere of sin, death, and condemnation to the sphere of the Spirit who bears witness to Christ. By finding freedom from sin, one finds freedom from the law as the perceived means of salvation rather than as the intended guide to holy living.[49] Paul is impassioned about the Galatians falling back into slavery under the law. He claims that it is for freedom that Christ set them free (Gal 5:1a). The message of hope that Christ brings is one of freedom *from* works-righteousness and freedom *to* love.

The sin problem has been solved once and for all by Christ's death and resurrection. The justified believer has been freed from the guilt and condemnation of sin, but Paul urges believers not to let the power of sin reign anymore because they have been raised with Christ (Rom 6:5–11). The Holy Spirit then makes this hope a reality (8:10–11) to those who do not let sin reign (8:13). And as believers are freed from the power of sin, they are freed

---

47. *Mē oun basileuetō hē hamartia*, a present imperative.

48. Ridderbos, *Epistle to the Churches of Galatia*, 186.

49. B. Martin states, "They [Christians] obey the law not to get saved, or to stay saved, but because they have been saved" (*Christ and the Law in Paul*, 156).

and empowered to obey the law as it was intended—as a guide to loving one's neighbor as oneself (13:8–10).

Believers, then, are empowered to fulfill the "law of Christ" (Gal 6:2). The Spirit-empowered person produces actions in keeping with the law (Gal 5:14, 22–23).[50] The law as a reflection of a gracious and loving God can become a tremendous tool for holy living when put in the sphere of Christ. The person who is "in Christ" uses the law as the sanctified tool of the conscience, showing the way how to be Christ-like (2 Cor 3:7–18).

The Tool of the Conscience

The Meaning of the Word

The Greek word translated "conscience," *syneidēsis*, occurs fifteen times in Romans and the Corinthian Correspondence (and of those, eight times in 1 Cor 8 and 10),[51] and six times in the Pastoral Epistles.[52] The etymology of *syneidēsis* helps unpack this rather difficult word. The word is made of two parts: *syn*, meaning "with," and *oidon*, meaning "to know." Hence, it is knowing something in agreement with another person or thing. Christian Maurer comments, "It is man aware of himself in perception and acknowledgment, in willing and acting."[53] Conscience can develop as a person becomes more aware of self and various issues, leading to the development of regulations or scruples.[54] The conscience serves as the guide in moral conduct (Rom 2:15).[55]

Although it can be found in Hellenistic moral teaching, the word "conscience" does not occur in the Gospels, suggesting that Paul introduced it to the Christian context by using a word from the Greek speaking world. The conscience functions as a judge for moral conduct. Paul can write to the

---

50. Commenting on Gal 5:14, Ridderbos says, "In this entire summary, Paul's purpose is both to let the law come into its own proper validity in the life of believers; and to graft its fulfillment upon a different principle from that of human self-validation through works—namely, the salvation brought by Christ. . . . Thus in this Epistle the apostle can on the one hand proclaim freedom from the law, and on the other can require love as the fulfillment of the law" (*Galatians*, 201).

51. Rom 2:15; 9:1; 13:5; 1 Cor 8:7, 10, 12; 10:25; 27, 28, 29 (twice); 2 Cor 1:12; 4:2; 5:11.

52. 1 Tim 1:5, 19; 3:9; 4:2; 2 Tim 1:3; Titus 1:15.

53. Christian Maurer, "*Synoida*," *TDNT*, 8:914.

54. For further discussion, see Pierce, *Conscience in the New Testament*; Jewett, *Paul's Anthropological Terms*, 402–46; Maurer, "*Synoida*," *TDNT*, 8:898–919.

55. Furnish, *Theology and Ethics in Paul*, 229.

Corinthians that his conscience testifies that his conduct in the world and in his relations to the Corinthians has been "in the purity and sincerity that are from God" (2 Cor 1:12).[56] Later, he confidently calls God as witness of his efforts to develop relationship with the Corinthians (1:23). In the same letter, Paul again defends his motives and ministry by demonstrating or commending himself "before every person's conscience in the presence of God" (4:2). Paul tries to convince the conscience of the Corinthians that his motives have been to persuade people about the gospel (5:2). In the context of 2 Corinthians, these are significant appeals for judgment from God and from the Corinthians that should vindicate Paul and his companions from any wrong doing in their relationship with this troubled church. This vindication happens because their consciences can judge Paul to be free from any type of malice or improper motive.

The conscience must rely upon some external norm as its basis for judgment. Law serves as this norm or standard and the conscience functions as the judge, guiding a person to act according to the revealed law or in disregard to it. The conscience can also be called as a witness to confirm that the behavior of a person is in agreement with the norm (Rom 9:1). A person's conscience is only as developed as the person's understanding of the norm, standard, or law. The conscience can speak no louder than what the person will allow. The witness of a person's conscience is valid for only that person, not for others (1 Cor 10:28–29). The conscience is not the norm because it can be misled, ill-informed, or underdeveloped. For Paul, God's law is the ultimate and final norm for the conscience (1 Cor 4:4).

Thus, one's conscience is limited to one's knowledge of the law, but it can be developed. An important passage for this idea is Paul's discussion about the weak brothers and sisters in 1 Corinthians 8–10, where the conscience serves as a major component in the argument. In this section, Paul is dealing with food that has been offered to idols and how eating this food can cause harm to those with weak or undeveloped consciences. He realizes that the problem and solution with eating idol food rest with knowledge. Like he does with the term *sophia* ("wisdom") in chapter 2, he will add his own definition to *gnōsis* ("knowledge") in 8:1—11:1. He has already proven that the Corinthians' wisdom is insufficient, and in this section, he shows that their knowledge is also incomplete. This so-called knowledge (8:1) is the basis for the strong Corinthians' ethical freedom (*exousia*, "freedom" or "authority"). The problem with this freedom is that it violates the conscience

---

56. Early reliable manuscripts give the word *hagiotēti*, "holiness." The editors of the Greek New Testament4 opt for *haplotēti* ("simplicity") because of the context. This word has the connotation of speaking with sincerity, uprightness, and frankness (see Eph 6:5; Col 3:22; BDAG, 85–86).

of the weaker brother or sister who has perhaps recently come from a polytheistic environment.

Therefore, Paul offers a different alternative in keeping with his paradigm of the cross (1:18—2:16). There was nothing essentially wrong with the knowledge that the strong had; that idols were only human-made objects and that there is only one God and one Lord. Their consciences had come to this awareness, so they adjusted their conduct in conformity to this new knowledge. The problem, however, was that some in the church had not yet come to this knowledge; they still attached the food sacrificed to idols with idol worship. The weak needed to grow up in their knowledge of idols, but the strong also had to grow up. The knowledge of the strong needed to conform to the higher law of love, and that love would then serve as the norm for their conscience. The assumption is that the conscience of both groups could be developed.

Moreover, one's conscience can be harmed. In the situation at Corinth, the conscience of the weak brother or sister was being damaged by the strong believers' use of a norm different than God's norm revealed on the cross, namely love (8:7). The strong were overlooking the spiritual needs of the weak, and by their behavior, the strong were causing the weak to question their relationship with Christ. By harming the conscience of the weak, the strong were in danger of causing the weak to fall back into a life of sin because the weak would no longer be following the norm of God's revealed law, in particular, the law of love exemplified on the cross (see 1:18–31; 13:1–13), but would be following the old norm of the world where idols were given more authority than they ought. Harming the conscience of the weak had serious consequences of falling into the trap of sin. The problem with the weak is that they lacked knowledge, thereby giving them a weak conscience. In chapter 8 Paul tells the strong, those with more developed consciences, not to let their awareness of the falsehood of idols cause the weaker brothers and sisters problems with their consciences (vv. 7, 11). In chapter 10 Paul tells the weaker brothers and sisters to "grow up," hence, to develop in knowledge about idols, leading to a more developed conscience (see 10:28).

The ethic Paul is expounding in this section is relative to the situation. He operates on principle in this passage. The most basic and essential norm for developing the conscience is the law of Christ, which is the law of love. In the context of 1 Corinthians, it is significant that Paul starts his letter with the paradigm of the cross. Chapter 13, the famous "love chapter," is a commentary on the way of the cross. The law of the cross, embodied in self-giving love, is the answer to the problems in Corinth (compare Rom 14:15–21; 1 Cor 10:31—11:1). Knowledge for Paul consists of being known by God in a relationship of love (8:1–2). This relationship is best summed up in Paul's concept of communion "in Christ" and "with Christ." Paul grounds the ethics of believers in love, and not knowledge, by redefining what knowledge is. Denaux comments, "Knowledge in itself is not a bad thing. But when knowledge about God is not informed by love for God, it leads to pride (*physiois*)."[57] Love and pride should not coexist in believers. Thus, the norm for the conscience is love, which is quite consistent with Jesus' statement in Matthew 22:37–40 about the two greatest commandments, loving God and loving one's neighbor.

First Timothy 1:5 is also noteworthy: "The aim of our charge is love that issues from a pure heart and a good conscience and a sincere faith." In the context, Paul is dealing with false teachers who had infiltrated the Ephesian church. His answer to this threat is to correct the false teaching. What is so critical about the threat of false doctrine is that it leads people's conscience astray by providing a norm different than the gospel. Paul gives the norm in this verse as love. Love is primary and serves as the goal (*telos*) of his message. Three things contribute to love. First, love comes from a pure heart. In the New Testament, a pure heart is the work of God by faith (Acts 15:8–9). Second, love comes from a good conscience. A good conscience results from following God's revealed will or law (2 Cor 1:12; 1 Tim 1:18–20). A conscience can be considered good when it testifies that a person has not violated the law of love. Serious consequence result from violating the conscience by breaking the law of love (see 1 Cor 8:11, 13; Rom 14:23). Third, love comes from a sincere faith. It is noteworthy that the conscience is paired with faith in this short list. There is a spiritual aspect to the conscience that will be explored in the following section. The conscience can help a person grow in love when it is coupled with faith in obedience to the Guide, the Holy Spirit. The responsibility lies with each person to develop one's conscience by becoming more aware of the norm and through careful and consistent living by this norm. God provides supernatural assistance in this task, a matter that needs careful consideration.

The Work of the Holy Spirit through the Conscience

A person is not left alone to develop the conscience. Paul says in Romans 9:1, "I tell you the truth in Christ, I am not lying, my conscience witnesses to me in the Holy Spirit." Two important but ambiguous prepositional phrases are used in this verse: "in Christ" and "in the Holy Spirit." Many translators

---

57. Adelbert Denaux, "Theology and Christology in 1 Cor 8:4–6," in Bieringer, *Corinthian Correspondence*, 598.

of the Greek New Testament know the challenge of interpreting the preposition *en* followed by the dative. This word can be instrumental, "by the aid of the Holy Spirit," and sometimes as locative, "in the presence of the Holy Spirit." Both possibilities offer an interesting interpretation of what Paul is saying in this verse. His purpose in this verse is to display his sincerity. To prove his sincerity, he calls upon two key witnesses and his relationship with these witnesses. First, he speaks the truth "in Christ." It is noteworthy that this verse comes after eight chapters detailing what this new life in Christ is like and how to experience it. Paul is a witness that life in Christ makes a difference in behavior.

Paul's second witness is the Holy Spirit who verifies both his sincerity and his relationship with Christ (see Rom 8:16). Significant here is the aspect of *inner* witness. For Paul, the Spirit can work completely only within those who have experienced transformed lives (12:1-2) "in Christ" (8:1-11). The first part of 9:1 provides the basis for the second part. Paul does not identify the conscience with the Holy Spirit but as the *instrument* of the Holy Spirit. The Spirit reminds us of certain truths, especially those in reference to Christ (John 14:26; 16:14-15). If the Holy Spirit told Paul's conscience that he was lacking the sincerity that a person "in Christ" should have, then Paul's sincerity in this letter could be questioned. He could call on no greater witness than the Holy Spirit. This witness is not, however, merely subjective but is based on the prior standard of relationship (the indicative mood), which can be objectified by lifestyle (the imperative mood).[58] By what means does the Holy Spirit communicate with our conscience? By grace, since all communication from the gracious God is in some aspect grace. The Spirit transmits grace to the believer to make the right choice in accordance with new life in Christ when the conscience is confronted with temptation (1 Cor 10:13).

Why do people, then, not always do good through the help of the Holy Spirit? The problem lies with the nature of sin and life in Adam. From an early age, people choose not to listen to their consciences. At that point, they choose to disobey whatever light they have been given and so become accountable to God. The law functions as the norm for the conscience; the conscience is thus linked with accountability. Sin is counted only when there is a law or norm guiding the conscience (Rom 5:13). The light by which the

---

58. The indicative mood generally indicates a statement of fact, and the imperative mood is used for a command or exhortation. Paul bases his ethics upon his theology. Furnish states that Paul's "ethic" is never formulated by himself, but "it is still present in the dynamic of the indicative and imperative which lies at the center of his thought" (*Theology and Ethics in Paul*, 211; see also 224-27; see Dennison, "Indicative and Imperative").

conscience makes judgements is based on many factors. Dunning makes this distinction: "We may say that formally conscience is the work of the Spirit (prevenient grace), but that materially it is the result of background, experience, and education."[59]

Since creation is in a fallen state, it is not difficult to conclude that the external influences upon the conscience only contribute to the dominance of sin. Simply stated, sin mars the conscience. People can reject the light that God shines on the conscience, giving sin more control over their lives. Heeding the conscience results in conviction, which brings the need for repentance. The Holy Spirit uses the law to convict people of sin. This law takes different forms. It is direct revelation through Scripture and indirect revelation through culture and other natural means for those who do not have access to the Scripture. By rejecting the Holy Spirit's guidance upon their conscience, people void the work of God's grace and end up in the dilemma of Romans 1: "God gave them up in the lusts of their heart . . . to dishonorable passions . . . to a debased mind" (vv. 24, 26, 28).

Two Options

The Holy Spirit works through the conscience in both a positive and a negative way. Positively, the Holy Spirit affirms to us that we are living the way God wants us to live. Jeremiah prophesied about a day when God would put his law on our minds and write it on our hearts (Jer 31:33). God does this through the Holy Spirit. Although Paul does not use the term "conscience" in Romans 8:16, the conscience may be involved in the Spirit's testifying with our spirit that we are children of God. Joy is the result of a conscience clear before God. God has given each person in the world an awareness of God's laws (for Jews, the Scripture; for Gentiles, the conscience; Rom 2:14–15). Negatively, the Holy Spirit convicts us when we do wrong and disobey God's standard of law. Jesus said that he would send the Holy Spirit who would convict the world of guilt about sin, righteousness, and judgment (John 16:8).

If a person heeds the guidance of the Holy Spirit, that person can develop in "the mind of Christ" (1 Cor 2:6–16). The world seeks power and wisdom, but those *in Christ* seek the mind of Christ. When God revealed his wisdom, he chose to do it on the cross (1:18–31). Divine wisdom can be known by those who are in fellowship with Christ through the Holy Spirit. Knowing the mind of Christ comes through the mediation of the Holy Spirit by whom God reveals his wisdom (2:10). This revelation is not simply

---

59. Dunning, *Grace, Faith, and Holiness*, 433.

cognitive (2:16) but also experiential. The Spirit serves as the eschatological power to make the ethic demanded by the cross possible in the lives of believers. The Spirit, as divine agent, is universally available to all who are in Christ (the *pneumakikon*). The Spirit is God's primary means of revealing the message of the cross.

The Corinthians were in danger of the other option: quenching the Spirit and hardening their hearts. What got in the way of their experiencing the full power of the cross were their worldly (*sarkikon*) attitudes and behaviors (3:1–3). They could not understand because they had hindered the Spirit from speaking to them. They were acting like the "unspiritual" (*psykikon*) who cannot understand the cross because of unbelief that rejects what the Spirit says to the conscience. They were living by the paradigm of Adam, as mere humans, by allowing the power of sin to control them, evidenced in their fleshly divisiveness. Paul urges them to be "spiritual" (*pneumakikon*) people who grow in understanding and appropriation of the message of the cross.

Paul writes to the Ephesians that they should not grieve the Holy Spirit (Eph 4:30) by participating in the negative behaviors mentioned in 4:25–29. The way to avoid grieving the Spirit is to become imitators of God by living a life of love (5:1–2), which results from new creation in the image of the righteous and holy God (4:23–24). When a person does not heed the conviction of the Spirit, the result is an insensitivity or a hardening of the heart. The Spirit speaks to the conscience, guiding people to fulfill the standard of the law of Christ—love. The will controlled by sin rejects this leading.

Having freedom of choice necessitates having a conscience. Thomas Oden writes, "Conscience is the capacity to judge oneself, present in all human beings, regardless of how acculturated."[60] A conscience that has become hardened is no longer free but has become a slave to the power of sin. By quenching the work of the Holy Spirit with their conscience, people make it more difficult to choose God's gift of grace. They replace the law of Christ with the law of self, flesh, the world, or any created other thing (Rom 1:18–32). Jesus warned that blasphemy against the Holy Spirit will not be forgiven (Matt 12:31–32). This sin is unforgivable because the Spirit is the one who gives life, and if one cuts out the Life-Giver, there is no possibility of life (John 3:6; 6:63). Thomas à Kempis (1380–1471) says of the calloused soul:

> Levity of heart and neglect of our faults make us insensible to the proper sorrows of the soul, and we often engage in empty laughter when we should rightly weep. There is no real liberty

---

60. Oden, *John Wesley's Scriptural Christianity*, 251.

and true joy, save in the fear of God with a quiet conscience. Happy is he who can set aside every hindering distraction, and recall himself to the single purpose of contrition. Happy is he who adjures whatever may stain or burden his conscience.[61]

There is only one solution to this helpless situation: new life in Christ. The law plays a significant role before and after one comes to faith in Christ.

Grace, Conscience, and Law

The Law and the Conscience

The revealed law (special revelation through the laws and commands of God through Scripture) serves as the highest guide for the conscience when the law is put under the sovereignty of Jesus Christ as Lord. The law can still be a valuable tool for the conscience even when a person is still bound by the power of sin. The problem, however, is that such a person becomes trapped by the law, and in this state, is unable to follow the gentle prodding of the Holy Spirit upon the conscience. This person is trapped like the "I" of Romans 7:14-24, who wants to do what is right but ends up doing what is wrong. When a person is "in Christ" through the Holy Spirit, the law becomes the positive guide for the conscience that it was meant to be. The highest goal for the conscience is to become like Christ and to be recreated in his likeness.

In Romans 1-3 Paul is building a deliberative case that no one can be justified by obeying the law. In chapter 2 he demonstrates that both Jew and Gentile alike are guilty before God for breaking the law. Lest Gentiles think they are exempt from guilt since they do not have the Old Testament filled with the commandments of God, Paul shows that they are guilty of breaking the law of the conscience written on their hearts. Verse 12 raises the issue of whether those who have received the lesser light of the "natural" conscience (norms gathered from nature or reason) will be saved. However, even "good" pagans cannot keep the law of their conscience enough to be saved. Both the written law and the law of the conscience are guides leading to righteousness, but obedience to them cannot save because no one can follow them perfectly to be counted righteous before God. The law of the conscience shows the need for a savior. As Oden comments, "In conscience we experience not a natural liberty to do the good, but to hope for it. In this way Christ who is the end of the law is being inscribed ever anew on our hearts by the preliminary discernment of the difference between good and

---

61. Thomas à Kempis, "On Contrition of Heart," in *Imitation of Christ*, 53.

evil."[62] The conscience helps confirm our guilt before God and the need for something or someone outside of ourselves to save us.

Paul essentially categorizes both Jews and Gentiles with the same problem: living in the sphere of sin. Nothing but divine power can save from the grip of sin. The revealed law and the law of the conscience function in the same way: to show people to be sinners in need of a savior. One might mistake the conscience as something of human origin, whether that be influenced by culture or personal choices, but it is the Holy Spirit working behind the scenes bringing conviction and awareness. The Holy Spirit brings grace that makes the choice to accept Christ possible.[63] Grace is God's initiative to offer the hope of eternal life to all who are otherwise bound by the condemnation and power of sin. Grace is the beginning with the law pointing the way.

Conscience is the link between grace and the law. It is the battleground between sin and grace. It is not the will but profoundly influence the choices a person makes. God takes the first step in salvation by enlightening the conscience which is otherwise dead in its rebellion against God. Negatively, the conscience declares all people guilty of breaking God's law and therefore condemned (Rom 3:23). Positively, the enlightened conscience allows the unbeliever the opportunity to respond in faith to the light, however small that light may be, towards salvation. Wiley comments, "There can be, therefore, no lack of harmony between the new law of Christ, and the old law of a fully redeemed and enlightened conscience."[64] The process begun with grace finds fulfillment when a person responds to God by believing in Jesus Christ.

In Pursuit of Holiness

There is no antithesis between law and grace because both have the same goal of conforming us to the image of Christ. Through the Holy Spirit, God quickens the conscience as it works with the law, which serves as the standard for the conscience. The law validates the decisions made by the conscience. A person's conscience can develop as one learns more about the law of God. This is not only a human endeavor but a response to the gracious work of the Holy Spirit. The conscience helps us conform to the will of God which, as Paul writes, is "our sanctification" (1 Thess 4:3). Holiness is first a gift of grace, but this gift necessitates the human response of obedience.

62. Oden, *Scriptural Christianity*, 252.
63. Wesley, *Explanatory Note*, 525.
64. Wiley, *Christian Theology*, 24.

The conscience, as the key tool of awareness of God's will, can experience the transforming grace in Christ. When God transforms our minds, the new standard of the conscience becomes Jesus Christ (Rom 12:2). We come to realize that our old ways are not consistent with the standard of Christ. Our conscience is the guide in every step of the sanctifying process. The Holy Spirit leads and convicts, refining us like gold until we are pure and holy. When the Holy Spirit speaks to our conscience, we are confronted with a choice of obedience or disobedience. Obedience leads to growth into the image of Christ. Disobedience leads to sin about which the Holy Spirit will convict us. When conviction comes and our consciences have become aware of the standard of Christ, we must be careful not to grieve the Holy Spirit by not repenting and continuing in sin (Eph 4:22–24, 30). When faced with temptation, God will provide a way out (1 Cor 10:13). How does he do this? The Holy Spirit speaks to our conscience, and the first thing our conscience does is rouse the will. Will we or will we not listen to the Holy Spirit, who will remind us of God's standard? Do we or do we not agree with God and choose his ways? We disobey the Holy Spirit by rejecting his leading in our lives. Disobedience results in a guilty conscience filled with fear and doubt. A conscience that heeds the law of Christ as revealed by the Holy Spirit (both objectively and subjectively) will conform more and more to the image of Christ. In theological terms, that person grows in holiness. Thus, the conscience is the critical link between the Holy Spirit and the standard or law of Christ, with the goal of developing the new self, "created to be like God in true righteousness and holiness" (Eph 4:24). P. T. Forsyth has said, "Unless there is within us that which is above us, we shall soon yield to that which is about us."

Having the Mind of Christ

Two tremendous events take place when a person enters into intimate relationship with Christ in the sanctifying experience "in Christ." One is that the law is liberated from the bondage of sin and becomes the guide to holiness that it was meant to be. The second is that the conscience can also be liberated from its bondage to the power of sin. This experience results in having "the mind of Christ." The Holy Spirit not only teaches us how to accept the law of Christ inwardly but also empowers us outwardly to live out the law in loving ways. Only the Holy Spirit, by transforming our wills, can give the power and freedom to gain victory over the law of sin and death (Rom 8:2). The life filled with the presence of the Spirit can bear fruit consistent with the law of love (Gal 5:22–23). As people become open and receptive to

God's grace through the Holy Spirit, their consciences can likewise grow in the grace and knowledge of Jesus Christ.

To have the mind of Christ necessitates openness to the leadership of the Holy Spirit who will conform us to the model of the self-giving love exemplified on the cross. To know the mind of Christ is to know the very thoughts of God. It is by no accident that in the same letter that Paul writes about having the mind of Christ (1 Cor 2:16), he also writes of the superiority of love (1 Cor 13). Love will be the primary result of having the mind of Christ. It would be impossible to live a life of love without the indwelling presence of the Holy Spirit who guides, convicts, and empowers those willing to submit to the divine prerogative. For believers, there is only one choice to make: to follow the Spirit who will guide and transform us into the image of Christ (2 Cor 3:18). The Spirit confirms that we are or are not living according to the law of Christ. Consistent nurture in the laws of God grows our conscience in its awareness of the standard of Christ (2 Tim 3:16–17). Listening to the Spirit brings growth and victory.

Conclusion

Paul's view of the law can be confusing on the surface. When read through the filter of new life "in Christ," the mystery of the law within Paul's thought becomes clearer. We should first see his letters as historical documents dealing with issues faced by the early church. But within these letters, Paul reveals his heart. At the center of his effort to provide meaning and guidance to early believers is his hope of transformation into the likeness of Christ, to begin to think like Christ and to act in holy love like Christ.

The law has a negative effect upon those still in the realm of Adam. The power of sin compels those who have not committed themselves totally to Christ to rebel against God, bringing further isolation from God and hardening of the conscience against the guidance of the Holy Spirit.

The law has a positive effect upon those in the realm of Christ. Those who let Christ be Lord will by doing this also open themselves to the guidance of the Holy Spirit upon the conscience. By living in obedience to the Holy Spirit, believers will keep in step with the Spirit (Gal 5:25), resulting in transformation at the fundamental level of the mind. The Holy Spirit can guide those who are willing to be guided and can empower those who have submitted in humility to being led.

5

Life in the Spirit

For those who are led by the Spirit of God are the children of God.
(ROMANS 8:14)

THE HOLY SPIRIT IS the one who makes life *in Christ* possible. One cannot be "in the Spirit" without being "in Christ." Likewise, one cannot be "in Christ" without the indwelling Holy Spirit. The Holy Spirit is the essential link that makes the experience of Christ actual in one's life. The Spirit's presence, however, may not be fully experienced but marginalized if a person remains attached to the values of the world. The Spirit is the essential link between believers that bonds them together as "church." If the priorities of the world replace the new life in Christ, the church suffers and may even degenerate into factionalism. In addition, its mission of sharing the good news is impaired when its members are not in relationship with the risen Jesus Christ. Without the Spirit, Paul's Christology becomes separated from real life and degenerates into an abstract mysticism like other religions of the first century. The Spirit is the vital link that allows believers' faith in Christ to be lived out in victory.

Christ and the Spirit

Paul's understanding of the Spirit is wrapped up in his understanding of Christ—the two are inseparable. The Spirit is the one who makes possible

"Christ in you, the hope of glory" (Col 1:27). The Spirit is the very presence of God among his people, empowering us to holy love. The word *pneuma* occurs 145 times in the canonical Pauline letters, most of which refer to the divine Holy Spirit. In three of those cases, the Spirit is directly connected to Christ in a genitive construction: "Spirit *of* Jesus/Christ/Son."

In Philippians 1:19, Paul links prayer to the Spirit of Christ: "for I know that through your prayers and the help of the Spirit of Jesus Christ this will turn out for my deliverance." Here, Paul shows that the Spirit provides help in response to the prayers of the Philippians. His specific hope is that Christ will be magnified through him (v. 20). Paul may connect the Spirit with Christ in this verse because the Spirit is the gift of God who works through Paul's suffering to bring glory to Christ. The genitive construction "of Jesus Christ" shows identification between Jesus Christ and the Spirit.[1] The Spirit will work powerfully through Paul in such a way that those around him in his imprisonment and those at a distance including the Philippians will give glory to Christ. Prayer is the crucial link that makes this happen.

Galatians 4:6 contains significant Trinitarian overtones: "And because you are sons, God has sent the Spirit of his Son into our hearts, crying, 'Abba! Father!'" The redemption through Christ's sacrifice results in adoption and is confirmed by the inner witness of the Holy Spirit. The gift of the Spirit is the evidence that we have been adopted as God's children (Rom 8:15–17). Those in Christ are free from the law as the way to be made righteous and are free to let the law lead to love (5:13–14). Paul connects the Spirit and the Son in two ways in this passage.[2]

First, he uses a "sending formula" with two parallel statements: God sent his Son (v. 4) and God sent the Spirit of his Son (v. 6). It is noteworthy that God the Father is the subject of both verbs. In order to be sent, the Son must have been pre-existent and divine, yet he became incarnate by being born to a woman. It is through the incarnate Son that God does the saving. It is through the Spirit that God actualizes the incarnation within each person.

Second, Paul connects the work of the Spirit to that of the Son through this grammatical construction. Paul wants to make sure that the Galatians see the clear connection between the work of the Spirit, described in 3:1–14, and the work of Christ, described in 4:5. He links the Galatians' experience of the Spirit with the historical salvation provided through Christ's sacrifice on the cross. The Spirit brings the past to the present. Fee writes, "The same Son whose death effected redemption and secured 'sonship' for them, now

---

1. Fee, *God's Empowering Presence*, 742.
2. Fee, *God's Empowering Presence*, 405.

indwells them by his Spirit, 'the Spirit *of the Son,*' whom God sent forth as he had the Son himself."[3] The Spirit actualizes the mission to all people *in Christ*, whether they be Jews, Greeks, slaves, free, males, or females (3:28). Adoption as the children of God comes not through works of the law or human standing but *in Christ* and *through the Spirit*, bringing new covenant relationship with God as *Abba*.

In Romans 8:9, Paul again mentions each person of the Trinity, connecting the Spirit to both God and Christ: "You, however, are not in the flesh but in the Spirit, if in fact the Spirit of God dwells in you. Anyone who does not have the Spirit of Christ does not belong to him."[4] The "Spirit of God" and the "Spirit of Christ" obviously refer to the Spirit spoken about throughout this context—the one and only Holy Spirit. The indwelling Spirit of God is experienced most fully by those who have committed themselves completely to Christ's supremacy in their lives. The Spirit of Christ removes someone from the control of the flesh and its capitulation to the power of sin. Paul's statement is exclusive here—there is no middle ground. The implied exhortation is that one cannot live in the flesh and at the same time have the Spirit of Christ.

The connection of Christ and the Spirit in 2 Corinthians 3:17 is less clear: "Now the Lord is the Spirit, and where the Spirit of the Lord is, there is freedom." "Lord" is ambiguous in the context and could refer to either God or Christ. Paul has been writing about how Moses reflected Yahweh's glory when he went up on Mount Sinai. Yet, Paul's purpose is to show how the present experience of the Corinthians' fellowship with Christ surpasses even Moses' experience of the Shekinah glory on the mount (v. 11). The key idea appears in verse 14 that only "in Christ" is the veil removed and the glory of the Lord reflected in a person's life. The phrase "when one turns to the Lord," in verse 16, strongly suggests that the "Lord" refers to Christ since the object of faith for Paul is Christ (Rom 3:22; Gal 2:16, 20; 3:22; Phil 3:9; Col 1:4; 2:5; 2 Tim 3:15; Acts 16:31). What is clearer is that the experience of the glory of God is most fully experienced in Christ through the Holy Spirit.

One other passage has often been discussed in relation to Christ and the Spirit. In 1 Corinthians 15:45 Paul writes that "the last Adam became a life-giving spirit." The question of interpretation in this phrase is to what the word "spirit" refers. Most modern English translations interpret the Greek *eis pneuma* with the lowercase "spirit," meaning that the resurrected Christ works within the spiritual realm to bring new life. A few translations (NLT,

---

3. Fee, *God's Empowering Presence*, 405.

4. The Spirit is attached to Jesus in other New Testament passages: John 7:38–39; 15:26; 16:7; 19:30; Acts 16:7; 1 Pet 1:11; Rev 3:1; 5:6.

GNT) capitalize "Spirit," implying a link here between Christ and the Holy Spirit. In verses 42–49 Paul is comparing two types of existence represented by Adam and Christ. God breathed *ruach*, "spirit," into Adam and he became a living, physical (*psychikon*, v. 46) being (Gen 2:7). Christ, however, is the giver of a new spiritual (*pneumatikon*) life to those who believe. It is stretching the grammar to equate Christ with the Holy Spirit here since *pneuma* does not have the Greek article. The outcome of the new spiritual life is bearing the image of Christ (v. 49). Paul's purpose here is not to describe how this life comes, which is through the Spirit, but the source of this life, Christ, who overcame the power of sin and death.

Paul's pneumatology is consistent with what Jesus taught as recorded in the Gospel of John. The Holy Spirit becomes the link between disciples and Jesus. The Spirit reminds believers of the teachings of Jesus (John 14:26; 16:13), just as the Spirit reveals the "mind of Christ" (1 Cor 2:10–16). The Spirit bears witness to Jesus (John 15:26) and glorifies him (John 16:14). It is by the Spirit that one can confess Jesus as Lord (1 Cor 12:3). Even with this close connection between the Spirit and Christ, however, the Holy Spirit is still distinguishable as a separate person from Christ.[5] All of these and more references indicate that Paul had a high Christology and Trinitarian understanding of the work of Christ. The Spirit connects new life in Christ to daily living and is the vital link between God the Father, God the Son, and creation. Stewart comments, "To be united with the risen Christ was to be united with the God who raised him."[6]

Christ is a living presence within believers, and this presence is experienced now through the Holy Spirit. Paul prays that the Ephesians will come to know Christ more and that Christ will take up more residence in their hearts through God's Spirit (Eph 3:16–17). God's gift of the Spirit strengthens the inner person so believers come to experience and know Christ's love more fully. Life in the Spirit is the experience of how life in Christ is lived out. As Dunn states, "It is 'having the Spirit' which defines and determines someone as being 'of Christ.'"[7] The Spirit is Jesus' mode of existence now with his people (Rom 1:4; 1 Cor 15:45; 1 Tim 3:16). To experience the Spirit is to experience Jesus. Dunn adds, "To be 'in Christ' and to have the Spirit indwelling were two sides of the one coin."[8]

---

5. Fee, *Paul, the Spirit*, 27–28.
6. Stewart, *Man in Christ*, 171.
7. Dunn, *Theology of Paul*, 423.
8. Dunn, *Theology of Paul*, 414.

Resolving the Fundamental Problem

New life in Christ is experienced most completely through full submission to the directives of the Holy Spirit. In his Letter to the Romans, Paul takes up the challenge of how believers may arrive at this point. The fundamental question is, who will be master, sin or Christ? This is the basic question Paul poses in chapter 6. He believed that his God-given mission was to preach the message of full salvation in Christ (1:16), strategically first to Jews and then to Gentiles. He hoped to stop in Rome and visit the believers there on his way to evangelize in Spain (1:11–13), though it is unclear whether he ever actually was able to carry out this plan.[9] His answer for the Romans, as for all his churches, is the promise of transformed life in Christ. This transformation impacts every aspect of our existence and is the basis for mission, fellowship, and ethics.

The emphasis in chapter 6 is on the surrender a believer must make in identification with Christ's own death. This chapter builds ("therefore," v. 1) on the argument begun particularly in 5:12, where Paul delves into the problem of sin. Sin entered the world through Adam's decision to rebel against God. Sin is like a disease that plagues all people (3:23) and leads to death (6:23). Chapter 6 is an important proof as Paul works his way to the high point of 8:1, that there is no condemnation for those who are in Christ Jesus. Paul uses diatribe to build his case against life controlled by the power of sin.[10] A key word in this chapter is "sin," *harmartia*. The singular noun is found only in Romans, with a concentrated forty-two times in chapters 5–8. The basic meaning is a failure to reach a standard, a deviation from the intended path, or a trespass against a law. In a religious sense, sin brings guilt before God for breaking God's laws. Because of human rebellion, represented "in Adam," sin has become "a ruling power that invades the world."[11]

Paul begins chapter 6 with the question, "Are we to continue in sin that grace may abound?" He is not simply referring to whether a believer should continue to do sinful actions. Many modern English translations mistakenly turn the Greek noun into a verb, "shall we go on sinning" (e.g., NIV). Paul repeatedly and significantly uses the dative case of the noun with the Greek article, literally, "the sin" (*tē hamartia*; 6:1, 2, 10, 11, 13).[12] The

---

9. See Ackerman, *1 & 2 Timothy, Titus*, 43.

10. Diatribe was a rhetorical tool by which a teacher dialogs by asking questions and give answers to bring new knowledge or change behavior. See Stowers, *Diatribe and Paul's Letter to the Romans*.

11. BDAG, 51.

12. The noun occurs with the nominative in vv. 12, 14, and the genitive in vv. 6 (twice), 16, 17, 18, 20, 22, 23.

dative case is often used in a sentence to designate the indirect object or is determined by a preposition before it, such as *en* ("in"), but there is no preposition used with "the sin" in these verses. In many English translations (e.g., NRSV) the "in" is added, making "in sin." The case syntax here is likely the dative locative of sphere. This usage of the dative often follows a verb, indicating the sphere or realm in which the action of the verb takes place.[13]

We must be cautious not to overinterpret the use of the article, but the context makes a strong case that Paul is referring to the sphere of sin's power,[14] the realm of living where sin is the controlling force, resulting in spiritual slavery that impacts daily living. Sin as a spiritual force enslaves our physical bodies ("members," *melos*, 6:13, 19; 7:5, 23) in unholy appetites and desires (vv. 19–20). Sin's dominion began its ensnaring power when Adam and Eve disobeyed God's simple command in the garden of Eden (5:12; Gen 2:16–17), bringing immediate spiritual death, experienced as shame before God (Gen 3:10), and physical death, evident in pain and suffering (Gen 3:16–19). To be "in Adam" is to exist in the realm of sin's control. Life "in Adam" is the antithesis to life "in Christ," with polar opposite results: sin brings death but Christ brings life (Rom 6:23). Paul's question in verse 1 could be paraphrased as, "Should we continue to live under the control of the power of sin so that we can experience more of God's grace?" If the problem of sin is not taken seriously, one cannot take seriously the solution found in Christ.

"Sin" occurs only one time as a verb in this whole chapter, in verse 15 in the rhetorical question, "Are we to sin because we are not under law but under grace?" As in verse 1, Paul answers his own question with the strong, "By no means!" If we are not under the control of the power of sin (the noun consistently used), then why should we commit the acts of sin? The answer is obvious for Paul—and should be for the Romans. The acts of sin are only the outgrowth of a person trapped under the power of sin. Paul dismantles the position of antinomianism by showing that sin has no place in the life of believers. Verse 15 and the following verses give support to the command in verse 12: *let not sin reign*.

Paul's next question in verse 2 is rhetorical and the answer should be obvious: "How can we who died to sin still live in it?" If we have died to the power of sin, then it no longer has power over us. If we live in the new sphere of "in Christ," sin should not be master anymore. A fundamental change of allegiance must take place. Paul is speaking in potentiality here because each person must make his or her own decision not to let sin reign,

---

13. Wallace, *Greek Grammar*, 153–54.
14. See Tannehill, *Dying and Rising with Christ*, 14–20.

a decision that becomes clear in verse 12. The metaphor of death represents the separation that must take place between the old life "in sin" and the new life "in Christ." Paul's logic is clear: if someone died, he or she is no longer part of our lives; the relationship has ended.[15] So also, dying to sin should bring separation and freedom from it. Since believers have died to sin, symbolically shown in baptism, sin should not be the controlling force that determines how we live. His next rhetorical question in verse 3 connects the metaphor to the Romans' experience of baptism: "Do you not know that all of us who have been baptized into Christ Jesus were baptized into his death?" The Romans should know the answer to this question because it was at the core of Paul's preaching (1 Cor 2:2).

In verse 4 Paul continues to explain the new life in Christ with language of union *with Christ* by using the Greek preposition *syn*, "with." Paul likely coined some of the resulting terms for this situation. The list makes a simple creed and shows the sequence necessary for one to find freedom from the power of sin:

> *synetaphēmen* (v. 4), burry with
> *symphytoi* (v. 5), identify with
> *synestaurōthē* (v. 6), crucify with
> *syn Christō* (v. 8), [died] with Christ
> *syzēsomen* (v. 8), live with.

To be united with Christ through these actions requires faith in what Christ has done and rejection of what the world offers. Stewart comments, "For to be united to Christ means to be *identified with Christ's attitude to sin*. It means seeing sin with Jesus' eyes, and opposing it with the something of the same passion with which Jesus at Calvary opposed it."[16]

This word series explains the fundamental choice symbolized in baptism: "We were buried therefore with him by baptism into death" (v. 4). Believers have died to sin in three ways.[17] Judicially, the penalty for committing sin is removed as one identifies with Christ's death on the cross. Paul has already established in the letter that those who trust in Christ's death as the means of atonement will be made right before God, resulting in eternal life (3:25; 4:24–25; 5:1). Faith requires that people recognize their utter in-

---

15. In Rom 7:2–3, Paul uses the image of death to illustrate the necessary separation from the law as master. Here, the key ideas are "release" and "freedom."

16. Stewart, *Man in Christ*, 196.

17. Cranfield, "Romans 6:1–14 Revisited," 40–41. He adds an eschatological sense but this is only weakly supported here. It will appear more significantly in Rom 8; see later discussion in this chapter.

ability to make themselves right before God by their own efforts of keeping the law; everyone has sinned and fallen short of God's glory (3:23). The only solution is to accept the free offer of grace provided through Christ's death.

Second, in baptism believers reject the old life of decay controlled by sin and become new creations in Christ. This act of faith through identifying with Christ's death is the visible acceptance of what Christ's death provides.[18] Greathouse comments, "Baptism objectifies and ratifies our death to sin; it removes the entire experience from the realm of pure subjectivity and ties it to an event in history."[19] Baptism confirms the decision made in faith to let Jesus be Lord. A different type of death is required—one that accepts Christ's death as our own death. We acknowledge the provision made by Christ's death and appropriate it in our own lives by the visible act of faith through baptism. Baptism is a sign of dying to sin (v. 10a) and a re-enactment of Christ's own total commitment to the will of the Father. The verb *synetaphēmen* (v. 4), "buried with," shows the decisive finality of this decision. Coming up from the water is the sign of new creation. Baptism as an expression of faith symbolizes a deeper spiritual decision of ownership.

Finally, death brings a moral change. The irony of the gospel is that new life comes through death. The resurrection power that raised Jesus from the dead also transforms those who put their trust in him (v. 5). Believers die to sin when they begin to embrace by faith the way of holiness. Baptism resources a person (note the purpose clause, *hina*, in v. 4) to walk in "newness of life." The term "newness" (*kainotēti*) is an abstract noun suggesting a state of extraordinary living or quality of life.[20] This newness is compared to the new life Christ experienced through his resurrection. The old person (*palaios anthrōpos*) was controlled by the power of sin and characterized by deceitful desires (Eph 4:22).

In verse 6 Paul describes sin's power with the phrase "the body of sin." The genitive *tēs harmartias* could be taken as a genitive of possession: the body that sin has control of and "owns." The physical body itself is not sinful but morally neutral and even blessed by God. It can be used for righteousness or wickedness. The body must not be harmed or destroyed through mutilation but rescued from the power of sin so it can be used for God's righteous purposes as God designed (6:13). Sin has control over the physical body because of the mind, which controls the actions of the body.

What happens on the outside is but a mere reflection of what happens on the inside (Matt 15:18; Luke 6:45). A person must be changed at the

---

18. Cranfield, *Romans*, 299.
19. Greathouse, *Romans*, 134.
20. BADG, 497.

deepest level—with the transformation of the mind. Believers are only able to live righteously because God has brought a fundamental change within them. The body that is dead to sin can no longer be used by sin. Sin is no longer a part of that person's life. The body as a living sacrifice is under the control of a new mind (Rom 12:1). Greathouse writes: "The self, having renounced its false and destructive organizing center, clings to its new and life-giving and sanctifying center—the Lord Jesus Christ."[21] The old way of life under sin's control has been put to death by the decision to accept Christ's supremacy. One control is exchanged for another. We become participants in the new creation that started with Christ and join with him in this new creation as members of his body, the church. The noun *kainotēti* occurs again in 7:6 and shows that this new life comes through the Holy Spirit.

The goal of this death is total freedom from the control of sin resulting in sanctification. Holiness is the primary characteristic of this new resurrection life in Christ. Christ's resurrection creates hope within believers and gives victory over sin in the present time. The same "glory of the Father" that raised Jesus is the same power that enables one to live free from sin's control. The "newness of life" experienced by believers is directly linked to and a result of Christ's own resurrection. By conquering death, Christ also conquered the power of sin (1 Cor 15:56–57). By identifying with Christ's resurrection by accepting his supremacy, believers experience this victory in the present moment. The resurrection of Jesus Christ completely removed sin's power over those who accept his sovereignty in every aspect of their lives.

Paul is dealing with the fundamental hope of the gospel with the repeated "we know" in verses 6 and 9 and "we believe" in verse 8. This realignment of one's life requires the commitment of faith. The aorist tense of the verb *apethanomen*, "we died," in verse 8 suggests a decisive decision of putting to death the old way of life under sin. The old life should not resurface and the decision remade, though the temptation to sin remains. The very reason Paul is writing this chapter is so that the church in Rome will not give in to temptation and commit the acts of sin (v. 15) but find total freedom in Christ.

Paul emphasizes the decisiveness of this death in verse 10: "For the death he died he died to sin." The unstated subject of the aorist verb *apethanen* most naturally refers to Christ of verse 9. But with believers' identification with Christ's death, the decisiveness of their own death (v. 6) is emphasized. The one who died, died to the sphere of sin once. Paul is

---

21. Greathouse, *Romans*, 136.

showing the radical break that took place when Christ died and the same break that must happen in those who identify with him. After this death comes resurrection to a new life of communion and fellowship with Christ. The future tense of *syzēsomen*, "we will live," in the same verse refers to the immediate future after the death to the old way of life. This is the down payment and assurance of the eschatological glory to be experienced when Christ comes again. This assurance is experienced now in this life through the transforming presence of the Holy Spirit (Eph 1:13–14).

Paul moves on in verse 11 to emphasize further this decision with the use of the first imperative verb in this chapter: "consider yourselves dead to sin and alive to God in Christ Jesus." Being in Christ does not guarantee that one will passively be holy without active faith expressed as total commitment. For Paul, those who are "in Christ" will live in obedient faith because of the new life the Holy Spirit is forming within them. A failure at this point calls into question one's commitment. Paul is essentially telling the Roman believers to be who they were recreated to be. The logic is clear: if one has indeed joined in Christ's death and resurrection by accepting his total sovereignty, symbolized in the act of faith in baptism, one has now entered a new type of existence where the power of sin does not need to control and lead one to committing any acts of sin. God has made us holy within and provides victory over the greatest human problem, sin, enabling us to live in the obedience of holiness.

Paul uses the metaphor of slavery to describe this change. The image of slavery first appears in the infinitive "to be enslaved" in verse 6. This is in essence what sin does to a person. Because all people are born "in Adam" (5:12), we have no choice about becoming slaves to sin. The law intensifies this slavery and closes the lock on sin's chain, as Paul later writes in 7:9, "when the commandment came, sin came alive and I died." The power of sin takes greater hold over a person over time, leading to more disobedience ("lawlessness," v. 19; see 1:18–31), influencing how one lives in the body. When the light of the gospel comes, one is given the choice of allowing sin to remain in this position of power or to replace it with a new source of power. Paul states in verse 16 that we are slaves to the one we obey. When the gospel is presented, one is given the choice of accepting the righteousness from God or the control of sin. The two paths offer two different results. Slavery to sin leads to death (v. 21), but slavery to obedience brings holiness with the promise of eternal life (v. 22). This was not a new teaching for the Romans but was at the heart of the gospel (v. 17).

Paul's teaching here could be misunderstood to mean that one simply must make the choice to obey God's laws and holiness will be the result, that holiness and freedom from sin's power are a matter of human obedience to the law. Just as in the Roman Empire of Paul's day, a high enough price must be paid to gain freedom from slavery. Paul will show in chapter 7, however, that freedom from spiritual slavery cannot come through human effort. The person who is a slave to sin is unable to obey God's laws well enough to be considered righteous (3:10). Paul moves on to argue that God has not created us to be torn by this conflict but to find wholeness and freedom in Christ.

The Human Struggle against Sin

After the theological height of chapter 6, Paul digresses in chapter 7 to discuss the struggle people have in obeying God's will resourced by their own strength. Paul vividly recounts the spiritual battle between the power of sin and a person's desire to do what is right, a battle that cannot be won by human effort. A high price must be paid to gain freedom from sin, a price no one can pay by his or her own efforts. The reason we are unable to do what God commands is because of a weak and fallen nature (8:3). We are born "in Adam" and unable to find release from this slavery except "in Christ."

The problem with the law of God is that it gives sin opportunity to enslave people. The law itself is not the problem. In verse 7 Paul asks, "Is the law sin?" He answers with an emphatic "No way!" In verse 12 he adds that "the law is holy and the commandment is holy righteous and good." The law is a reflection of the divine will and reveals the grace of God. The law helps us be honest about the human problem and lets us know we are sinners (v. 13), but it cannot solve the problem. The struggle results when people try to obey the law by their own strength (v. 18).

As an example, Paul quotes the Tenth Commandment using the Septuagint of Exodus 20:17: *ouk epithymēseis*. Most modern translations interpret the verb *epithymēseis* as "covet." Although the word is neutral and can even have positive connotations in the New Testament of good desire or longing (Luke 22:15), in some usages it has the sensual sense of "lust" (Matt 5:28). Greathouse comments on the word, "It is the overweening desire for the heights of self-exaltation."[22] The act of covetousness is the manifestation of the deeper heart problem of a person controlled by the power of sin. The law arouses sinful passions that seek to please the "flesh" (v. 5).

There are two different orientations vying for control, mentioned in verse 14 with the words *pneumatikos* and *sarkinos*. These two terms represent two ways of living later described in chapter 8 and Galatians 5:19–23. "Flesh" (*sarx*) is the problem. Paul uses this word in two major ways in his

---

22. Greathouse, *Romans*, 149.

letters. Literally, it refers to the physical existence in the body. The "flesh and blood" are temporary, part of this earthly existence, and will not inherit eternal life (1 Cor 15:50). The "mortal flesh" is weak but is the only sphere in which we can live out our life in Christ from this side of the grave (2 Cor 4:11). By extension, the word has a special theological connotation referring to seeing our existence as if this world is all there is, and so people can do whatever they want to fulfill the desires that are part of living in this world. Paul's quotation in 1 Corinthians 15:32 displays the empty pursuit of the flesh: "Let us eat, drink, and be merry, for tomorrow we die."[23] When used in this way, the word has a negative sense and refers to living without any reference to God. Living by the flesh is self-focused and fulfills pleasures that are distorted because of sin. Fleshly living follows in the path of Adam in the descent into rebellion against God. The flesh is the primary tool sin uses to enslave people, primarily because people satisfy the appetites (in many cases, natural instincts) of the body in ways that are contrary to God's will revealed in God's laws.

A person may still be enslaved by the flesh while having at least a beginning faith that Jesus is the source of salvation. Paul is writing to believers in Rome, prodding them forward in their relationship with God. The reality of life, however, is that this journey is not always easy. For first-century Christians, the shift from their old worldview and the lifestyles that went with it to the new way of life in Christ was not easy. For Gentiles, the temptations from their pagan environment and the pull of the flesh were powerful. Romans 6 tackles this issue. For Jews, the temptation was to see obedience to God's laws as the way to prove their own righteousness. Romans 7 deals with this challenge. Paul is quite aware of the reality of the human struggle, evidenced by his use of the first-person "I" beginning in 7:7 until the end of the chapter. By involving himself in the struggle, he is indicating that any human effort to overcome the pull of the flesh will ultimately fail without God's intervention. In verses 14–24 Paul describes the person controlled by the power of sin and how this is a losing battle without God's help. Verse 18 highlights the problem: "For I have the desire to do what is right, but not the ability to carry it out." The situation is so bad that he ends up even doing what is evil because of the control of sin.

The clue for understanding Paul's argument is the "sin that dwells within me" (v. 20). When sin has control, we cannot do what we want because we do not have the power to overcome temptation. The pull of the flesh is strong, and the weakened conscience is unable to choose the way

---

23. The source of this quote is debated. It may be Isa 22:13 but also sounds similar to the desolate life described in Plutarch, *Moralia* 1098C, 1100D, 1125D, cited by Fee, *First Corinthians*, 770.

of righteousness. Obedience to the law cannot help but just makes the situation worse by bringing further bondage through the subtlety of legalism. It is a struggle to live in the sphere of Christ within a fallen world without allowing Christ to be supreme. A radical change must take place at the core of our beings, at the level of our will and thinking. The inner person (*ton esō anthrōpon*, v. 22) may even believe in the Messiah, but rest of a person's life continues to struggle against the flesh. The mind (*noos*, v. 23), moreover, continues to struggle against the power of sin and the bondage of the law. The defeat in the voice of the "I" reaches its peak with the question of verse 24: "Wretched man that I am! Who will deliver me from this body of death?"

Just like the "old self" of 6:6 was enslaved by the power of sin, the person struggling to gain victory from sin by obedience to the law ends up further enslaved to sin. Instead of bringing liberation, the law increases sin's hold on a person. The result is a spiritual battle that more often than not results in defeat to the power of sin. The law cannot rescue from slavery to the power of sin because it is weakened by our fallen condition (8:3). There is no inner power to change a person's thinking and to guide the conscience to the right choice when confronted with temptation. Paul has logically and thoroughly shown the need for an outside source to help people overcome this battle that defeats us all. There is only one answer emphatically given in verse 25 without a verb: "Thanks be to God through Jesus Christ our Lord!" Paul has one major part of his argument to give: how is the inner person transformed so that there is victory over the allure of the flesh and the pull of inner sin?

Freedom through the Holy Spirit

The deep change required to live the holy life cannot be accomplished by human ability but only through God's recreative presence. Chapter 8 is Paul's answer to the problems of sin's control in chapter 6 and the inability to keep the law in chapter 7. God's response to the anguished cry of 7:24 is "no condemnation for those who are in Christ Jesus" (8:1). Humans have a two-part problem but there is only one solution: Jesus Christ, who "loved us and gave himself up for us, a fragrant offering and sacrifice to God" (Eph 5:2), and "who gave himself for us to redeem us from all lawlessness and to purify for himself a people for his own possession" (Titus 2:13). Only those who are "in Christ Jesus" are released from condemnation brought by sin and the law. The answer to freedom from bondage to the law is the same as finding freedom from sin—namely, death (6:6; 7:1–3).

Death to sin marks the end of the dominion of Adam in a person's life and the inauguration of the new life in Christ. The age of sin's control over the human race was decisively ended with Jesus' resurrection. Each person, however, remains bound to this age until he or she accepts in faith a new master. Paul uses different terms to describe sin's dominion such as "enslaved" (6:6), "reign" (6:12), "rule" or "dominion" (6:14), and "slaves" (6:16). How does one die to sin and the life in Adam that sin represents? The metaphor of death is played out in real life through a change of allegiance. Paul personifies sin as a power, but it can be described more precisely as a spiritual condition of pleasing or preserving oneself resulting from misplaced worship. Worship that was misdirected to things of this world is refocused upon God (1:21; 12:1–2). A person must allow a new master to take control, and this master begins to redirect everything about the person's life, beginning with the mind and values.

The critical point of chapter 8 is how this redirection and reformation of the self takes place and the results in a believer's life. The answer to this dilemma of sin is the *life controlled by the Holy Spirit*. Paul briefly mentioned this in 7:6, echoing 6:4: "so that we might serve in the newness [*kainotēti*] of the Spirit and not the old way of the law" (lit.). A new law takes the place of the old law. "For the law of the Spirit of life has set you free in Christ Jesus from the law of sin and death" (8:2). This verse reveals several important ideas. One exegetical question is the purpose of the prepositional phrase "in Christ Jesus." The word order in the Greek places it directly after "Spirit of life." It could modify the Holy Spirit, the new life that comes through the Holy Spirit, or the means by which someone is set free from the law of sin and death.

Theologically, all three are true. The Spirit is able to bring the new life to those who have aligned themselves totally with Christ, and this brings freedom from the control of sin and hope against the power of death. Käsemann writes, "The law of the Spirit is nothing more than the Spirit himself in his ruling function in the sphere of Christ."[24] Being in Christ is the prerequisite for the Spirit's full work in one's life. Paul describes the Holy Spirit here as the "Spirit of life." The genitive "of life" is subjective, meaning that the Spirit is the source of life: the new life that the Spirit produces in those who are in Christ. The Spirit was present and active at creation, breathing life (*ruach*) into Adam (Gen 2:7) and is now present at the recreation, breathing new life into those who submit to the lordship of Christ (see John 3:5–6). The Holy Spirit makes the new existence in Christ a reality in the life of those who have given themselves totally over to Christ's supremacy.

---

24. Käsemann, *Romans*, 215–16.

Fee comments, "God's saving work in behalf of his people is brought about through Christ and the Spirit—Christ effects it; the Spirit appropriates it to the life of the believer."[25]

Obedience to the law could never bring the inner change required to overcome the power of sin's pull upon our fleshly existence. God intervened by sending his Son as a descendant of Adam, bound to the weakness of the flesh (8:3). Yet, where Adam and all other humans failed in their disobedience, Christ overcame temptation (Heb 4:15) and did not turn his back on worshipping God alone (Matt 4:10). His power over fleshly existence was confirmed by his resurrection from the dead (Rom 1:4). Christ's victory over the power of sin and the flesh enables the Holy Spirit to take God's holy and righteous law and write it on our hearts (Jer 31:31–34). Christ accomplished through his life, death, and resurrection what the law could not do.

There are two primary results of the Spirit's work in a person's life. First, the Spirit brings love in reflection of God's love shown through Christ (Rom 5:5). By "walking by the Spirit," believers are empowered to serve one another through love (Gal 5:13, 16). The Spirit conforms us into the likeness of Christ by filling our hearts with love for others (Rom 13:8; Gal 5:22). Second, the Spirit brings victory over the temptation of the weakened flesh and the "fleshly" desires that come with it.

In 8:4–17 Paul compares two different ways of life, characterized by two different mindsets: "For those who live according to the flesh set their minds on the things of the flesh, but those who live according to the Spirit set their minds on the things of the Spirit" (v. 5). The word for "mind" here is *phroneo*. This word is used for the seat of the will, the place of the spirit. It describes having "something as the prevailing mood of mind, habit of thought, or direction of moral interest. What are you really interested in?"[26] Paul uses this word in Philippians 2:5: "Have this mind in you that was also in Christ Jesus." The life controlled by the flesh gives value to things that replace God in our life. It is a life oriented to what this world offers. Paul gives a long but not complete list of acts of the flesh in Galatians 5:16–21. This type of life allows something other than God to serve as the guide to our conscience. As we begin to follow these alternative "laws" (or values), we may find ourselves consumed by them, unable to break free (vv. 7–8). The person turned inward to self and flesh is not able to love God or others. The eventual result is death (v. 6).

The Holy Spirit grows within believers the love of Christ by transforming worldly values into the values of Christ (1 Cor 2:16). A life of love results

---

25. Fee, *God's Empowering Presence*, 501.
26. Archer, *Romans*, 45.

by walking with and by the Spirit (Gal 5:25). Only in Christ do we become the people we were created to be. Only when we have put ourselves under his full authority as led by the Spirit do we experience God's purposes for us (Eph 1:4). The Spirit gives us all the grace we need to love and be complete in Christ (Eph 3:16–19; Col 2:10).

The flesh bound by sin wages war against the grace offered through the Holy Spirit experienced through one's conscience and thinking. This results in an inner conflict about who will be in control of one's life. "For the mind that is set on the flesh is hostile to God" (Rom 8:7). Such a mind may try to please God but is unable because of its weakness. The only answer is God's assistance. The fundamental question raised in chapter 6 is implied in chapter 8: who or what will control our lives? When God is at the center of a person's life, God can then direct that life. "Being filled with the Spirit" is another way to describe this control issue. To be "filled" requires one to be "submitted" in worship. Paul sets up a conditional statement in verse 9, that believers are "in the Spirit" and not "in the flesh" *if indeed* they have the indwelling Spirit. Being "in the Spirit" is how to experience "Christ in you" (v. 10), which is our hope for glory (Col 1:27). Life in the Spirit is indistinguishable from life in Christ. "At best we may speak of Christ as the context and the Spirit as the power."[27]

A change of mind brings a change of behavior. When we are filled with the Spirit of Christ in total submission, there is no room for sin. God has provided the way of escape from temptation (1 Cor 10:13) by transforming the mind, resulting in a new way of life characterized by the ability to make the choice for righteousness. Although God provides grace through the Spirit, each person must choose to accept this help. The requirement is "put to death the deeds of the body" (Rom 8:13), the inclinations that come when our attention is drawn to fulfilling the *epithymia* ("desires") of living in this fallen world. Paul tells the Philippians to "work out your own salvation with fear and trembling, for it is God who works in you, both to will and to work for his good pleasure" (Phil 2:12–13). The required human response of "fear and trembling" recalls the required attitude of submissive worship. "God's work in you" surely indicates the work of the Holy Spirit to guide the conscience, leading one to "think this way in yourselves with the thinking which is in Christ Jesus" (2:5; author's translation). This is the only choice that will transfer our desires from the futility of satisfying the flesh to bringing glory to God. Greathouse makes clear, "Settling this issue is of

---

27. Dunn, *Theology of Paul*, 408.

urgent importance for every believer. It is a call for moral decision—to let God be God!"[28]

The sequence in this section of Romans is significant. First, believers must make the decision to offer themselves completely to God by identifying with Christ's death and resurrection, testified through the submissive act of worship in baptism (6:11; 8:13; Gal 5:16). God's responds by sanctifying us through the Holy Spirit (6:22; 7:6; 8:10). Significantly, Paul writes in 1 Corinthians 1:30 that Christ Jesus is our sanctification. He is the source (8:9) and goal (2 Cor 3:18; Rom 8:29; Gal 4:19; Col 3:10) of our sanctification. The Spirit makes real in our lives what Christ did on the cross. The result of this is victory over the temptations of the flesh (8:9). The Spirit-filled life relies upon the resources of God in complete devotion to God. The Spirit of holiness comes to a person, urging that person to respond to God's offer of salvation. As the person responds in submission and commitment, God takes the mundane and changes it into something that will bring him glory.

The Spirit-Filled New Life in Christ

Paul urges the Roman believers to act like who they are becoming as new creations in Christ. Because of the work of the Spirit within them, they are now part of a new existence and are given divine help through the Holy Spirit to live victoriously over sin and the flesh. Beginning in 8:12 with the "so then" (*ara oun*) until the end of the chapter, Paul turns his focus to how to live the eschatological tension in this life free from sin's control. If indeed a believer is living in obedience to the Spirit, that person is not obligated (*opheiletai*) to please the flesh. While all people are bound to a weakened physical condition because of our frail bodies that constantly fight off death and various instincts that drive this fight, we do not need to be controlled by these but can sanctify them for God's use. This assertion does not mean a person cannot or will not sin but that God provides a resource to overcome sin's dominating force while in this earth-bound life.

The new existence in Christ is breaking into this fallen age through those who believe and have committed themselves to his lordship. The result is an ever-increasing hope of the glory that marks this new life (5:2; 2 Cor 3:18). Paul offers the fundamental choice in verse 13: what kind of death does a person want to experience: death now to one's old self controlled by sin or death for eternity? The Spirit enables believers to live out continually their decision to identify with Christ's death and resurrection (6:4; 7:6).[29]

28. Greathouse, *Wholeness in Christ*, 102.
29. Tannehill, *Dying and Rising with Christ*, 81.

Living by the flesh leads to death but living by the Spirit requires death. Believers no longer live by the old life (Rom 7:4–6) but the new. Bruce comments, "The Spirit is the sanctifying agency in the lives of believers: he wages perpetual warfare against the flesh, but he is more powerful than the flesh, and can put the flesh progressively out of action in those lives which are yielded to his control."[30] The challenge is that, although free from the control of sin, believers are not free from the presence of sin or the temptations that come from this world. We must still live in the physical flesh but do not need to be controlled by it (Gal 2:20; 2 Cor 10:3). Paul makes this clear in 1 Corinthians 9:27: "I discipline my body and keep it under control."

This idea has significant impact on ethics. The crucial component in this for Paul is the presence of the Holy Spirit with the required response of our obedience in faith to the leading of the Spirit (Rom 8:14; Gal 5:25). God's gift of the Spirit is the proof that believers have been "removed from out of the natural state of existence and transferred into the supernatural."[31] The Spirit confirms our adoption into the family of God. This new relationship with God in Christ through the Spirit brings confidence and intimacy (Rom 8:15). The Spirit confirms our identification with Christ's death and resurrection, that we are indeed the children of God, and that our consciences are clear and nothing stands between God and us in this relationship (v. 16). Ridderbos adds, "Those who by virtue of the corporate bond have been united with Christ as the second Adam, have died and been buried with him, may know themselves to be dead to sin and alive to God, may also know themselves to be 'in the Spirit.'"[32]

When we allow the Spirit to take control, we step back from our struggle to follow God's will and allow God to lead us. Ridderbos adds, "Thus, for the mystical doctrine of the being-in-Christ, ethics is nothing else than the Spirit's working."[33] Obedience must be the response of faith lest it degenerate into the failure of legalism described in chapter 7. It is no coincidence that Paul begins and ends this letter with the theme of the obedience of faith (1:5; 16:26). This is the heart of the divine mystery prophesied in the Hebrew Scriptures and now fulfilled in Christ. Fee adds, "Life in the Spirit is ethical realism, life lived in the already/not yet by the power of the Spirit."[34] The ethical change begins with a renewing of the mind (Rom 12:1-2; Eph 1:17; Col 1:9). Our ears hear and our hearts obey. Our minds conform and

---

30. Bruce, *Paul*, 210.
31. Schweitzer, *Mysticism of Paul*, 167.
32. Ridderbos, *Paul*, 221.
33. Ridderbos, *Paul*, 294.
34. Fee, *Paul, the Spirit*, 107.

our bodies perform. This brings a new dynamic way of living, not by the letter of the law but by the guidance of the Spirit (Gal 5:18), leading to the fulfillment of the law (Rom 10:4).

Because of the overlap between the "now" and "not yet," Paul warns the Romans in 8:17 of the inevitability of suffering that comes because of our union with Christ. It is not coincidental that Paul includes the topic of suffering in the context of victory over the flesh. He uses another word with the preposition *syn* ("with") used as a prefix, *sympaschomen*, meaning "suffer with." To be in Christ means to join in his suffering by putting ourselves on the cross. This ends the control of the flesh and allows the resurrected life of Christ to gain more influence over us. This impacts every aspect of a believer's life now, in this present evil age.

Significantly, Paul uses the perfect tense for the verb *gegonamen* in Romans 6:5: "we have been united with him in a death like his." Similarly, he uses perfect tense verbs in Galatians 2:19, "I have been crucified with Christ" (*synestaurōmai*), and Galatians 6:14, "the world has been crucified to me" (*estaurōtai*). The perfect tense is rich in meaning in the Greek. An author would choose this tense for a specific reason. Its significance here is that the crucifying of the old life under the flesh was a decision made in the past but must be continually renewed. The old self was crucified, never to come off the cross. Paul says something similar in 2 Corinthians 4:10: "always carrying in the body the death of Jesus, so that the life of Jesus may also be manifested in our bodies." This is a significant clue of what life *in Christ* must be like in order to experience the freedom about which Paul writes in Romans 8. To become like Christ in love and holiness, one must die to the old life.

Suffering with Christ involves more than the aches and pains common to all humans. Although Paul is not clear in 8:17 what this suffering entails, the open door to suffering comes as a result of aligning ourselves with Christ. If his will becomes our will, we join in his battle against sin, not only for our own persons but in intercession for others. Paul believed his suffering for the sake of Christ had an impact on the life of other believers. In Colossians 1:24 he writes how his sufferings fill up what is lacking in Christ's afflictions for the sake of the church. This is not an easy verse to interpret. The clue may be found in Paul's understanding of union with Christ. Paul may have viewed Christ's suffering as incomplete because Paul still had to live an imperfect life in this fallen age; he was still on the journey and Christ still had more transformation to do in him (Phil 3:12). Dunn comments, "Since Christ's death is the means by which the sinful flesh is killed off, it is incomplete till the whole entail of sinful flesh is brought to an end. Since

Christ's death is the means by which death is conquered, it is incomplete until the final destruction of the last enemy (1 Cor 15:26)."[35]

Victory through suffering takes the same route as victory over sin: experiencing the resurrection life of Christ. Paul writes to the Corinthians, "So we do not lose heart. Though our outer self is wasting away, our inner self is being renewed day by day. For this light momentary affliction is preparing for us an eternal weight of glory beyond all comparison" (2 Cor 4:16–17). We begin to experience resurrection power now through the indwelling Spirit who births hope within us, even though there may be physical suffering because of union with Christ. We need the Holy Spirit while we are away from the Lord because the Spirit is the link between us and the Lord.

God has given us the Spirit as the "firstfruits" (Rom 8:23) or down payment (2 Cor 1:21–22) that guarantees that the sanctifying work he began in us will be completed at the coming of Jesus Christ (Phil 1:6; 1 Thess 5:23–24). The Spirit helps us now in our weakened condition (Rom 8:26). This unfolding of the eschatological hope is expressed again in 2 Corinthians 5:4: "while we are still in this tent, we groan, being burdened—not that we would be unclothed, but that we would be further clothed, so that what is mortal may be swallowed up by life. He who has prepared us for this very thing is God, who has given us the Spirit as a guarantee."

New life in Christ is driven by hope. To be "in the Spirit" shows that one has been brought to a new sphere of existence with this new hope for the future driving life in the present. Paul ends the body of Romans with a prayer wish in 15:13: "May the God of hope fill you with all joy and peace in believing, so that by the power of the Holy Spirit you may abound in hope." There are two noteworthy phrases in this verse. First, this hope is experienced through the act of believing (articular infinitive *en tō pisteuein*). Faith is the required response of the crucified life. As Paul states in Galatians 2:20, "the life I now live in the flesh I live by faith in the Son of God, who loved me and gave himself for me." It all comes back to where one will put his or her trust: in things of this world, which sin manipulates to satisfy the flesh resulting in death, or in Christ, who brings new life through the Spirit who transforms us through this crucified life. The second significant thought here is that the result of life through the Spirit is joy and peace, characteristics of victory and not defeat.

---

35. Dunn, *Theology of Paul*, 486.

Conclusion

To experience new life in Christ in its fullness, one must follow the course that this new life requires. Jesus talked of two paths in Matthew 7:13–14: the easy and popular way through the broad gate ending in destruction, and the hard way few follow through the narrow gate leading to life. Paul also reflects on two ways. All people are bound to the way of Adam which leads to slavery to the power of sin. This is vividly portrayed by living to please the flesh, in whatever forms this may manifest in a person's life (Gal 5:19–21). Trying to gain freedom from the power of the flesh by obedience to the law only ends in failure. Living by the flesh turns one inward to satisfy selfish instincts and desires that eventually result in death.

The other way in Christ requires that a person reject the popular way of the flesh and embrace the consecrated way of the Spirit. The prerequisite to experiencing new life is dying to the old way of bondage to sin, flesh, and the law. There is no resurrection without crucifixion. The simple requirement is the response of faith that accepts the supremacy of Christ as Lord. When early Christians were baptized, they made the confession that Jesus Christ is Lord. Baptism is the symbolic act of crucifying the old self (Col 2:11–12). For this confession to be life transforming, it must be spoken through the work of the Holy Spirit in one's life (1 Cor 12:3).

The Son and the Spirit are linked in Paul's thinking. To experience salvation in the Son not only from one's past in sin (justification) but freedom from sin's control in the present (sanctification), one must embrace fully the Spirit's convicting guidance. Those who have become slaves to Christ are able to do what God commands because they have the indwelling Spirit to prompt them and guide them into Christ's way of thinking. This will be shown experientially by agreeing with the Holy Spirit who will transform and conform our thinking into the mind of Christ (Rom 12:1–2). This new way is marked by cruciformity, where one follows the pattern of Christ through co-crucifixion with him.

The Spirit is sufficient to give us victory now in this world. The Spirit teaches the mind of Christ and enables believers to fulfill the law of love. The Spirit gives all the grace we need to love and be complete in Christ (Eph 3:16–19; Col 2:10). The Spirit is also God's guarantee that we are indeed his children and participants in the eternal hope of transformation into the likeness of the Son (Rom 8:23–25, 29). Those who have their hope in Christ because of union with him do not need to live in fear of condemnation (vv. 33–34). Nothing can separate those *in Christ* from "the love of God in Christ Jesus our Lord" (v. 39) because the Spirit who lives within believers connects them to this love. To be *in Christ* is both transactional and transformational.

6

The Missional Community in Christ

In him you also are being built together into a dwelling place for God by the Spirit.

(EPHESIANS 2:22)

THE CHURCH CANNOT EXIST outside of Christ, nor can believers find victory over sin outside of one another. Paul offers an alternative community that crosses ethnic barriers, is bound together in fellowship with the triune God, and fulfills its purpose of holiness before God. Paul's letters reveal his efforts to form alternative communities primarily characterized by the new life made possible through fellowship with Christ through the Holy Spirit. Paul saw God's grace and peace at work as believers joined together for prayer, worship, fellowship, and mission to the world. The Letter to the Ephesians offers one of the most developed expressions of the church in the New Testament. In this letter, Paul brings theology to bear on the practical needs of the church, anchoring the life of the church to the foundation of relationship with Christ. Paul offers a radical vision of the church that compels believers to mission. Ephesians represents the development of his thinking about the church and its purpose in the world.

The Foundation *in Christ*

Fundamentally, the church cannot exist without being *in Christ*. Paul uses the word "church" (*ekklēsia*) to designate the holy ones (1:1) who have been adopted into God's family (1:5). Although the word *ekklēsia* occurs only nine times in the letter, there are other expressions, images, and implicit references to the people of God.[1] The meaning and origin of this word has been debated, but the more likely background comes from Judaism and the Septuagint, where it refers to the gathered assembly of God's people, the *qāhāl*.[2] Paul uses the term in his early letters to designate the gathering of believers in a particular location (Gal 1:2; 1 Thess 1:1). The church is described by a location indicator ("of the Thessalonians") and identified in its relationship to "God the Father and the Lord Jesus Christ." The church is not abstract but a specific gathered community of believers. Paul uses this same idea in Ephesians but connects the local community with the cosmic purposes of God. He consistently uses the singular "church" with the article. Through our local connection with other believers, we become participants in God's greater purposes for humanity through our fellowship with Jesus Christ. The many gathered communities become one in purpose because of their bond with Christ through the Holy Spirit.

Ekklēsia is defined primarily in its association with and response to Jesus Christ. Paul begins this letter with a self-description, marking his calling as "an apostle of Christ Jesus by the will of God" (v. 1). The letter is then addressed to "the saints who . . . are faithful *in Christ Jesus*." The phrase *in Christ Jesus* specifically associates this gathered community with Christ and sets the theological tone for all that follows. New life with Christ is the primary identity of the church and one of the key messages of Ephesians.

God's Will for Us in Christ

A Relationship Defined by Holiness and Love

In the opening section of the letter, known as the *Berakah* (the "Blessing") and famous for being one of the longest sentences in Greek literature, Paul begins with his typical statement of praise to the God and Father of our Lord Jesus Christ (1:3), setting the tone for the rest of the letter. This praise springs from the fact that God has "blessed us in Christ with every spiritual blessing in the heavenly places." Paul does not immediately define what these spiritual blessings are. Markus Barth suggests that they involve the "decision, action, and revelation of God which has culminated and been 'sealed' when the 'Holy Spirit' was given to both Gentiles and Jews (1:13-14;

---

1. See George Lyons, "Church and Holiness in Ephesians," in Brower and Johnson, *Holiness and Ecclesiology*, 238–56.

2. Schmidt, "*Ekklēsia*," *TDNT*, 3:501–36.

4:30)."[3] These blessings are spiritual in nature, implying the inner work of the Holy Spirit, in anticipation of the eschatological life of heaven, and are experienced "in Christ." Paul uses a prepositional phrase with some designation for Christ fourteen times from verses 3 to 14, drawing the readers' focus to the source of all that God intends for humanity: "in Christ" (v. 3); "in him" (vv. 4, 9, 10); "in the Christ" (vv. 10, 12); "before him" (v. 4); "through Jesus Christ" (v. 5); "into him" (v. 5); "in the Beloved" (v. 6); "in whom" (vv. 7, 11, and twice in v. 13).

The purpose of the blessings is given in the purpose clause in verse 4: God chose us in Christ before the world was created *in order that we might be* holy and blameless before him in love.[4] God's plan for humanity was for a certain quality of life that would enable people to be in relationship with the Holy One. In 1 Samuel 6:20 the men of Beth-Shemesh asked, "Who is able to stand before the Lord, this holy God?" Only those with clean hands and pure hearts can come before God's holy presence (Ps 24:3-4; Matt 5:8). Without holiness, no one can see God (Heb 12:14b). The eschatological promise of dwelling with God (Jer 31:33; Rev 21:3) comes as a direct result of being *in Christ*. This is no afterthought but God's very purpose in creating the universe. Jesus' death and resurrection were not a solution to the sin problem that God thought up after Adam and Eve fell into sin but were the plan from the start (see 2 Tim 1:9-10; 1 Pet 1:19-20; Rev 13:8). The requirement of holiness to enter into God's presence is provided through Christ to those bonded to him by grace. This is both moral and relational.

The phrase "in love" is difficult to interpret because what it modifies is unclear. Should it be taken with the earlier purpose clause, that we will live out our holiness before him in love, or with the phrase that follows, "in love he predestined"? The word order would suggest that the first is the intended meaning, which is quite significant in light of Paul's other references to love in this letter. In 4:24 he writes of being recreated in the holy image of God, and then he goes on in 5:1-2 to anchor this holiness in imitation of the love of Christ. Holiness and love are essential partners (see 1 Thess 3:12-13) that mark the quality of life of those in Christ and enable them to be in relationship with the holy God who planned it all this way from the beginning. God's plan in Christ is that all people be adopted as his children and become part of his people and family (Eph 1:6; Rom 8:16). The final result of this plan is that God will be glorified for how he has planned for the salvation of the world (Eph 1:7). From the world's perspective, it is foolishness, but it actually shows how glorious, gracious, and wise God is (1 Cor 1:18-25).

---

3. Barth, *Ephesians*, 1:101.
4. The purpose specifically appears in the infinitive clause *einai hēmas*.

The Goal of Knowing God

Paul offers two prayers in this letter. The first is given in 1:17–23 and has the expressed purpose that God may grant the readers "the Spirit of wisdom and of revelation in the knowledge of him" (v. 17). In the Greek, there is no article before "Spirit." Some translations treat this generically, like we might use the word "attitude" or "disposition" (e.g., KJV, NRSV). This use is seen later in 4:23. However, there could be a more specific intention here. The change of outlook that God intends for humans comes through the transforming power of the Holy Spirit. The way God will give this wisdom is through his Holy Spirit who will transform us into the image of Christ (2 Cor 3:18) by teaching us the mind of Christ (1 Cor 2:16; Rom 12:1–2). The ultimate goal of God's plan in Christ is that people will come to know God in his fullness. The word "revelation" assumes that something has been hidden, which is often described as a "mystery," a word Paul uses many times in this letter to describe God's plan for the salvation of all people through Christ (1:9; 3:3, 4, 6, 9; 5:32; 6:19). God reveals knowledge about himself through the Holy Spirit. We come to know more about God's eternal plan in Christ through the Spirit. Paul is praying that the Ephesians will participate more in this eternal plan of God. The object of this knowledge is God, and it is not abstract knowledge but personal and relational knowledge (*epignōsei*) that comes "in Christ."

The reason for our creation is to see God for who God is: wise, gracious, and loving towards us as revealed through Jesus Christ. This revelation offers hope for eternal life, expressed in 1:18 as "the riches of his glorious inheritance in the saints," and in 2:5–6 as being raised up with Christ and seated with him in the heavenly places. The more we know about God, the more our hope in his grace grows. The source of this knowledge is God's specific revelation in Christ's death, resurrection, and exaltation (1:20). This is powerfully expressed in Paul's second prayer in 3:14–21, which also has the goal of knowing the love of Christ shown to us and grown in us by the Holy Spirit. Knowledge of God comes through Christ in partnership with the Holy Spirit.

The Cross as the Means for God's Plan

The problem of sin, however, ensnares and keeps people from experiencing God's perfect plan for them. At several points in the letter, Paul speaks of the "before" and "after" situation of believers. Before salvation, believers were spiritually dead because of their disobedience, evidenced in living by the passions of the flesh (2:2-3). When sin comes, death is soon to follow (Gen 2:17; Rom 7:9). In Romans 5:12-21 Paul compares the two opposite states of being "in Christ" and being "in Adam," with Christ and Adam representing two ways of living.[5] Adam serves as the archetype for sinful humanity in rebellion against God.[6] Through Adam's disobedience, sin and death entered the world, resulting in condemnation and bondage for all people to the power of sin. This power, as James Dunn comments, "turns humankind in upon itself in preoccupation with satisfying and compensating for its own weakness as flesh."[7]

Although Paul does not use the phrase "in Adam" in Ephesians, every person (including the "we" of 2:3) follows the pattern of disobedience begun by Adam as the archetype in the garden and ends with the same consequence of death, which comes as a result of "trespasses and sins" (2:1). These two terms are used to express the one idea of the exertion of the self-will against the divine commandments. Paul does not refer to the power of sin in Ephesians, like he does in Romans 6, but the evidence of this deeper problem shows up in the acts of sin. It is not the power of sin that leads to our personal death but the acts of disobedience. We each die like Adam when we break the commandments of God (Rom 7:9). Lincoln writes, "Trespasses and sins both bring about the condition of death and characterize the existence of those who are spiritually dead."[8] Disobedience also leads to divine wrath (2:3), expressed in Romans 1:24, 26, and 28 with the terrifying words, "God gave them up." Sin as idolatry turns one's self inward in fulfillment of fleshly passions (Rom 8:5-8; Gal 5:19-22).

If left unchecked, the result will be hardness of heart and callousness to the grace of God that is experienced through the inviting presence of the Holy Spirit (4:17-19, 30). This way of life characterizes the world, which is compelled by "the prince of the power of the air" (2:2) and evidenced in a futile and darkened way of thinking (4:18). Without God's presence, the result is a fractured world full of brokenness and without any hope for community. Sin alienates us from God and from one another (2:11-14). For the Corinthian church, their fleshly living left them divided and unable to develop the mind of Christ within them (1 Cor 2:16—3:3). Living in

---

5. Paul uses "in Adam" in 1 Cor 15:22. It is possible that Adam stands behind Phil 2:5-11. See Dunn, *Christology in the Making*, 114-15; R. Martin, *Hymn of Christ*, 116-19.

6. Life "in Adam" is illustrated in Rom 6:1-14 with enslavement to the power of sin and is manifested in 6:15-23 in the acts of sin.

7. Dunn, *Theology of Paul*, 112.

8. Lincoln, *Ephesians*, 93.

imitation of Adam will always erect walls of separation within the church and between the church and the world.

God's answer for the alienation of sin is the "blood of Christ" (1:7). The way by which we can participate in God's plan is through the redemption (*apolytrōsin*) that comes through Christ's death and resurrection. God's love expressed through the "Beloved" Son is the source for redemption (1:6; John 3:16). The phrase "forgiveness of trespasses" is used in 1:7 in apposition to the word "redemption." The word *apolytrōsin* has the connotation of having been owned or enslaved by someone or something, and a price must be paid to buy freedom. Slavery to the power of death results from disobeying God (2:1). All people have fallen short of God's glory, resulting in death (Rom 6:23), and so all are in need of redemption (Rom 3:23). We are bound "in Adam" to self-focused and depraved living, without any source of rescue from within this world. Dead people cannot resurrect themselves. There is only one answer: being *in Christ* (Rom 7:25—8:1). Redemption provides the solution for the problem created by our trespasses by releasing us from the guilt incurred because of our sins. Thus, justification is closely linked to redemption and can be understood as the result of God's forgiveness of our sins.

The very power of God is revealed in Christ's resurrection. Paul bursts forth in praise of this essential truth in 1:19-20, declaring "the immeasurable greatness of his power toward us who believe, according to the working of his great might that he worked in Christ when he raised him from the dead" (2:19-20). The same power that created the world with the spoken word (Gen 1:3) is the same power that works in us through Christ (Col 1:16) to enable us to know God in relationship (Eph 1:17). Christ's sacrifice of himself in love for us (5:2) opens the way for us to become participants in the household of God (2:22). The alienation caused by sin is removed by Christ's death and resurrection, and we become participants in Christ of the spiritual blessings for which we have been created. Holiness and love become possible as new creation comes in the lives of believers (4:23-24). Paul uses the key prepositional phrases *hyper hēmōn* ("for us") in 5:2 and *hyper autēs* ("for it" referring to the church) in 5:25 to speak of Christ's sacrifice and how it enables love and holiness within the church as an example and enabling power. Christ's death and resurrection make it possible for us to participate in kingdom life here on earth. Just as spiritual death is the prelude to eternal death (2:1-3), new spiritual life is a foretaste of eternal life (2:5). We are participants now in the age to come because we have been raised to newness of life (see Rom 6:4). Paul goes as far as to claim that believers are already seated with Christ in the heavenly places (2:6). Christ's victory over sin and death guarantee our own victory which awaits the "fullness of time" (1:10), when Christ will hand over the conquered kingdom to the Father (1 Cor 15:24-28). Meanwhile, we await the total triumph of God with assurance that comes by being in Christ.

God's plan for the whole created order and its restoration was revealed through the suffering and victory of Christ at "just the right time" (Rom 5:6). In 1:9-10 Paul expands our view of Christ by showing that his death had cosmic significance. All things will be united in Christ by experiencing the purpose for which they were created. The word used in verse 10 for "to unite" (*anakephalaiōsasthai*) has at its root the word "head," implying that all things will be brought under one head, Christ, who is the ruler of all creation (see Col 1:15-20), resulting in perfect harmony and the completion of God's plan "that we should be holy and blameless in love" (1:4). Paul describes this plan as the mystery of God's will (v. 9). At the very core of God's being is the love shown on the cross (Rom 5:8). The word "mystery" conveys that what needed to be revealed is God's plan that all who trust in Christ, both Jew and Gentile, will experience the promised salvation (3:3, 6).[9] Paul expresses this in 1:11 with the word "inheritance," which has the idea of something planned and promised as a gift to the next generation. What is this inheritance? First Peter 1:3-7 uses the word "inheritance" for eternal life. In the context of Ephesians 1:11-14, the word is associated with receiving the gospel of salvation. This experience of the fullness of God's plan is the reason for our creation, expressed in 1:11 with the word "predestined." The final result of our salvation in Christ is given in verse 12: that we might be to the praise of the glory of God.[10]

This leaves us with an expanded view of what Christ has done. Salvation is much more than walking on golden streets or living in a mansion on a hilltop, as the popular gospel songs say. It reveals the very gracious character of the triune God. Viewing salvation as an individual union card to heaven brings no glory to God but only shows the selfish nature of humanity. The gospel is about more than "getting in." *All things* were created *in order to experience* the gospel! Christ brought change to the very core of the existence of all things. The church does not exist primarily to disciple people into a holy ethic but first and foremost to connect people to God's cosmic purposes of transformation in Christ. The church stands at the intersection of God's cosmic plan and a world lost in sin. Through our experience of

---

9. Paul refers to the gospel as mystery also in Rom 16:25-26. The prophets had a glimpse into this mystery of God's plan but it was only revealed in its fullness in Christ (1 Pet 1:10-12).

10. The antecedent for the pronoun *autou* in the phrase "his glory" is vague. The context of the verse suggests God the Father, whose will is being fulfilled. The issues are similar in v. 6, where the primary actor is God but the one in whom God acts is Christ.

transformation in Christ, the holy ethic will emerge as we become who we were created to be.

Experiencing the Blessing through Grace

How humanity experiences God's plan in Christ is best characterized by the word "grace." Grace is one of the central themes in this letter, with the word *charis* occurring eleven strategic times.[11] This word basically means a kindness, goodwill, gift, or favor shown to another person. Etymologically, it is related to "joy" (*chara*) and "thanksgiving" (*eucharisteō*). When one receives an undeserved gift, the response is a sense of both joy and gratitude. Grace is a favorite word for Paul and captures in part God's response in Christ to the sinful condition of humanity.

Paul uses the imagery of death to characterize the inability of people to save themselves through human effort. Sin ensnares people and leaves them unable to fulfill God's purposes for them (Rom 7:14–20). Instead of responding to our trespasses with wrath, God shows love, which we experience as mercy when we are lost in sin (Eph 2:4–5; Rom 5:8). Both "love" and "mercy" translate the Hebrew *chesed* in the Septuagint. God's essential nature of love (Exod 34:6; Deut 7:7–9) is experienced on the human side as mercy and is the cause (*dia tēn pollen agapēn autou*, 2:4) of life in Christ. Grace comes through Christ's death on the cross (1:6) and leads to life with Christ. There is no other source or means by which we can experience God's purposes for us in this life and for eternity. No human effort can bring reconciliation and end the alienation between us and God that profoundly affects every aspect and relationship in this world. Grace opens the door to the "riches" (1:7; 2:7) of God's love that we will share "in the saints" (1:18).

The Necessary Human Response

This offer is not irresistible because it comes through the open door of faith (2:8). Faith is the acceptance and appropriation of God's gift in Christ. Faith for Paul involves trust and a change of allegiance from self or anything or anyone in this world to dependence upon God. Faith acknowledges that there is no other source of life than what God provides in Christ. Because we are dead in sin and have no other alternative but self-destruction, we need someone from outside of our doomed existence to extend a helping hand. Faith itself is a result of grace. Grace is the hand extended through

---

11. 1:2, 6, 7; 2:5, 7, 8; 3:2, 7, 8; 4:7; 6:24.

hopeless darkness, and faith is the action of trusting the one who offers the hand and embracing it out of the desperation of repentance. God planned for salvation before creation (1:4) and took the initiative in Christ (1:5), but he still leaves the reception of salvation up to each person. God took the initiative by predestining that the salvation of humanity would lead to his glory (1:11).

Two groups participate in this plan. The first are the believers who have already "put their hope" (*proēlpikotas*) in Christ (1:12). Hope generates faith and involves trusting for something not yet experienced. In this case, hope is expressed in a perfect participle implying that hope began in the past and remains to this moment. The second group includes those who heard the message (*akousantes*) from the first group and believed in it (*pisteusantes*, 1:13). Believers become participants in God's purpose by offering hope to those who have not yet believed (Rom 10:14–15). This is expressed again in 1:18–19, where Paul prays that the Ephesians will become participants in this hope and "the immeasurable greatness of [God's] power toward us who believe." The goal of Paul's second prayer in 3:17 is that "Christ may dwell in your hearts through faith." Faith is the expression of hope that leads to participation in God's plan in Christ. The destiny of the church is to believe in the message of Christ and share that message with others to the glory of God.

The Appropriation of the Mystery of Christ through the Spirit

Two key events unfold God's plan for humanity and give the church its identity: the death and resurrection of Christ and the gift of the promised Holy Spirit. Paul anchors all spiritual blessings in the triune God. First, Christ sets the pattern for God's eternal plan for us by living a life of love (5:1–2). His life not only sets the pattern for living but provides the inner resource for being filled with the fullness of God (3:19). Christ is the center and focus of all we should be about because in him we experience the divine plan that leads to the praise of God's glory (1:9, 14). Second, the Spirit is the source of all blessings in Christ (1:3) with the goal of us being blameless in holiness before God (1:4).

Faith in Christ opens the floodgate of grace and all God can and wants to do in and through the church (3:17). The result is receiving the "seal" or "down payment" (*arrabōn*) of the Holy Spirit (1:14; 2 Cor 1:21–22; Gal 3:14). The purpose of this sealing is our ultimate redemption (Eph 4:30). Those who belong to this family can be assured of their salvation through the abiding presence of the Holy Spirit. The Spirit bears witness with our spirits that we are indeed the children of God (Rom 8:16). The Holy Spirit confirms the truth of the gospel by bringing freedom from sin (Rom 8:1-13) and transformation into the holy image of Christ (2 Cor 3:18). The Holy Spirit inaugurates and appropriates the new age in Christ for each believer in the present moment and instills a deepening desire to experience the fullness of Christ in the age to come (Eph 1:10). The presence of the Holy Spirit is the evidence that life in Christ has already begun. Though our faith may be weak now (1 Cor 13:9-12), because its object is Christ, we can be assured that it is not in vain and that our hope will certainly be fulfilled (Eph 1:18).

In addition, the Spirit brings a deeper knowledge of the holy and loving nature of God best seen in the person of Christ (1:17-18). The Holy Spirit works in our inner person with the specific goal of helping us to know better the love of Christ (3:16). The natural result of the Spirit's work is recreation into the image of Christ. Although the Spirit is not specifically mentioned in 4:23-24, the passive voice of the verb "to be made" (*ananeousthai*) indicates that someone outside of ourselves is restoring us into God's image of "true righteousness and holiness." This is not simply cognitive or intellectual but change at the core of our being (Col 1:27). In 3:20 Paul mentions a "power that works within us." This power is described in 3:16-19 as coming from the Holy Spirit who enables us to experience the love of Christ more in our inner person. In other words, the Spirit enables us to grasp and experience the gospel in ever increasing ways. Simply stated, the Spirit opens the way to experience all that God has predestined for us through Christ (1:3-4; 2:18). The imperative of 5:18, "Be filled with the Spirit," implies that we must respond to the Spirit with the obedience of faith. We must not grieve the Spirit by allowing any of the old life controlled by desires of the flesh to creep back in (4:23, 30; Gal 5:25). The significance of the work of the Spirit to implant the love of Christ deeply in our hearts cannot be overstated.

The Mission of the Church

Experiencing the depth of grace can only happen in community. Grace creates a new people of God who transcend barriers erected within this world. New creation (2 Cor 5:17) not only opens our hearts to receive more fully God's love in Christ but also enables this love to flow out to those around us as we participate in God's purposes in this world. An agreed mission statement or list of objectives is not adequate for any group of people to be called "church." Unity results as Christ is allowed to reign supreme through obedience to the leading of the Holy Spirit. The church nurtures individuals who then participate in community by being catalysts for new creation in the lives of others. The church is the place where the new age of Christ breaks into the old age of sin. New creation involves a transformation of devotion from the objects of the world to the person of Christ.

The Church in Relationship with Christ

The ecclesiology of Ephesians is firmly christologically focused but Trinitarian resourced. The church gets its identity in its relationship to Christ, and from this identity comes its mission. The mission of the church rests solidly on the supremacy of the resurrected and exalted Christ (1:20-21) who is "head over all things to the church, his body, the fullness of him who fills all in all" (1:22-23). If he is not supreme over every aspect of the church, the church is not being his body.[12] As the sovereign one, Christ gives the church all the resources needed to fulfill its mission (4:11-13). The church is not a function but a communion. Anything the church does must flow out of its relationship with Christ. Anything else will have the wrong source of power and ultimately fail. Paul uses several images to describe this relationship.

The Body of Christ

One of the most frequent images of the church is as the body of Christ (2:3, 16; 3:6, 4:4, 12; 5:23, 30; see Rom 12:5). The background for this image is debated, but Paul is using a well-known image to illustrate how the church ought to live out its relationship with Christ especially symbolized through the Lord's Supper and baptism.[13] There are two related themes stated in 1:22-23. First, Christ is described as the "head over all things." The Greek *kephalē* often translates the Hebrew *rōš* to signify a ruler or leader, with the nuance of authority because of priority. Christ as head has supreme authority over all creation (*panta*, 1:22) since through him all things were created (Col 1:15-16). God confirmed Christ's supremacy by raising him from the dead and exalting him to the highest place (1:20; see Phil 2:8-11). Christ's supremacy assures the church that it has the same power available through the presence of the Holy Spirit to fulfill its mission in Christ (1 Thess 5:23-24). Christ as the head is preeminent and the source of life and growth for the body (Eph 4:15-16).

---

12. John 15:4; see Küng, *Church*, 235-36.

13. It has often been pointed out that Paul's body language in 1 Cor 12:12-31 and Rom 12:4-8 resembles the fable of Aesop as used by Menenius Agrippa. The eucharastic imagery for the body can be seen in 1 Cor 10:16-17 and 11:23-24. Baptismal traditions may lie behind Rom 7:4. See Grieb, "People of God," 234-35.

From the image of Christ as head emerges the solidarity of believers as a body. First, the church as the body is described as "the *fullness* of the one who fulfills all things in everything" (1:23). This phrase is difficult to interpret but gives the stylistic impression of the completeness that is in Christ. The meaning of *plēroma* carries the connotation of Christ as the incarnation of the glory of God (John 1:14; Eph 3:19; Col 1:19; 2:9). Ideally, the church is the embodiment of Christ, the presence of Christ on earth, and the proof of the resurrection power of Christ. The mission of the church as the body of Christ is to incarnate the redemptive purposes of God's grace in Christ and to continue what Christ started. To be "in Christ" involves becoming participants of this "fullness" through the Holy Spirit. As the creation of God, the church exists for the mission of God so that when people see the church, they see God's love lived out in obedient faith. The church becomes the channel by which unbelievers receive the transforming grace of God in Christ. The church as the incarnation of Christ is still distinct from Christ: Christ fills the church, not the church filling Christ. Christ the exalted one becomes intimately and immanently involved with his people.

Second, union with Christ through the Spirit results in union with one another as one body. The goal of each individual believer is expressed in Paul's second prayer in 3:14-21, that each person may be strengthened by the Spirit to know and experience the fullness of the love of Christ.[14] Interestingly, one does not experience God's fullness alone but "with all the saints" (v. 18). We come to know the love of Christ together because this love must by nature be shown to others. As each person comes to know the love of Christ through the indwelling Spirit, the bond of unity within the church results.[15] God provides the source of unity through the Holy Spirit but this unity must be maintained through peace (4:3). As channels of love, believers become agents of reconciliation (Gal 5:22; Rom 8:6; 14:17; 15:13; 2 Cor 5). This unity is expressed in 4:4-6 in a series of seven theological affirmations: one body, one Spirit, one hope, one Lord, one faith, one baptism, and one God and Father of all. The "calling" of the Ephesians (4:1) is the hope expressed in the prayer of 3:14-21, that the well of God's love in Christ will never run dry (3:20; Rom 8:38-39). Being worthy of this call creates a sense of obligation met through obedient faith.

---

14. There are two parallel infinitives in vv. 19-20 that imply that this knowledge is not simply cognitive but active and experiential: *katalabesthai* ("to grasp") and *gnōnai* ("to know"). The phrase *agapēn tou Christou* can be both an objective (love for Christ) or subjective (Christ's love for us) genitive. Since we love only because he first loved us (1 John 4:19), both are possible theologically in this passage.

15. This is one of the major themes of 1 Corinthians.

Each member of the body is given special gifts by the Spirit to help the body grow in unity, faith, and dependence upon Christ (4:7; 1 Cor 12:7, 27). Five specific leadership positions have the special calling of equipping believers for works of service (4:11-12). Significantly, the goal of body life, both the individual gifts and leadership, is to grow "in the knowledge of the Son of God and become mature, attaining to the whole measure of the fullness of Christ" (4:13, NIV). What takes place within each person's life and within the gathered community ought to lead to becoming more and more participants of God's eternal plan in Christ. This relationship with God in Christ through the Holy Spirit gives strength to face the challenges of the day (4:14) and to fulfill the purpose of the church to be perfected in love (4:15-16).

Third, the church as one body is a tangible entity sustained by spiritual power. The argument of Ephesians rests upon the assumption that the church is a spiritual entity experienced in local community. Each local fellowship is part of the universal church, but life in Christ can be lived out only in a local community, where love can be tangibly expressed and where holiness is visible (4:1, 4:24-6:9). Each local church is part of the universal church that spans time, culture, location, and language. What makes a particular group of people the church of God is that it shares in the essence and mission of the universal church of new life in Christ in all its fullness.

The Temple

A second important image is the church as a building formed into the temple of God. The church as a building is a common comparison in the New Testament. Paul uses the image to describe a people not a place. The essential characteristic of these people is holiness, which makes them a fit dwelling for God, the Holy One (1 Cor 3:16; 6:19). This image has a number of similarities with the body of Christ and addresses the same desire of unity within the church.

Two keys themes emerge in Ephesians with this image. The first is the unity of believers as they become united with Christ. In Christ, a new humanity is created that bridges the separations that polarize and divide people because of sin (2:15; Gal 3:28). The problem is that the law creates division among people by allowing sin to exert itself against the sovereignty of God (2:14; Rom 7:8-9). Sin makes us enemies against God by rejecting his will for us, and it makes us enemies with other people by replacing love with selfishness and self-gratification (2:3; 4:19). This universal problem has a complete answer in God's grace in Christ (2:5), who removed through his death on the cross the effects of sin caused by the law (2:15; 1 Cor 15:56). The result of what Christ has done is reconciliation, first with God (Rom 5:10; 2 Cor 5:18–19) and then with other people (5:21). With the barrier of sin removed, believers become reconciled with one another as they become united with Christ, resulting in peace. The good news of the mystery of the gospel is that this involves both Jews and Gentiles. It does not matter how "far away" one is (2:13), all who believe become one in Christ Jesus. In a world full of ethnic and political division, this is powerfully good news. God calls forth through all of creation a people from every culture and economic and social status to create human community based on love. Through the Spirit, the promises of the new covenant are fulfilled in Pentecostal power (Joel 2:28–32; Acts 2:17–21).

The other theme is that God is present in the building through the indwelling Holy Spirit (2:22). This building has the special purpose of being a house of worship, a temple, and the place where human and divine meet. It is holy because God's presence is there. The church as God's temple is built on the foundation of the gospel proclaimed by the prophets and apostles with Christ as the cornerstone (2:20). What makes the church holy and different than any community in the world is the abiding presence of the triune God through the Holy Spirit. Christ as the cornerstone determines the quality and strength of the building. The temple exists *in Christ* with all the implications this phrase involves. The members are in the ongoing process (present tense) of being joined together through love (4:16; Col 3:14) because the Holy Spirit is recreating the image of Christ in each person with "righteousness and holiness" (4:24). The Spirit makes believers holy in order to make them fit vessels of God's love in Christ. This is the essence of what it means to be church in this world as we anticipate being in God's presence fully in eternity. The Spirit brings us into conformity with Christ's holy image of perfect love as we live in the obedience of faith, which involves total commitment to the supremacy of Christ (5:1–2; 1 Cor 2:16; 2 Cor 3:18). This has profound and tangible impact on community life.

The Church United in Mission

From these images emerges the mission of the church as Christ's ambassador of grace and channel of his love. The church engages the world with the grace and reconciling power of God in Christ and embodies the eschatological hope to which God purposes all creation (see 1 Pet. 2:9). The mission of the church is an extension of the Trinity. All three persons of the Godhead are mentioned numerous times throughout the epistle. The prayer of 3:14–21 is one of the most revealing passages where Paul prays that God the Father may reveal his love to humanity through Christ Jesus, and this is experienced through the Holy Spirit. God intends this love to flow through the church to the world.

The only way the church can sustain its mission is through the fellowship of love. This mission can only be fully experienced within a gathered community of believers because that is where incarnation can take place. The broad concept of the universal church compels us to be involved in the cosmic purposes of God but we cannot do this without the local fellowship. It starts at the individual level. Individualism, isolation, and lack of integrity keep the church from fulfilling its mission. Egotism or anything that is inconsistent with life in Christ by violating the law of love will keep the church from growing and removes the vital ingredient that keeps it together. The world leaves fragmented lives in its wake, but in the church, the bond of peace in Christ brings diversity into unity (2:14–15, 17; 4:3; 6:15). With Spirit-filled leaders training the body to seek after the love of Christ, the church becomes an unstoppable force because it has tapped into the power source of the God of the universe. The church must not be interpreted with hierarchy, with the laity somehow inferior, but as a living organism with each part mutually dependent upon the other and contributing to the wellness of the whole (4:16; 1 Cor 12:14–26).

This unity does not come through human ability but only as the church is in fellowship "with Christ." This communion begins with being crucified with Christ by "putting to death" (Rom 6:5–7) or "putting off" (Eph 4:22) the old life controlled by sin. God has promised to raise us to new life in Christ (2:5; 4:23–24; Rom 6:4, 8–11). These images summarize the moment of entire sanctification when a person changes allegiance from sin as master to Jesus as Lord. This change happens when one opens oneself totally in faith to God's transforming grace (Gal 2:20). Transformation in Christ is the only sustaining power for the church to carry out its mission. If individuals within a local church are not being remade into the image of Christ, not only are they not fulfilling God's purposes for them, but collectively they keep that church from fulfilling its mission and are missing out on what God is doing on the cosmic level in bringing all things together in unity under Christ (1:10).

The church is reminded of its relationship with Christ through the sacraments. The gathered church is a worshipping community filled with the Spirit where music rises from the heart to the Lord (5:19–20), prayers are offered for all people (1 Cor 1:2; 1 Tim 2:1–7), the Scriptures are read (1 Tim 4:13), and the saints are trained up in the Lord (Eph 4:12). The sacraments of baptism and the Lord's Supper engage the church in its purpose and bring the community together in unity.

Baptism is specifically mentioned only once in Ephesians, in 4:5, as one of the elements that unites the church. The common baptismal confession "Jesus Christ is Lord" unites all believers together in a common faith (1 Cor 12:3, 13), but this is deeper than simply a verbal confession. It is the initiation into the body of Christ but also marks the commitment of faith necessary for life in Christ. Baptism serves as the visible testimony of the inner transformation that the Spirit makes within the believer. The early Christians had the practice at least as early as the second century of putting on new clothing after baptism.[16] Though it is impossible to know when this started, all the elements for this can be found in Paul's letters and offer some important theological insights for the church. In Galatians 3:27 Paul mentions that those baptized into Christ are clothed with Christ. Romans 13:14 also exhorts believers to be clothed with Christ as a mark of their life in Christ. Romans 6:1–11 uses the image of old and new in the context of baptism and provides an important synthesis for Ephesians. Baptism serves as the visible act of dying to the old way of life controlled by the power of sin. As one comes out of the water, one assumes a new life marked by freedom from sin and commitment to the lordship of Christ (6:4). Thus, baptism serves at the initial symbol of new life in Christ and the mark of the sanctifying process of the Holy Spirit.

There are two allusions to baptism in Ephesians that support this idea. In 4:22–24 Paul again refers to the change from the old self to the new self in a similar way to Romans 6:3–4. God recreates the new believer into his image of "true righteousness and holiness." The new life is visibly marked with holiness and a separation from sin (see also Col 2:12). This new life comes in the total commitment that baptism ought to mark. Baptism is not only the mark of initiation but should mark the committed faith of entire sanctification, which should be the identifying lifestyle of one in Christ. In 5:25–27 Paul uses the relationship of Christ and the church as an illustration of marriage. Christ "loved the church and gave himself up for her in order to make her holy by cleansing her by the washing with water through the word." It is impossible to tell if Paul means here water baptism or a spiritual baptism through the Holy Spirit. This verse draws us back to the vicarious love of Christ (*hyper autēs*) on the cross as the source of sanctification, and this is experienced through the washing away of the old life and the renewal of the Holy Spirit in making the church holy (1 Cor 6:11). Christ continues to show love to the church by caring for it as his body (Eph 5:29).

---

16. Meeks, *First Urban Christians*, 155.

The Lord's Supper continues the symbolism of new life in Christ found in baptism. Although there is no specific mention of the Lord's Supper in this letter, the theme of the unity of the church through Christ's sacrificial giving of himself on the cross (2:13; 5:1-2, 25) provides an important theological connection. The Lord's Supper is more than a memorial; it is a means of grace and cause for unity on a far deeper level than humanly possible. The Supper brings believers together in unity because all share in the same cup and loaf (1 Cor 10:16-17). This means more than everyone dipping from the same cup of wine or breaking apart one loaf of bread. The physical elements represent the choice one makes to be united with Christ (*koinōnia*) in one's will and purpose through agreement with the conviction of the Holy Spirit. When believers come together at the Supper, they commit as the body of Christ to the mission of his death. It is the opportunity for love to be renewed among the individuals within the community. Individualism, selfishness, or a lack of love stops the grace of the Supper from sanctifying the church. The Supper is a celebration of the love and unity that Christ enables through the indwelling Holy Spirit. To eat it in a worthy manner (1 Cor 11:27) begins with total allegiance to Christ (and not sharing this loyalty with any other being, such as demons, 1 Cor 10:21) and must be shown by the renewed commitment of total submission to him by dying to self in sanctification. Each time the Supper is eaten, the church is given opportunity to renew the commitment of total consecration involved in putting on the new person (Eph 4:24) and fulfilling its purpose of being holy and blameless (1:4).

Proclaiming the Good News

As the church lives out resurrection life as an extension of its relationship with Christ, it must become engaged in the mission of incarnation that compels it in love to embrace every movement of God in this world. Our identity cannot be determined by this mission, but the mission must be a result of the identity. The response in faith to the work of the Spirit impacts how the church acts both internally and externally.

Ethics: Living Out the New Life in Christ

Because believers have been transformed into new people in Christ (4:23-24), they follow two driving standards for their conduct. First, they imitate the love of God that Christ showed on the cross (5:1-2), and second, they do what pleases God by living consistently with his holy character (5:10).

Paul gives many examples in 4:25—6:9 in response to specific needs of the first-century context. It is possible to reach these two standards in cooperation with the indwelling Spirit, who enables believers to bear fruit consistent with the character of Christ (Gal 5:24–25) and to live in victory over the temptations of the flesh (Rom 8:9–13; 1 Cor 10:13). Alfred Wikenhauser comments that "the Spirit is the vital influence which gives the new life its quality."[17] Without the transforming assistance of the Spirit, any effort to live by these standards eventually degenerates into legalism, which poisons the unity and mission of the church (Gal 5:1–15). These standards are successfully fulfilled not simply between the Spirit and each individual believer but in community, where edification, worship, and accountability take place. Only as "church" is new life fully possible.

Eschatology: Participating in Something Greater

The church exists in the tension of the already and not yet. The church is called to embody in the present age the new creation in Christ promised in the eschaton, but yet it still lives with a sense of not having arrived because of the ongoing battle with the forces of evil. The church participates in the eternal, spiritual sphere of existence in its relationship with Christ (1:21–22), but this connection does not isolate the church from the need to be the instrument through which God brings about his purpose in this world. This engagement can be messy as new people are incorporated into the church and their growth from sin to new life is enabled. Lincoln writes, "Yet the distinctive behavior required of the new humanity, of the children of light, is not achieved by flight from the world but by living responsibly in the world, in the ordinary structures of human life—husband-wife, parent-children, and master-slave relationships (cf. 5:21–6:9)."[18] The church is constantly drawn towards eschatological life in Christ because Christ gave himself to make the church radiant, pure, holy, and blameless (5:27). This happens as believers embrace Christ's way of thinking (Rom 12:1–2; 1 Cor 2:16) because he dwells within them through the Holy Spirit, not overpowering their personhood, but recreating it in the image it was meant to be. Paul was confident that he "who began a good work in you, will bring it to completion at the day of Jesus Christ" (Phil. 1:6; see 1 Thess 5:23–24).

---

17. Wikenhauser, *Pauline Mysticism*, 55.
18. Lincoln, *Ephesians*, xcv.

Enemies: Victorious Living

Although the church is in the process of being made holy in Christ as each person embraces the movement of the Spirit, it still lives in conflict with "the ruler of the power of the air," who, with his evil forces, wages war against people, enticing them into disobedience against God (2:2; 6:11–12). The church as an alternative community finds itself at odds against a world decaying because of sin and death and dominated by evil. Because the power of sin has been broken by the death and resurrection of Christ, believers can have victory over these evil powers (1:19–23; 4:8–10; see ch. 7 below). Through the church God is progressively reordering the cosmos against these forces. The church represents a new order that counters the divisiveness of the devil. God has provided the church spiritual armor to battle these forces. The list of the armor in 6:13–20 is a summary of life in Christ: truth which is found in Christ (4:21), righteousness (4:24), the gospel of peace (2:14), faith (3:17), salvation (2:8), the word of God (4:13), and prayer in the Spirit (3:14–21). Each believer must keep awake and connected to Christ through prayer. Believers are already seated with Christ (2:6) and are assured victory because of Christ's resurrection (Rom 6:5, 8).

Ecclesiology and Ecology in Romans 8

What God does in Christ not only impacts individual believers but creates community which participates in his kingdom on earth. God's kingdom is breaking into this earth with the restoration of all creation in Christ, as expressed in Romans 8 and other passages in Paul's letters. Creation suffers decay in the same way that humans experience suffering in this world. Sin is more than a violation of a code of law but involves a subordination of creation to human selfishness and idolatry. Sin results in the decay and suffering of humanity and all of creation with it. In Christ, we find freedom from continued inward decay but the effects of sin continue through outward suffering. Through this suffering, we become one with creation which longs for full restoration. The church embodies in this world God's purpose for all creation. Believers are in the privileged position of fellowship with the one who creates and holds all things together. Since we are in Christ, we participate in part in God's eschatological kingdom breaking into earthly existence. Creation longs for the full glorification in which believers now participate. Because we are now in Christ, our goal is to form restored community that increasingly becomes more like Christ. We can then view creation not as an object to be used but as a participant in the journey from decay to restoration in Christ. The church becomes the catalyst for creation renewal, for in this renewal, we become participants in the emergence of God's kingdom here on earth with an anticipation of the kingdom's fullness at Christ's return.

Conclusion

Ephesians sets forth the ideal for the church: living entirely sanctified by the Holy Spirit in total commitment to the lordship of Jesus Christ. In Christ, the temporal and the eternal are joined at the juncture of the church. This begins on the individual level as each believer finds victory over sin and new life in Christ. The result is an ever-increasing love for God and for other people that is shown in a holy ethic consistent with the character of Christ. God provides the resources for this victory, first and foremost through the Holy Spirit, but also by means of spiritual disciplines that help us embrace the leading of the Spirit (6:13–18). New life is then best lived out with other believers, with each person equipped with the teachings of Christ, worship that is supported by the sacraments, and love that is learned to be expressed. This corporate life lived in holiness and love is God's ideal for humanity and a foretaste of what heaven will be like. Every local fellowship becomes part of this heavenly vision and finds itself part of the cosmic people of God.

7

Victory in Christ over the Forces of Evil

And the peace of God, which surpasses all understanding, will guard your hearts and your minds in Christ Jesus.
(Philippians 4:7)

The central message of Scripture is that humans were created for relationship with the eternal God. Creation in the image of God (Gen 1:27) involves primarily the possibility of communion with the *Holy One*. God alone is *holy*, and any other holiness is derived in relationship with God (1 Sam 6:20; Isa 5:16; 40:25).[1] Only that which is holy can be in relationship with the holy God (1 Sam 6:20; Matt 5:8; Heb 12:14). God's holiness excludes all that is unholy or profane. God's holiness, however, is not exclusionary but inviting because God comes in love, seeking a relationship with his creatures.

A significant challenge when reading the Bible is to understand what lies behind human struggle to be holy before God. The reality of life, as we see and experience it, is that this world is dominated by brokenness, decay, sickness, and death. No matter how hard we try, we cannot hypothesize the bad away. Does that mean God is distant, unknowable, or uninvolved with the human predicament? To the contrary, the good news is that God Incarnate came and lived among people (John 1:14), making relationship with him possible, offering victory over sin and hope against evil. Human

---

1. Snaith, *Distinctive Ideas*, 42–50.

struggle against the power of sin has not changed. The immorality of the Canaanites or the Corinthians can be found with the click of the computer mouse. Optimism has been replaced with skepticism and uncertainty. The Enlightenment and the emergence of the scientific world-view have challenged the simplistic perceptions about the supernatural held by the cultures of the biblical era.

The struggles on the surface against poverty, war, freedom, and disease distract from the deeper spiritual needs that empower these issues. The basic human need has not changed. The same discouragement and doubt that reigned in the hearts of Adam and Eve as they stood facing the cherubim holding a flaming sword east of the garden of Eden blocking the way to the Tree of Life (Gen 3:24) also rages in people today. The presence of sin and evil block the way to the source of life. Many in the world today live in fear, not only of human-made troubles, but also of supernatural forces.

Paul was not concerned in his letters about naming and describing the spiritual foes of humanity. In a general sense, he was an existentialist, concerned with the more evident problems of sin and death. He shared much in common with his Jewish context, including his understanding of the forces of evil, but he put all this through his experience of Jesus Christ. As Dunn suggests, Paul's concern was more pastoral than speculative: "whatever names his readers give to the nameless forces which threaten the Creator's work and purpose, they are in the end impotent before him who is God over all."[2]

The Relation of Sin to Satan and the Forces of Evil

The Adversary

Although Satan was involved as the deceiver in the fall of Adam and Eve,[3] ultimately the human race is to blame for its problems. The proverbial "The devil made me do it" fails to account for the sin problem. However, there are forces at war against humanity, compelling us to rebel against the things of God. Paul's most common designation for the enemy of the human race is "Satan." "Satan" is a transliteration of the Hebrew word *sâtân*, meaning "adversary." Paul consistently uses the definite article with this word, suggesting a specific adversary to God and the people of God, "*the* adversary."

The first canonical location in Paul's letters where the word *ho satanas* occurs is Romans 16:20. Paul is closing out his letter at this point, giving

---

2. Dunn, *Romans 1–8*, 513.

3. Although there is no explicit connection of the serpent as Satan in the Genesis account, see Ezek 28:12–19; Rev 12:9, 20:2.

his final instructions to the believers in Rome. He is giving his last appeal to watch out for people who cause divisions and create obstacles to sound teaching, who serve their own "belly" (appetite), and who deceive the naïve (16:17–18). The context would suggest that these people are "adversaries," in a general sense, to the believers in Rome. These believers have several weapons in their battle against these foes: obedience, wisdom, and avoidance of evil things (v. 19). Yet, they are not left on their own in this struggle. Paul reminds them that the God of peace is on their side in their battle against Satan, and they have the grace of the Lord Jesus Christ with them.

Why did Paul bring Satan into the conversation in verse 20? One reason might be the association of smooth but deceitful talk in verse 18 and obedience in rejection of evil in verse 19. Deceit and compromise were problems in the garden of Eden for Adam and Eve. The smooth-talking serpent deceived them into being disobedient. The very actions of the troublemakers in Rome were also characteristic of the chief troublemaker, Satan. Satan and these foes were involved in the same type of devious activities.

Satan can serve as a tool of the sovereign God for spiritual discipline. In 1 Corinthians 5:1–13 Paul deals with the disturbing issue of a man associated with the Corinthian church who was having sexual relations with his father's wife, and the church was not doing anything about it. Paul's answer for the church is to kick the man out (v. 13; note that Paul cannot even call him a "brother"). Paul's answer for the man is for him to be delivered to Satan for "the destruction of his flesh, in order that his spirit might be saved on the day of the Lord" (v. 5). This is a difficult phrase to interpret. Fee suggests, "What Paul was desiring by the man's being put outside the believing community was the destruction of what was 'carnal' in him, so that he might be 'saved' eschatologically."[4] The man's flesh represents his sinfulness that resulted from his selfish lusts. This man needed to crucify the flesh with its deceitful desires. Satan serves as the means by which the man could realize his improper behavior. Paul does not say how Satan will accomplish this, but those who seek after things that satisfy the flesh will only find emptiness. Satan's cunningness reveals the broken human heart. Expulsion from the community would also add a shaming affect to the whole matter. Paul is reminding the Corinthians that God's grace and sovereignty are at work even when Satan seems to be having his way.

In later correspondence with the Corinthians, Paul exhorts the church to accept back an erring brother (2 Cor 2:5–11). Many interpreters view this brother to be the same man mentioned in 1 Corinthians 5. If he is not, the situation seems to be at least one of exclusion from the community ("the

---

4. Fee, *God's Empowering Presence*, 126; Fee, *First Corinthians*, 209–13.

many" in v. 6) for some wrong done. The church is to forgive and accept this brother back lest he be overcome by sorrow. Apparently, the community's shaming of this brother had the intended positive effect. In this situation, Satan serves again as a problem to the church. The Corinthians needed to forgive this man *so that* (a purpose clause) "we might not be outwitted by Satan; for we are not ignorant of his designs" (v. 11). Satan could use the wedge of an unforgiving heart to trouble this church. Paul is silent about what Satan might do. The context suggests that Satan exploits the lack of love in the church and obedience to the Lord's purposes (vv. 8–9). Satan here is characterized with "wit." The Greek word comes from *pleoneteō*, which basically means "to covet." In this context, it has the connotation of being overpowered or taken advantage of.[5] Both covetousness and taking advantage of people belittle them and make them objects to be used and abused. Paul, however, knows Satan's schemes and will not be caught off guard.

In another passage Paul associates Satan with improper sexual gratification outside of the bonds of marriage. In 1 Corinthians 7:1–5 Paul deals with the matter of sexual fulfillment within the marriage relationship. In 7:5 he writes that depriving the other marriage partner from sexual fulfillment opens the door for Satan to tempt that person because of the person's lack of self-control. The answer to sexual gratification is to be married to one person, according to God's design. Satan exploits sexual desire and the blessings of marriage by making sexual satisfaction a matter of fulfilling the desires of the flesh, a selfish motive, rather than meeting the needs of the partner, a motive of unselfish love. There are two key words at the end of verse 5: "tempt" and "self-control." Satan has the power to tempt sexually, and he tempts in areas of vulnerability, especially in lives that are not exhibiting the fruits of the Spirit (see Gal 5:19–22).

Paul mentions another attribute of Satan in 2 Corinthians 11:14. Satan disguises himself as an angel of light. In the context, Paul is dealing with his opponents who had come to Corinth with deceit, teaching a different interpretation of Jesus than he preached (2 Cor 11:3). These false apostles were disguising themselves as apostles of Christ. Paul associates these false, deceiving apostles with Satan as "his servants" in verse 15. Just as the serpent led Eve astray in the garden, these false apostles fell in line with the same deception in Corinth. Satan is mentioned here only in passive comparison, but the passage does indicate that one of his attributes is deception. Satan can have human "ministers" (*diakonoi*) who follow in his footsteps, even people who appear to be doing the work of God. The primary issues are message

---

5. Delling, "*Plenazō*," *TDNT*, 6:266–74.

and motivation. These false apostles came boasting in their abilities, which undermined the gospel of the crucified Christ. Those who preach the gospel from impure motives may find themselves in the companionship of Satan.

Paul knows personally what it means to be harassed by Satan. In 2 Corinthians 12:7 Paul mentions his "thorn in the flesh." It is impossible to know what this "thorn" was, but more significant here is to note the following phrase. Standing in apposition to "thorn" is "a messenger of Satan." Whether this was a physical or emotional challenge ("the flesh"), Satan's messenger used this as a way to harass Paul and keep him humble. Although Satan intended this thorn for Paul's demise, God turned it for Paul's good. God would not take it away but instead provided grace for Paul to endure through it (v. 9). This passage reveals several important things about Satan. One, Satan is against the servants of Christ, trying to force them to lose heart while living in these "earthen vessels" (2 Cor 4:7, 16). Second, Satan does not have the ultimate say because God's grace works in believers "to show the surpassing power which is of God and not from us" (4:7). There is danger in not being dependent upon the grace of God in Christ. The unsanctified heart will be discouraged with the struggles of life, and Satan is standing in the wings ready to exploit human frailties.

First Thessalonians 2:18 records another battle Paul had with Satan, who had hindered him from seeing the Thessalonians as he had intended. He left Thessalonica under difficult circumstances (Acts 17:1–9) and wanted to check up on this new church. We see the heart of Paul as pastor in this letter, concerned for his young flock lest they grow weary from persecution. He does not say how Satan hindered him but simply that Satan did. This verse implies that Satan fights against the growth of the church by putting roadblocks in the way of the servants of Christ.

Paul further aligns Satan in opposition to the things of God in an eschatological passage in 2 Thessalonians 2. In this chapter Paul writes to the Thessalonians in response to some questions they had about the *parousia* ("appearance," the second coming) of Jesus Christ (2:1). Because of persecution, they may have thought the end was near. Paul writes that before Christ's appearance, there will be a rebellion and revelation of "the lawless one" (v. 3). Who is this lawless one? Paul appears not to be too concerned with an exact identification but rather with the characteristics. In verse 9 he says that this person comes "by the activity of Satan with all power and false signs and wonders." This person follows the example of Satan and so can be identified with Satan. Charles Wanamaker notes that the phrase *ho anthrōpos tēs anomias* ("man of rebellion") "describes this individual's blatant disregard for and opposition to the will of God."⁶ Paul calls him the son of destruction, who exalts himself above all gods and sits in the temple of God and proclaims himself to be God. This self-idolatry and blasphemy are blatant manifestations of the power of sin. Paul in his apocalyptic thinking saw the same type of disregard for God at work in his day. Wanamaker comments, "The process of rebellion was known to be at work already by the community of faith, but it would only become manifest with the revealing of the person of rebellion."⁷ The depravity of this person will be enhanced by Satan, who will enable this person to perform miracles. The purpose of these "false" signs (*pseudous*, v. 9) is to lead people astray. Those who refuse to love the truth are deceived.

The answer to this problem is to be aware of and prepared for the deception. The work of the lawless one is ultimately under the sovereign control of God (v. 11). Jesus will destroy this person with a breath (v. 8). It is noteworthy that in the very next passage, Paul goes on to speak of those loved by the Lord, chosen to be saved "through sanctification by the Spirit and belief in truth" (v. 13). The answer to the problem of Satan and all the problems Satan can create through his agents has already been provided "from the beginning" through the sanctifying work of the Holy Spirit. The necessary human response for avoiding the threats of Satan and receiving the power of God is "belief in the truth." The gospel calls us to obtain the glory of our Lord Jesus Christ (v. 14). Paul provides his readers the clear way to experience hope in this fallen world.

In 1 Timothy Paul mentions two different groups facing possible battles with Satan. The first group is Hymenaeus and Alexander, who had shipwrecked their faith by rejecting faith and a good conscience (1 Tim 1:19-20). Paul handed these two over to Satan so that they might learn not to blaspheme. As in 1 Corinthians 5, the one positive thing here is that Satan helps people realize the wretchedness of sin. A possible conclusion is that faith and a good conscience are weapons and protection against the attacks of Satan. Both qualities are characteristics of those who trust in Jesus as Lord and walk in obedience to the Spirit. The other group of people are young widows who were in danger of being drawn away from Christ because of their "passions" (5:11-16). The word *katastrēniasōsin* in 5:11 describes being drawn away by one's sensuous impulses. The use of the word in this context may have a negative connotation of sexual lust. What also contributes to this problem are their idleness, gossiping, being busybodies, and bad talk (v. 14). Paul implies that these are lures of Satan to pull young

---

6. Wanamaker, *Epistles to the Thessalonians*, 245.
7. Wanamaker, *Epistles to the Thessalonians*, 255.

widows from their faith in Christ, which, in fact, some had already done (v. 15). It is better for these women to remarry and be in a family situation, where this passion can be fulfilled in a positive and God-ordained way. In both situations, Satan seeks to pull believers away from Christ, but also in both situations, believers' active response in faith to Christ provides the way out.

Paul uses other terms to describe this "adversary." In 2 Corinthians 4:4, he writes that the "god of this age" has blinded the eyes of unbelievers, keeping them from seeing the light of the gospel of the glory of Christ. Paul gives this statement in an apologetic and defensive context. His language is dualistic, which would leave this "god" to be none other than the adversary of God, namely, Satan.[8] This present evil age will come to an end, but until then, Satan has a degree of power and influence over the world. The primary reason for this is that sin and death are still present to plague humanity. Satan has a goal, described with the infinitive clause "to stop unbelievers from seeing" (*eis to mēs augasai*). The verb *augazō* is found only here in the New Testament and has three connotations: "to shine," "to illuminate," or "to see clearly."[9] Like the serpent in the garden of Eden, Satan takes human attention away from God's love and places it on things of this world. Consequently, it does not take much for idolatry to set in.

These verses come right after Paul's significant statement of transformation into the image of the Lord in 3:18. The "god of this age" draws people into darkness and away from Christ, blinding hearts and hindering believers from experiencing the glory of God. Thus, transformation back into the glory of God is hindered or stopped. Paul describes those who are blinded by Satan as perishing in verse 3, a vivid opposite to the positive change God intends to make in our lives. Paul and his companions, however, have renounced this world by renouncing disgraceful, underhanded ways and rejecting cunning practices or tampering with God's word (v. 2). God's light is available, but people need outside helpers to show them this light. This shining of God's light was one of Paul's primary goals in life as an apostle.

Later in the letter, Paul uses another term for Satan in 6:15: "What has Christ in common with Beliar?" This phrase is given in a series of parallels:

Believers	Unbelievers
Righteousness	Lawlessness
Light	Darkness
Christ	Beliar
Temple of God	Idols

---

8. Barrett, *Second Corinthians*, 131.
9. R. Martin, *2 Corinthians*, 79.

This opposition shows that commitment to Christ cannot be compromised. There are many interpretive challenges with 6:14—7:1, one being the identity and meaning of the term "Beliar" or "Belial." This term is found only here in the New Testament, but in intertestamental Jewish literature Belial represents a personalized force opposed to God.[10] Noteworthy in this list is the term "unequally yoked" in 6:14. The comparison between Christ and Belial here is not an equality but an opposition. Although Satan seems to have influence in this age, his power is limited. Satan and all that he does to harm followers of Christ cannot stand up to the presence of God in them (vv. 16–18).

The answer to the problem of Satan is given in the exhortation of 7:1, the strategic end to this section: "let us cleanse ourselves from every defilement of body and spirit, bringing holiness to completion in the fear of God." This significant statement puts the responsibility of victory on those who believe. On the negative side, people need to crucify the "old person" and put off sin that tries to be master over the members of the body (Rom 6:6; Eph 4:22). On the positive side, people should fear God by worshiping him and honoring him as supreme. By this act of consecration and dedication, believers make the conscious choice to avoid sin by placing their lives before God in consecration. The result will be completing God's purpose for us in holiness. The present tense of the participle *epitelountes* ("perfecting," "fulfilling," hence "reaching our goal") shows the attainability but also growth of holiness in this life. God's purpose for believers is fulfilled as they are perfected in holiness.

In Ephesians 2:2, Paul mentions the "prince of the power of the air, the spirit that is now at work in the sons of disobedience." The context of this phrase is negative and contrastive, with Paul speaking about the old way of life before coming to faith in Christ. This life is characterized by trespasses and sins (2:1) and with following the passions and desires of the flesh and mind (2:3). There are three parallel clauses found in this verse. The first clause is literally "according to the age of this world." Andrew Lincoln notes that this clause is "a way of talking about both spatial and temporal aspects of fallen human existence. Instead of being oriented to the life of the age to come and the heavenly realm, the past lives of the readers had been dominated by this present evil age and this world. Their sinful activities were simply in line with the norms and values of a spatio-temporal complex wholly hostile to God."[11]

---

10. See R. Martin, *2 Corinthians*, 199–200, for the ancient texts and discussion of the Jewish and early Christian use of this term.

11. Lincoln, *Ephesians*, 95.

The second clause is literally, "according to the ruler of the authority of the air." One issue to resolve here is to whom "ruler" refers. This ruler is not given any name here, but the context of Ephesians indicates this to be none other than "the devil" of 4:27 and 6:11, and "the evil one" of 6:16. The location of the ruler's authority is the "air." Lincoln suggests this could refer to the lower reaches of the heavens, thus emphasizing the proximity of this evil ruler to the world that he influences.[12] Paul as an apocalyptic Jew believed in levels of heaven, where "the lower heavens were populated by various hostile powers or that the hostile heavenly powers mounted a kind of roadblock to prevent access to the higher heavens (paradise being in the third heaven—2 Cor 12:3)."[13]

The third phrase reads, "the spirit now at work in the sons of disobedience." In Greek grammar, a genitive word is usually attached to another word before it. In the case of this verse, it is difficult to determine with which word the genitive *tou pneumatos* ("the spirit") goes. It could be part of the string of genitives that come after "ruler," making "ruler" and "spirit" separate entities: "according to the ruler . . . of the spirit which is now at work in the sons of disobedience" (lit.).[14] The ruler here seems to be personal and the spirit the impersonal force and attitude within the sons of disobedience. We need not worry about the identity of these two enemies of God's people because the outcome is the same. There is solidarity among the forces of evil to keep people from experiencing God's purposes in Christ. Those who follow Satan are characterized by disobedience and rebellion. Satan will pull down and hold captive as many as possible.

Paul uses the adverb *pote* ("now") in this verse, indicating that now is the age of the influence of Satan; but this is not the end of the story. In 1:20–22 the supremacy of Christ in this age is clear because of his resurrection from the dead. The answer to the problem of Satan is given in 2:4–7: the great God of love who makes us alive with Christ and exalts us with him in the heavenly places. Believers are now citizens of heaven and no longer dominated by trespasses or sins (v. 1) or harassed by Satan (v. 2).

Another term for the adversary is "the tempter," used in 1 Thessalonians 3:5. The context indicates that this tempter is Satan (2:18). The tempter could pull these new believers away from the gospel, making all of Paul's efforts and their struggles meaningless. Again, one of Satan's goals of pulling believers away from Christ is evident. The temptation in this situation emerged from being troubled by afflictions (3:3), referring to the

---

12. Lincoln, *Ephesians*, 96.
13. Dunn, *Theology of Paul*, 108.
14. See Lincoln, *Ephesians*, 96.

suffering that the Thessalonians had experienced because of their faith in Christ (2:14). The temptation was similar to the one Jesus encountered in the garden of Gethsemane when faced with impending suffering and death (Matt 26:36–46).

In 2 Thessalonians 3:1–5 Paul expresses his confidence that the Lord will establish and guard the Thessalonians against *tou ponērou*. This Greek word is an adjective used as a substantive with two possible meanings. It could be taken as a neuter meaning "evil" in the sense of the opposite of good (Rom 12:9), or as masculine for "the evil one" (1 Cor 5:13). If the latter is the case, then it could refer to "the evil man," one of the people Paul mentions in verse 2, or *the evil one*, namely, Satan. In either case, Paul states that God can protect against this evil. There is a sequence with the imagery implied in verse 3. The word *stērixei* has the connotation of supporting from below to enable one to stand. The word *pylaxei* has the connotation of guarding alongside of through protection. Paul does not say here how God will do this, but he has already written to the Thessalonians that the Lord could establish their hearts blameless in holiness (1 Thess 3:13) and in every good work and word (2 Thess 2:17).

Another term Paul uses for the adversary is "devil." This term is found in Ephesians and 1 and 2 Timothy. Ephesians 4:27 exhorts the reader not to give the devil an opportunity. This is part of a series of prohibitions that should help guide believers to live out God's purposes for them expressed in 4:22–24 by putting off the old, corrupted self and putting on the new self, created to be in God's likeness of righteousness and holiness. The construction of verses 26b–27 (*mē . . . mēde*, "neither let the sun go down . . . nor give the devil opportunity") shows that there is a link between being angry and giving the devil an opportunity. The devil takes advantage of angry people. Something about letting anger fester makes people vulnerable to the devil's attempt to get them to sin. Part of the answer to this dilemma is found in 2 Corinthians 2:11, where Paul writes about the need to forgive the erring brother lest Satan be given an opportunity. Forgiveness is the necessary response to anger for those who want to be Christ-like. Paul goes on to write in Ephesians 5:1–2 that as new creations we must become imitators of God and live a life of love.

A noteworthy passage filled with imagery referring to the battle with the devil is Ephesians 6:10–20, where Paul writes of putting on the full armor of God to stand against the schemes of the devil (6:11). This armor is provided by God (the genitive *tou theou*). In 2 Corinthians 10:4 Paul writes about weapons not of the flesh but of divine power used to destroy strongholds. This would suggest that the armor is not simply defensive but also offensive. Since we have God on our side and he is the source of our protection, the battle is not ours to fight. Lincoln writes,

> The decisive victory has already been won by God in Christ, and the task of believers is not to win but to stand, that is, to preserve and maintain what has been won . . . the call to the readers to stand against the powers is also a reminder of their liberation from the tyranny of these powers. The major victory has been achieved, but the eschatological tension with its indicative and imperative characteristic of Paul's thought remains.[15]

Paul also writes that the devil schemes against believers, suggesting that the devil is cunning in his efforts to pull believers away from Christ. In verse 16 Paul urges the readers of the letter to take up the shield of faith, which will enable them to extinguish the arrows of "the evil one." The future tense of the verb *dynēsesthe* ("will be able") shows the certainty of faith's protection. The devil also has his allies in this battle with God's people (see the next section).

Paul also refers to the devil in his letters to Timothy. At the end of the list of credentials for overseers in 1 Timothy 3:1–7, Paul gives two qualifications that counter the trap of the devil. The inner quality of overseers is that they must be mature Christians and not recent converts lest they fall into condemnation with the devil because of pride (3:6). Pride could result from many things in spiritually immature leaders but is especially an indicator of the power of sin in one's life. The way to avoid this trap is to be humble, which comes with maturity in the Spirit (see Eph 4:2–3).

The external quality is that overseers must have a good reputation with outsiders lest they fall into disgrace and into a snare of the devil. Reputation and shame were significant social forces in the first century.[16] The Greek word *oneidismon* has the connotation of abuse and could be taken here not simply as a psychological embarrassment but ridicule by others.[17] If Paul is referring to the potential of persecution, then overseers might find themselves in a similar situation as the Thessalonians in 1 Thessalonians 3:5 (see below). Paul has already told Timothy to pray for government leadership so that "we may live peaceful and quiet lives in all godliness and holiness" (2:2; NIV). Being rejected by society for our own faults rather than for the sake of Christ (Matt 5:11) not only harms our testimony but puts us in a place of vulnerability because we are living on our own resources rather than God's grace. The earthly direction of this suffering will only lead to defeat.

15. Lincoln, *Ephesians*, 442–43.
16. Malina, *New Testament World*; deSilva, *Honor, Patronage, Kinship, and Purity*.
17. Schneider, "*Oneidos*," *TDNT*, 5:238–42.

In 2 Timothy 2:22–26 Paul exhorts Timothy about being a worker approved by God. One quality of such a worker is the ability to correct one's opponents with the result that they repent and come to a knowledge of the truth of God (2:24–25). These unnamed opponents are in danger of being captured by the devil to do his will. The word for "capture" here is *ezōgrēmenoi*, "to be captured alive," a perfect passive participle with emphasis on the present results. This metaphoric language shows the ongoing danger of giving the devil a foothold (Eph 4:27). Seeking the help of God through repentance is the answer to finding freedom from the trap of the devil.

Battling the Forces of Evil

Satan has an entourage of forces that aid in the sabotage of the followers of Christ. It is difficult to determine what Paul and the rest of the New Testament say about these entities. One problem appears at the linguistic level of trying to understand the words and concepts in the way the ancients did. It is also difficult for those from modern cultures to understand how those in the preindustrialized cultures of the first century would have interpreted the evil that plagued their lives. How organized and intentional are these evil forces in the demise of God's people?

In Romans 8:38–39, Paul gives a triumphant benediction that nothing human or supernatural can separate believers from God's love in Christ. These verses conclude a section of Romans where Paul shows that the power of grace in Christ overcomes the power of sin and death. With the God of grace on our side, we have nothing to fear—victory is possible for those who rely on God, demonstrated by faithful obedience (8:31). Paul describes this in pairs: death and life, angels and rulers, things present and things to come, and height and depth. He deals with human adversaries in verses 31–37 and cosmic entities in verses 38–39. Wink comments, "Paul's readers would probably assume that he is referring primarily to evil powers, since only such would be likely to try to separate them from Christ. But even the good, made absolute, becomes evil. Even the best can be perverted by idolatry (the Law, the Temple, religion itself). None is immune to apostasy. None is able, however apostate, to negate the work of Christ."[18]

Paul begins his list with death, the great enemy of people since the days of Adam (5:12). Three other terms are noteworthy here: angels, rulers, and powers. It is impossible to determine what connotations these angels, rulers, and authorities have based only on this context. "Angels" has a positive

---

18. Wink, *Naming the Powers*, 49.

connotation in Paul's letters (1 Cor 4:9; 6:3; 13:1) but can serve as a potential barrier between God and people if worshipped.[19] "Ruler" is used several times for the authorities with an evil nature (Eph 1:21; 3:10; 6:12; Col 1:16, 2:10, 15). "Powers" has no pair in Paul's list. Several times Paul uses "powers" with "rulers" to denote spiritual beings (1 Cor 15:24; Eph 1:21). Douglas Moo offers two interpretations for the pair "height and depth." The first views these in an astronomical sense for space below and above the horizon with the connotation of celestial powers, thus spiritual beings, but there is no other use of these terms in this way in the New Testament. The other interpretation is a spatial sense to cover all above and beneath the earth.[20] As a catchall, Paul ends the list with "anything created."

These verses provide strong assurance to those "in Christ." In verse 37 Paul reminds the Romans that they are more than conquerors through the one who loves them. He begins the verse with "all these things," referring to tribulation, distress, persecution, famine, nakedness, danger or sword—things that characterize a fallen world. Since God is for us, and we experience his love for us in Christ, no one can be against us (v. 31). This is security as strong as the love of God. The source of victory is "through him who loved us" (v. 37) and the "love of God in Christ Jesus our Lord" (v. 39). On our own power, victory in this life is impossible (7:24). Victory only comes from God's side and is available only in Christ.

Paul was not a dualist; Satan and the forces of evil are never equal to God and Christ. The supremacy of Christ can be seen in Ephesians 1:20-21, where Paul writes that God has exalted Christ above all rule and authority and power and dominion. Paul also proclaims Christ as victor in Colossians 1:15-20. Verse 16 states, "For by him all things were created, in heaven and on earth, visible and invisible, whether thrones or dominions or rulers or authorities—all things were created through him and for him." All earthly and heavenly beings have been created through and for Christ. By his death on the cross, Jesus Christ has and will reconcile all things to himself, whether on earth or in heaven (1:20). Christ is Lord even over the cosmic, unseen forces of good or evil. All spiritual forces fall under his sovereignty. Paul shares the same perspective found in the four Gospels, where Satan and demons always acknowledge the supremacy of Jesus, and in the Old Testament, where Satan and the forces of evil fall under the sovereign control of God. The conclusion one may draw from Colossians 1 is that the forces of evil are limited, and those who put their trust in Christ should have no fear. Wink comments, "Like a cancer dependent on the host organism for its

---

19. Dunn, *Romans 1-8*, 407.
20. Moo, *Epistle to the Romans*, 546.

very destructive energies, evil remains inescapably parasitic of the whole. Try as they will to become autonomous and set up their own interest as the highest good, the Powers must inevitably come to terms with the Power of the Powers."[21]

Paul speaks of a triad in 1 Corinthians 15:24 of "rule, authority and power." He does not identify these powers, but the term "enemies" in verse 25 implies opposition. These powers somehow hinder God's kingdom in this present age of spiritual warfare, but their fate is sealed by Christ's own resurrection, just like the outcome for death. By neutralizing or destroying the powers,[22] Christ will bring about a cosmic restitution that will include the physical universe (see Rev 21:1). Nothing in this age can stop God's plan of full redemption from being carried out. Meanwhile, believers must battle against these powers.

In Galatians 4:3 and 9, Paul writes about enslavement to the "elementary principles of the world" (*stoicheia*). There have been many different interpretations of the term *stoicheia* over the course of church history. The basic meaning of this term is something placed in a row and came to refer to the alphabet, and hence the basic principles in education. It is used in different ways and with different connotations in the New Testament. In the context of Galatians 4:3, Paul uses the term to refer to how the Galatians were enslaved by the law and in danger of using it as the way to be righteous. They could be free from the law as bondage and be free to serve God as sons and daughters.

The use of the term in 4:9 is slightly different in that Paul is not referring to the law but to being enslaved to "beings which by nature are not gods" (v. 8). Just as the Jews were trapped by life under the law, the Gentiles were trapped by their pagan worship of the "gods." There is some debate about what Paul means by "gods" and the term *stoicheia* in verse 8. Charles Cousar suggests that Paul could have in mind demonic forces or elemental spirits. What is more significant, however, is that he puts both Jews and Gentiles in the same category. "He is depicting the predicament of any person who is not set free by Christ."[23] In both situations, the Galatians were in danger of becoming enslaved by their former way of life. The *stoicheia* are powerless over those in Christ, for as Bruce comments, "they cannot

---

21. Wink, *Naming the Powers*, 64.

22. There is some debate on how to take the word *katargēsē* in v. 24: as "destroy," in the sense of annihilate, or "neutralize," as in leave in existence but take away the ability to operate. The latter seems to cohere better with Rev 20:7–10, where Satan will be tormented forever. For a discussion of this, see Wink, *Naming the Powers*, 50–51.

23. Cousar, *Galatians*, 93.

reassert their authority over them unless these deliberately put themselves back under their power."[24]

Paul uses the term *stoicheia* in a similar way in Colossians 2:8 and 20. In verse 8 the term is used alongside philosophy, deceit, and human tradition to refer to things that can hold us captive and are opposite to life in Christ. In verse 20 Paul uses the term in the context of regulations of human precepts and teachings that are characteristic of self-made religion, asceticism, and bodily mutilation. These represent human effort to suppress the cravings of the flesh but cannot take care of the deeper problem. The various "mysticisms" of the ancient world of Paul could not satisfy the deep longing for which people sought answers. The only way to take care of this conflict is by dying to these principles and rising to new life with Christ (3:1). Although there are many ways to take these references to *stoicheia*, the principle is clear: there is hope and freedom in Christ for those who are enslaved to principles or principalities, whether these be abstract or of a more spiritual nature.

Paul writes about this battle with evil in Ephesians 6:12. This verse intensifies the battle between believers and the devil described in verse 11 by adding as foes "the rulers, authorities, cosmic powers of this darkness, and the spiritual forces of evil in the heavens." This verse poses several problems to the interpreter. One is the meaning of "flesh and blood." Paul is not contradicting his theology about the struggle with the flesh in Romans 6 and 8. "Flesh and blood" here is likely describing human beings in their earthly, bodily existence.

Another challenge is with the identification of the other entities used in this verse. The context implies that these are evil supporters of the devil and are not easily detected like flesh and blood, suggesting that they are of a spiritual nature. As Dunn writes, Paul has in mind here "heavenly beings, subordinate to God and his Christ, with the potential to intervene between God and his creation, and hostile to his purposes and people."[25] The threat of these forces is real and present, but so is God's presence and protection. Those in Christ are not left to struggle against the forces of evil but are assured of victory with the full armor of God.

In 1 Timothy, Paul encourages young Timothy to hold strong against his opponents and the heresy present in Ephesus. In 1 Timothy 4:1–3 Paul writes that in the last days people will depart from the faith by devoting themselves to deceitful spirits and teachings of demons. Whatever the heresy was in Ephesus, at its root lay Satan and his entourage. The true enemy

---

24. Bruce, *Galatians*, 204.
25. Dunn, *Theology of Paul*, 106.

was more than simply the heretics in Ephesus but the power behind them (like Eph 6:12). This force, though, used liars whose consciences were seared, who could no longer hear the prompting of the Holy Spirit (v. 2; Rom 1:32). As William Mounce writes, "They bear the brand of Satan on their conscience and yet pretend to be servants of God."[26] The key word in verse 1 is *apostēsontai*, to apostatize or rebel against God. This deceitful and demonic power at work in the liars posed the real danger of leading these believers away from their faith.

The Weakness of the Flesh

There are many ethical implications stemming from the battle with the forces of darkness. Paul's letters show Satan and the forces of evil battling against the servants of God, trying to set them off course from their walk with Christ. Satan takes advantage of people who take their eyes off God (Rom 1:21). When God is not the focus of life, a person becomes vulnerable to spiritual attack.

Genesis 3 offers a good illustration of this. In the garden of Eden, the serpent took advantage of Eve's curiosity. Evidently, Adam and Eve were in the center of the garden, close to the tree of knowledge. They had placed themselves in a dangerous position of vulnerability. The serpent took advantage of this weakness by tempting them to eat of the forbidden fruit. Why did God not put the tree in the far corner, out of sight and out of mind? It would have saved a lot of trouble, at least for a time. The application is clear: if we put ourselves in vulnerable positions of compromise, Satan will take advantage by drawing our attention away from the things of God.

Two perspectives need to be kept in balance. First, the human problem cannot simply be attributed to supernatural forces. Paul is very practical and not philosophical when it comes to dealing with the human condition. Nowhere in his letters does he say that people are mere pawns in a cosmic duel between God and Satan. People are to blame in their rebellion against God. According to Dunn, Paul demythologized the more ontological forces of evil and devoted more effort to the existential powers of sin and death. Dunn states, "In each case it would seem that Paul refers to such heavenly beings as opposed to God's purposes, not so much because he had clear beliefs about them himself, but because he needed terms to speak of the all too real supraindividaul, suprasocial forces of evil which he experienced and saw at work and because these were the terms which expressed widely held

---

26. Mounce, *Pastoral Epistles*, 237.

current beliefs."[27] Wink says in a similar way, "Paul for his part developed a quite unique manner of dealing with the determinants of human existence, substituting such quasi-hypostatized words as sin, law, flesh and death for the terms more frequently encountered in Jewish apocalyptic: Satan, Azazel, Beliar, evil spirits, demons."[28]

Although these insights of Dunn and Wink are helpful, we must not force Paul into a twenty-first century, demythologized mold. These powers cannot simply be explained away as first-century mythology.[29] This leads to the other perspective. The powers of evil cannot be reduced to only the outgrowth of human sin, nor can human sin account for all evil. Paul's letters, as well as the rest of the New Testament, consistently describe a force that battles humans utilizing the propensity of humans to sin. These two perspectives must be kept in balance.

Paul teaches, then, that our fallen condition is an open door for Satan. Satan does not gain victory in people's lives just arbitrarily. Sin involves volition and exemplifies itself in rebellion. The word *harmartia* describes a "violation in the sense of falling short of a specified duty or goal, generally through a *willfully wrong aim*."[30] The root of sin is misguided human desire (James 1:13–15). Satan takes advantage of the pull of the *sarx* ("flesh"), with its passions and desires. This dark side to human nature has a power compelling its decent into self-destruction.

An example of this is the immoral man of 1 Corinthians 5, who was to be handed over to Satan for the destruction of the flesh. Fee writes, "In contrast to the gathered community of believers, where the Spirit, as the power of the Lord Jesus, is to be visibly manifest in edifying gifts and loving concern for one another, this man is to be put back out into the world, where Satan and his 'principalities and powers' still hold sway over people's lives to destroy them."[31] Furnish adds, "The flesh thus seeks to exercise control over man's life, and while it is not a power *outside of* and *over against* man in the same way as are sin and death, it threatens always to become the quisling tyrant, holding man in bondage to the demonic forces of the world. Since

---

27. Dunn, *Theology of Paul*, 109–10.

28. Wink, *Naming the Powers*, 100; for a criticism of Wink, see Lincoln, *Ephesians*, 64.

29. Rudolf Bultmann is one example of a Bible scholar demythologizing the New Testament and arguing that evil is the result of our sins and not of any forces or beings. See Bultmann, *Jesus and Mythology*, 16.

30. Purkiser et al., *God, Man, and Salvation*, 272.

31. Fee, *God's Empowering Presence*, 126.

this quisling power itself provides death its opportunity, it is no less God's enemy, 'hostile' to him (Rom 8:6–7) and to his Spirit (Gal 6:8)."[32]

Victory in Christ

The answer to the desperate condition of fallen humanity is found in the resurrected Jesus Christ. By his victory over death, Jesus conquered the power of sin and gives victory over the forces of evil. This world of death and decay is one area of human experience that Satan and the forces of evil can exploit. Irenaeus wrote that Christ as the second Adam resisted and conquered Satan where the first Adam failed. Where the first Adam gave into sin and the temptation of Satan, the second Adam became what we are yet was victorious over sin and Satan, making it possible for us also to experience victory.[33]

The Lordship of Christ

When believers proclaim the resurrected Jesus as "Lord," they tap into divine resources beyond comprehension. The word *kyrios* connotes one who is master and in a superior position. The use of the word assumes that those who say it are in the position of service to this lord or master. The word was used in the ancient world to refer to both divine and human figures. To call someone "Lord" is to give that person allegiance and honor. This submission requires the loss of some freedom because people now answer to a higher authority; they are not free to do as they want. It is a word rich in theological meaning, being the primary Greek equivalent in the Septuagint for the divine name, YHWH.[34] Paul calls Jesus "Lord" over two hundred times, many of these interchangeable with the name Jesus or Christ. When Paul called Jesus "Lord," many of the above ideas are implied or explicit.

In Philippians 2:5–11, the humble, crucified Christ is exalted by God and given the highest name of all, Jesus, "Savior." Every knee will bow before him, "in heaven and on earth and under the earth" and confess, "Jesus is Lord." This honorary designation points to Jesus' position above all else, his power over all creation, and his personal qualification of being divine. By calling Jesus "Lord," one attributes to him the same qualities as Yahweh of the Old Testament. To call him Lord also signifies his supreme position in

---

32. Furnish, *Theology and Ethics in Paul*, 117.
33. Irenaeus, *Against Heresies* 3.18.7.
34. Foerster and Quell, "*Kyrios*," *TDNT*, 3:1039–98.

one's life. His lordship requires the willful decision to crucify the old self, which attempts to pull away from God into idolatry. Accepting his lordship results in a new person who is being transformed into his likeness.

Therefore, accepting Jesus as Lord allows God's grace to transform people into God's holy image. Several things happen as a result. First, when accompanied by faith, this confession leads to salvation (Rom 10:8-9). Even demons must acknowledge the lordship of Jesus, but that does not mean they put their faith in him as master (Mark 1:24; 5:7; see Jas 2:19). Second, this confession allows the Holy Spirit to begin changing believers into the holy image of God (1 Cor 12:3). The Spirit binds believers together in love as one body in unity under the same confession of faith (12:12). Third, acknowledging the supremacy of Jesus changes the orientation of one's life. The primary motivation becomes the "love of Christ" (2 Cor 5:14). Christ's love shown on the cross enables those who trust in him to love him in return by dying on their own crosses, enabling new life in Christ to develop (Rom 6:4).

Putting one's self under the supremacy of Christ puts one in a place of protection against Satan. Satan cannot take advantage of the desires of fleshly living because self is no longer in control of the believer. When Satan tempted him in the desert, Jesus demonstrated his full submission to the Father by rejecting personal satisfaction, popularity, and power—things that are part of fleshly living (Matt 4:1-11). He proved his supremacy over Adamic living through his resurrection from the dead (1 Cor 15:21-22). Everyone is cursed with death because of the transgression of Adam (Rom 3:23; 5:12), but those in union with Christ are promised eternal life (3:24; 6:23). The curse of death is universal, but the gift of life is available for all who are "in Christ" (see 1 Thess 4:16). By being united with Christ in death and resurrection through baptism (Rom 6:4), believers experience spiritual resurrection now and bodily resurrection when Christ returns. There are two alternatives in Paul's mind: the unavoidable decision to follow in the way of Adam, ending in death, or the conscious identification with Christ through death to self, bringing life by the grace of God.

God's hidden plan in Christ will be completed when death as the last enemy is conquered, signifying that Christ reigns supreme and that there is nothing, not even death, that he has not conquered. When this happens, Christ will hand over the conquered kingdom to God so that God can be "all in all" (1 Cor 15:28). Christ's lordship will be finally and fully evident when he comes again. His resurrection as the "first-fruits" guarantees the outcome of his battle with all the "rulers, authorities, and powers" (v. 24), of which death is representative. His reign may not seem evident in the present age because death still plagues those in Christ. However, his supremacy will be proven when death is finally vanquished (v. 26). The completion (*telos*, v. 24) of the divine plan will occur at Christ's *parousia*, after he hands over the conquered kingdom to God once and for all. Fee comments, "Therefore, the inevitable chain of events set in motion by Christ's resurrection has ultimately to do with God's own absolute authority over *all things*, especially death."[35] God stands as the supreme power responsible for the destruction of the power of death. Fee adds,

> God Himself stands as both the source and goal of all that is; and since he has set in motion the final destruction of death, when that occurs he will be "all in all." Christ's role is to bring about this destruction through the resurrection, which is inherently tied to his own. When that occurs, all of God's enemies will be subjected to Christ, so that in turn he may be made subject to God, who, it turns out, has been the one who subjected all things to Him in any case.[36]

For Paul, the eschatological kingdom has already come because of Christ's resurrection. A. D. Hill writes, "Paul understands the kingdom of Christ in 1 Corinthians 15:24–28 to be Christ's present, cosmic lordship which he exercises from heaven. It does not await the *parousia* for its inauguration, it is not a kingdom of this world . . . but began with the resurrection of and acquisition of life-giving prerogatives by the Last Adam."[37] The cross marks Christ's subjection to the power of death, and his resurrection removed the power of death. By faith, those in Christ have now become participants in the new resurrection age. The sting of sin and death has been removed because of "the victory through our Lord Jesus Christ" (15:56–57). Sin as a cosmic force has been decisively dealt with by the resurrected Jesus Christ. Jesus as Lord opens the door for full and complete victory.

The Present Evil Age

Before the blessed moment of Christ's return, believers struggle on in a fallen, dying, and decaying world, what Paul calls "this present evil age" (Gal 1:4), a time that is passing away (1 Cor 7:31). Death and its affects are still around, though the end of death has been guaranteed by Christ's resurrection. Walking in newness of life does not completely remove one from the curse of Adam and the temptations of this corrupt world. Paul was not a

---

35. Fee, *First Corinthians*, 747.
36. Fee, *First Corinthians*, 755.
37. Hill, "Paul's Understanding of Christ's Kingdom," 317.

dualist in a Gnostic or Platonic sense; the battle between the way of the flesh and new life in the Holy Spirit for those in Christ is not between two equals. Temptation remains but God provides the way of escape through the power of the Spirit (1 Cor 10:14). Christ's death and resurrection forever altered the human situation. The possibility for new life in Christ exists in this age, but so does the veracity of sin and death. Those "in Christ" are part of this age but not bound by it.

A motif in Jewish apocalyptic literature is Adam's fall and the hopes for a return to the primal paradise (*4 Ezra* 3:5-7, 20-21; 4:30-31; 7:118-119; *2 Bar.* 17:2-3; 23:4; 48:42-43; 54:14, 19.) Adam's sin brought death for all who follow him. This present age is one of death but the age to come will be one of life.[38] Before his fall, Adam is seen as a heavenly creature on earth (*L.A.E.* 4:2; 10:4; and 16:3). He will be restored to this heavenly existence and become like one of the angels (*1 En.* 69:11; *2 En.* 30:11; *Apoc. Mos.* 7:2; *Jub.* 3:15). The hope for humanity is to experience this same restoration (*2 En.* 22:6). Paul shared similar ideas but believed Christ as the second Adam makes this restoration possible, beginning in this life through faith in Christ demonstrated through holy living in his likeness. The Spirit is the source of strength that makes this possible (2 Cor 3:18).

The battle against sin began with the fall of Adam when existence "in Adam" became the universal curse of humanity. With this fallen condition emerged a battle between the idolatrous state of being controlled by sin and the draw of God's prevenient grace. In this weakened condition, humanity becomes more vulnerable to the forces of evil because of the weakness and self-direction of the "flesh." This battle with sin and the forces of evil will continue until Christ comes again and takes away death, thus ending forever the power of sin. Satan and his forces will experience a decisive and final defeat (Rev 20:7-10). Meanwhile, is there any hope in this present evil age, or are people left to battle continuously the forces of evil?

Paul would respond that there is indeed victory for those who are in Christ. He writes in Colossians 2:14-15 that on the cross God canceled the debt of our trespasses and "disarmed the rulers and authorities and put them to open shame, by triumphing over them in him." Christ's resurrection completes the first part of God's plan of redemption. The second part involves believers living in fellowship with Christ in the present age by acknowledging his supremacy in their lives (Rom 6:4-11). The third part and completion of the plan will take place when Christ returns and all those who have lived in union with him will be raised from the dead and fully transformed into the image of Christ as God intended.

---

38. Lincoln, *Paradise Now and Not Yet*, 46-50.

Victory over the power of sin and the flesh also bring victory over the forces of evil. Believers must deal with three types of evil. The first comes as a direct result of human sinfulness, including our own and the sins of others. As long as people interact with one another, they will be receivers of others' sinful actions. Paul's letters often deal with the suffering believers experience because of the sins of others both in and outside of the church. Believers cannot be completely free from human evil in this life but can escape much of it by carefully choosing where they go and with whom they fellowship. Those in Christ, however, should expect persecution because of the evil choices people make (2 Tim 3:11).

The second type of evil is more systemic and impersonal in nature and comes as a result of the fall of Adam and Eve. The easiest way to understand this is simply that bad things happen to all people. We live in an imperfect world that groans against decay and death (Rom 8:20–21). Only hope in God's presence, peace, and promise in Christ's return can counter this type of evil (v. 23). As long as we are part of this present evil age, we can expect suffering. This suffering comes to those "in Adam" as well as to those "in Christ" (Matt 5:45).

The third type of evil takes advantage of the other two and can be attributed to Satan and the forces of evil. Satan takes advantage of our sinful condition and uses the problems of the present evil age to draw our attention away from the things of God. While we cannot totally disregard the presence of this more personal type of evil, this evil does not need to hold power over those who are in Christ. As long as our attention and devotion are on God (with the "full armor" on), we can rest secure against the schemes of the devil (Eph 6:11). As part of this age, we will have to battle the god of this age, but we are assured of victory through the love of God in Christ Jesus (Rom 8:38–39). As long as we are part of this fallen creation, we will battle Satan and the forces of evil, but if our trust is in God, we are assured of victory.

Fellowship with One's "Lord"

Being in Christ does not free one from temptation or the attacks of the devil. The deep issue for Paul is who one's "lord" is. He writes about fellowship with one's "lord" in 1 Corinthians 10:14–22. In the wider context of chapters 8–10, he is dealing with the problem of eating food sacrificed to idols and the affect this has upon the church community (8:1). Some Corinthians who had "strong" consciences were eating such food without concern because they recognized that idols are nothing but human-made objects (8:4) and that there is one God and one Lord (8:6). The problem was that when some with a weak conscience saw the strong eating idol food, the weak might be tempted to fall back into idolatry (8:11). Beginning with 10:14, Paul gives the most significant reason why the Corinthians should avoid idol food—because of the exclusive demand of loyalty to Christ. In this passage, he uses language of communion. The word *koinōnia* used in this verse denotes a relationship of two or more people who share in some type of common bond or interest. It can mean both "fellowship" and "participation."[39]

Paul deals with two issues related to the fellowship that takes place at sacred meals. The first is theological and results from the spiritual dangers inherent in eating idol meat. Sacrificial ceremonies in both ancient Israelite and pagan religions involved a meal, after the offering of a sacrifice, when the sacrificed food was eaten. Those who ate the meal entered into fellowship with the god being honored or worshiped and with those sharing in the meal. The focus of these meals was the deity who was considered to be present among the worshipers.[40] Paul, as a monotheistic Jew (8:4), understood that idols are only human-made objects of stone and metal and eating food sacrificed to non-entities is not sinful. Although the idol may not be a "god" in the sense that the pagan Corinthians may have understood it to be such, the idol still represented a supernatural power that could pull believers away from Christ. When pagans offer a sacrifice to an idol, they are actually offering it to demons (10:19). Evil supernatural powers lay behind these pagan worship practices.

Participating in anyway with this religious practice could compromise the allegiance of believers to Christ. Paul stresses the total incompatibility between Christian and pagan sacred meals. Verse 21 is a call to exclusive loyalty without compromise. Smit comments, "All participants in the Lord's Supper, without exception, enter into an alliance with the one Lord and may not enter into additional relationships with other so-called 'lords.'"[41] Paul's call to be loyal to Christ here is similar to Exodus 20:32 and Deuteronomy 6:4. There is total incompatibility between Christ and participation in idol worship. God demands exclusive devotion (v. 22, see v. 5). Participation in idolatry leads to fellowship with demons and results in God's jealousy. Like the Israelites, the Corinthians could miss out in God's grace and the prize of salvation (9:27; 10:12). Paul does not want the Corinthians to slip back into idolatry and thereby apostatize.[42] Like ancient Israel, by compromising with

---

39. Kauch, "*Koinōnia*," TDNT, 3:798–809.
40. Fee, *First Corinthians*, 466.
41. Smit, 'Do Not Be Idolaters," 45.
42. Willis, *Idol Meat in Corinth*, 160.

their culture, the Corinthians put themselves in a place of spiritual vulnerability. Adherence to Christ as Lord symbolized in the visible partaking of the bread and cup could provide the security of communion with the Lord of all.

The second challenge deals with the moral level of relationship within the community and results from the theological crisis. The cup and the bread unite believers with Christ (10:17) and with one other (v. 18). If the "strong" of the community participated in eating meat sacrificed to idols, the fellowship of the church would breakdown because the conscience of the "weak brothers" would be violated, causing them to sin against Christ (8:7–12). Participating in pagan feasts hindered the church from being community.

Paul is arguing for complete allegiance to Christ, which enables believers to participate in the new covenant promise of perfect love. When one eats the bread and drinks the cup, one participates in the new covenant community in Christ (11:25). What binds the community together is the common bond of love from and for Christ (Col 3:14). Demons fight against the formation of the church as community. With the loss of unity comes a loss of being church. Demons play on the inclination of humans to be lovers of self rather than lovers of others.

Joining in fellowship with Christ involves appropriating the benefits of the new covenant. The new covenant sealed by the blood of Christ brings the hope of victory over sin, Satan, and the forces of evil. The power of worship in word and sacrament keeps us in fellowship with Christ and keeps us secure from the ploys of Satan. The community that worships together is drawn together in force against Satan, and the gates of hell cannot prevail against it (Matt 16:18).

Victory over Temptation

For Paul, to be "in Christ" is to have undergone a crucifixion of the old self controlled by earthly desires (the "flesh") or desires for earthly things ("idolatry"), to identify with Christ in baptism, and to be filled with the Holy Spirit in new life. The presence of the triune God provides the power for transformation from the sinful self to the redeemed new creation resulting in protection against the enemy. This victory through the Spirit is not simply defensive and protective but active by providing new direction for living.

The Holy Spirit brings victory over temptation for those who are in Christ. The Corinthians faced a serious temptation with what to do with idol food. Their relationship with Christ and one another in the church was at stake. Paul uses the example of ancient Israel to warn them to flee idolatry and its temptations (1 Cor 10:1–14). The critical problem with the Israelites and the danger for the Corinthians rested in their desire for evil (v. 6). The Greek word for "desire" (*epithymētas*) is morally neutral but often in the New Testament denotes desire that leads to disobedience and sin.

By their participation in idol festivities, the Corinthian believers were tempted to compromise their exclusive loyalty to Christ. Since they were not strong in Christ but still immature and living to please their flesh (3:1–3), the idolatry and sensuality around them could pull them away from Christ. Satan and his demons (10:20) could exploit their spiritual weakness, break apart the fellowship in the church, and pull the "weak brothers" away from Christ (8:11). The influence of evil was enticing because of the Corinthians' fleshly living (*sarkinois*, 3:1). They needed a fundamental transformation that comes only in submission to the Spirit's desire to form within them the mind of Christ (2:16). The Israelites had special privileges that they forfeited because of their disobedience, and the Corinthians were at a similar point of decision. They were in danger of falling like the Israelites if they did not change the fundamental focus of their lives. With what paradigm they aligned themselves would determine how they would be treated by God.

The "way of escape" (10:13) comes as one identifies with Christ's death and resurrection symbolized in sharing the bread and cup (v. 16). Saying "yes" to Christ and "no" to the flesh takes away Satan's primary way to entice people away from God. This is essentially what Jesus did when he emptied himself and became obedient to death (Phil 2:6, 8). He rejected the easy way of escape and embraced the cup of suffering (Matt 4:9–10; 26:39–42). The Holy Spirit is the critical link by making communion with Christ possible on the personal and communal level (Rom 8:9). Crucifying the "flesh with its passions and desires" allows the voice of the Spirit to be heard in one's conscience, which results in loving obedience to God (Gal 5:24–25) in imitation of Christ (Eph 5:1–2).

Conclusion

When we are in Christ and allow the Holy Spirit to be our guide, we experience freedom from the power of sin and victory over the forces of evil. In Romans 6:4–11 Paul describes the significant change of ownership that takes place when one is co-crucified with Christ and rises to newness of life with him. The pivotal verse is 6:11: "So you also must consider yourselves dead to sin and alive to God in Christ Jesus." *In Christ* we find the source of new life. Paul uses the illustration of putting off the "old person" and putting on the "new person" (Rom 6:6; Col 3:9-10; Eph 2:15; 4:22-24). The old person is a slave to the power of sin and death symbolized by life *in Adam*. A fundamental change of disposition takes place as we die to the old way of life through total surrender to God and rise to newness of life, a life in the process of being recreated in the image of the perfect Second Adam.

In Romans 8, Paul gives the divine resource for victorious living through the Holy Spirit. When believers enter the sphere of Christ and place themselves under the lordship of Christ, Christ then dwells within them through the Holy Spirit. Albert Schweitzer wrote, "The possession of the Spirit proves to believers that they are already removed out of the natural state of existence and transferred into the supernatural. They are 'in the Spirit,' which means that they are no longer in the flesh. For being in the Spirit is only a form of manifestation of the being-in-Christ. Both are descriptions of one and the same state."[43]

Paul shows that the promise of sanctification offers the answer to the forces of evil. The hope of a new, Christlike life, the presence of the Holy Spirit, and the empowerment to love give believers hope from the control of sin. This new orientation not only solves the sin problem, it also takes away one of the key tools Satan uses to pull us away from God. If Satan tries to tempt us with things that might satisfy our earthly desires, God has provided the resource of his Holy Spirit. When we put our lives into his protection, we find life, liberation, and love.

---

43. Schweitzer, *Mysticism of Paul*, 167; see also Phil 3:3; 2 Cor 3:6; Gal 4:6; 5:16-26; Rom 7:6; 8:14-16.

Conclusion

PAUL'S LETTERS CALL READERS to respond in faith to Jesus as the Messiah and Lord of Old Testament prophecy. Paul's message was simple and compelling enough that it attracted people of all walks of life. There was something more powerful at work in his message than simply words that pleased or tickled the imagination, like the popular sophists of his day. When the message of new life in Christ reached people's ears and penetrated their hearts, a spark of hope ignited within them. Paul calls this message a mystery because it was long hidden but now revealed to those who believe (Rom 16:25; 1 Cor 2:7; Col 1:26). *This mystery is Christ* (Col 4:3; 1 Tim 3:16). Paul believed this mystery was revealed to him through revelation (Eph 3:3). God called him to proclaim the revelation of this mystery to Gentiles (Eph 3:6). People experience this mystery as new relationship with God through the presence of Christ within them (Col 1:27). The Holy Spirit is the instrument through whom the mystery is revealed in the hearts and lives of people (1 Cor 2:10).

Christ's presence profoundly affects all of one's life. It brings encouragement, unity in love, and a deeper understanding of God (Col 2:2). Christ in us produces love that binds the church together in united purpose and mission. His presence is a gift of grace that produces godliness evident in loving actions and holy living through the power of the Holy Spirit (2 Tim 1:7, 9). Paul experienced firsthand this transforming grace of God (1 Tim 1:12–16) and urged the readers of his letters to open their lives fully to God's purposes for them in Christ Jesus. Paul did not dwell in the past of his old life, though he used it conveniently to show the greatness of God's grace, but looked forward to experiencing life in its fullness when either he died or Christ returns (2 Cor 5:8; Phil 1:21).

Paul's message met a need in the lives of first-century Greco-Roman and Jewish people. Literature and archaeological discoveries suggest that people of that time were looking for deeper meaning to their lives through mystical experiences. Early Christian thought stands out in the first-century religious milieu with the belief that God's plan for the salvation of the world was revealed in the life, death, and resurrection of Jesus of Nazareth. Paul claimed that his message about this plan of salvation came by way of revelation (Gal 1:11–17), though what he preached had its foundation in the Hebrew Scriptures and the teaching and experience of the early church. His experience was "mystical" because he encountered the risen Savior in a vision and continued to experience the Savior through the Holy Spirit. He used terms that were common in other religions but filled these with his own content based upon his experience of the risen and exalted Lord Jesus Christ.

Paul's initial experience of Christ was unique but his ongoing relationship with Christ through the Holy Spirit had universal possibilities for those who also believe. The "mystery of God" was not something to be experienced only by certain elite Christians who had undergone certain rituals. It was available to all who crucify the "old person," symbolized in the act of baptism, and rise to a new life in the Spirit. This communion with and in Christ was where believers should live. This was God's plan since the creation of the universe and the new "normal" for Christian living. The divine mystery of sanctified life in Christ is for all people (Gal 3:28). The exhortations found in Paul's letters and the rest of the New Testament urge believers to live out this new existence of faith in Christ.

The struggles of the early church to live out their faith in Christ in the midst of pagan and hostile contexts prompted the New Testament writers to explain Christian ethics and mission. Paul understood that experiencing the presence of God cannot come through purely human effort but only in response to God's initiating grace. Romans 7 shows that trying to obey God's laws without the help of the Holy Spirit ends in spiritual defeat or empty legalism. Living by human effort leads to moral defeat because we cannot overcome the power of sin without God's intervention. Because Christ rose from the dead, ending the reign of sin and death, we can have freedom from the power and control of sin, which distorts the intentions of God's laws and urges us to disobey them. Human response is required for grace to have its transforming effect in a person's life. The conscience that is being transformed by God's grace through submission to Christ's lordship is open to the leading of the Holy Spirit. The new life "in Christ" allows the law to be the guide for the conscience, transforming the mind into Christ's likeness.

The new life "in Christ" is best experienced in community. The Holy Spirit grows the fruit of love within the hearts of those who have crucified the flesh in total commitment to Christ as Lord and binds them together in united mission. The Spirit works within both individuals and churches to bring about God's purpose of transformation into Christlikeness. The community of faith provides the nurturing context where people learn to listen to the Spirit in worship and through equipping. The primary task of the church is to lead people to transformation in Christ. The ways this mission is accomplished varies but there are common essentials to all situations. Holiness and love are nurtured through worship where Jesus is confessed as Lord and sacraments provide means for grace, and spiritual disciplines by which individuals learn to express their worship through faithful obedience. As believers are transformed *in Christ*, their actions begin to model Christ's mission of revealing God's *mystery* of redemption for all people. Believers become participants in the transforming process through their submission to the Spirit, knowledge of the teachings of Christ and Scripture, and engagement with others in the church and world.

New life in Christ brings freedom from the control of sin and victory over the forces of evil and deception. The old life *in Adam* is no longer in control since it has been symbolically crucified through baptism which is confirmed with the ongoing confession that Jesus Christ is Lord. Believers become participants in a new existence that continues after physical death with the assurance of resurrection and eternal life. Although Satan and the forces of evil still seek to destroy God's people, God provides the way of escape through the presence and power of the Holy Spirit. Being *in Christ* enables one to be *in the Spirit*, where the presence of the triune God points to an alternative way of life characterized by unconditional love and obedient holiness.

The major question of this study has appeared numerous times in reflection of Paul's experience of the divine mystery of being in Christ. The fundamental choice with which the gospel of Jesus Christ confronts a person is, who will be in control? How we answer this question will have a profound influence on how we live in this life and our eternal destiny. Our answer will overflow into our relationships in our families, churches, and communities. If we choose to remain bound by the things of this world, the so-called flesh, we take upon ourselves a burden that offers false promises but ends in misery, emptiness, and struggle. If we choose to make Christ our Lord and live in obedience to the leading of the Holy Spirit, we will experience transformation leading to love, joy, peace, patience, kindness, goodness, faithfulness, gentleness, and self-control (Gal 5:22–23). This life of being totally sanctified by the Holy Spirit is God's will for us and the very purpose for our existence. It is in this expected fullness that we find the deep relationship with the triune God for which we have been created. Although Paul's theology is profound, the simplicity of it can be summarized in the simple word "yes," which marks the life of obedient faith.

Bibliography

Ackerman, David A. *1 & 2 Timothy, Titus*. New Beacon Bible Commentary. Kansas City: Beacon Hill, 2016.
Alexander, Philip A., editor and translator. *Textual Sources for the Study of Judaism*. Manchester: Manchester University Press, 1984.
Archer, Leonard Gleason. *The Epistle to the Romans*. Grand Rapids: Baker, 1974.
Baird, William. "Visions, Revelation, and Ministry: Reflections on 2 Cor 12:1-5 and Gal 1:11-17." *Journal of Biblical Literature* 104 (1985) 651-62.
Barclay, William. *The Mind of St. Paul*. New York: Harper and Row, 1958.
Barrett, Charles Kingsley. *From First Adam to Last: A Study in Pauline Theology*. New York: Scribner's, 1962.
———. "New Testament Eschatology." *Scottish Journal of Theology* 6 (1953) 136-55.
———. *The Second Epistle to the Corinthians*. London: A. & C. Black, 1973.
Barth, Karl. *The Epistle to the Romans*. Translated from the 6th edition by Edwin C. Hoskyns. London: Oxford University Press, 1933.
Barth, Markus. *Ephesians*. Anchor Bible 1. New York: Double Day, 1974.
Bauer, Walter. *Rechtgläubigkeit und Ketzerei im ältesten Christentum*. Tübingen: Mohr, 1934.
Bauer, Walter, Frederick W. Danker, W. F. Arndt, and F. Wilbur Gingrich. *A Greek-English Lexicon of the New Testament and Other Early Christian Literature*. 3rd ed. Chicago: University of Chicago Press, 2000.
Beck, Dwight M. "Paul as Mystic." *Methodist Review* 108 (1925) 431-41.
Beker, Johan Christiann. *Heirs of Paul: Paul's Legacy in the New Testament and in the Church Today*. Minneapolis: Fortress, 1991.
———. *Paul the Apostle: The Triumph of God in Life and Thought*. Minneapolis: Fortress, 1980.
Benoit, Pierre. "Qumran and the New Testament." In *Paul and Qumran*, edited by Jerome Murphy-O'Connor, 1-30. Chicago: Priory, 1968.
Best, Ernest. *One Body in Christ*. London: SPCK, 1955.
Betz, Hans Dieter. *Der Apostel Paulus und die sokratische Tradition; eine exegetische Untersuchung zu seiner Apologie 2 Korinther 10-13*. Tübingen: Mohr, 1972.
———. *Galatians: A Commentary on Paul's Letters to the Churches in Galatia*. Philadelphia: Fortress, 1979.
Bieringer, Reimund, editor. *The Corinthian Correspondence*. Leuven: Leuven University Press, 1996.

Black, Michael. "The Pauline Doctrine of the Second Adam." *Scottish Journal of Theology* 7 (June 1954) 170–79.
Bouttier, Michel. *En Christ: Etude D'Exegese et de Theologie Pauliniennes.* Paris: University of France, 1962.
Brainard, F. Samuel. "Defining 'Mystical Experience.'" *Journal of the American Academy of Religion* 64 (1996) 359–93.
Brower, Kent E., and Andy Johnson, editors. *Holiness and Ecclesiology in the New Testament.* Grand Rapids: Eerdmans, 2007.
Brown, Alexander R. *The Cross and Human Transformation: Paul's Apocalyptic Word in 1 Corinthians.* Minneapolis: Fortress, 1995.
Brown, Colin, editor. *The New International Dictionary of New Testament Theology.* Vol. 3. Grand Rapids: Zondervan, 1986.
Brown, Raymond E. *The Semitic Background of the Term "Mystery" in the New Testament.* Facet Books Biblical Series 21. Philadelphia: Fortress, 1968.
Bruce, F. F. *Biblical Exegesis in the Qumran Texts.* London: Tyndale, 1960.
———. *The Epistle to the Galatians.* Grand Rapids: Eerdmans, 1982.
———. *The Letter of Paul to the Romans.* Grand Rapids: Eerdmans, 1985.
———. *Paul: Apostle of the Heart Set Free.* Grand Rapids: Eerdmans, 1986.
Büchsel, Friedrich. "'In Christus' bei Paulus." *Zeitschrift für die neutestamentliche Wissenschaft und die Kunde der älteren Kirche* 42 (1949) 141–58.
Bultmann, Rudolf. *Jesus Christ and Mythology.* New York: Scribner's, 1958.
Burkert, Walter. *Ancient Mystery Cults.* Cambridge: Harvard University Press, 1987.
———. *Greek Religion.* Cambridge: Harvard University Press, 1985.
Campbell, Constantine R. *Paul and Union with Christ: An Exegetical and Theological Study.* Grand Rapids: Zondervan, 2012.
Carr, Wesley. *Angels and Principalities: The Background, Meaning and Development of the Pauline Phrase* hai archai kai hai exousiai. Society for New Testament Studies Monograph Series 42. Cambridge: University Press, 1981.
Charlesworth, James H. *Old Testament Pseudepigrapha.* Vol. 1. Garden City, NY: Doubleday, 1983.
Collins, John J., editor. *Apocalypse: The Morphology of a Genre.* Semeia 14. Missoula: Scholars, 1979.
———. *The Apocalyptic Imagination: An Introduction to the Jewish Matrix of Christianity.* New York: Crossroads, 1992.
Cousar, Charles B. *Galatians.* Interpretation. Louisville: John Knox, 1982.
Cranfield, C. E. B. *A Critical and Exegetical Commentary on the Epistle to the Romans.* International Critical Commentary 32. Edinburgh: T. & T. Clark, 1979.
———. "Romans 6:1–14 Revisited." *Expository Times* 106 (1994) 40–43.
———. "St. Paul and the Law." *Scottish Journal of Theology* 17 (1964) 42–68.
Cullmann, Oscar. *Christ and Time: The Primitive Christian Conception of Time and History.* Translated by Floyd V. Filson. Philadelphia: Westminster, 1964.
Dan, Joseph. *The Revelation of the Secret of the World: The Beginning of Jewish Mysticism in Late Antiquity.* Occasional Paper 2. Providence, RI: Brown University Program in Judaic Studies, 1992.
Davies, D. R. *Down Peacock's Feathers.* London: Centenary, 1942.
Davies, William David. *Jewish and Pauline Studies.* Philadelphia: Fortress, 1984.
———. *Paul and Rabbinic Judaism: Some Rabbinic Elements in Pauline Theology.* London: SPCK, 1980.

Davis, Christopher A. "The Trust which Is the Gospel: The Coherent Center of Paul's Theology." PhD diss., Union Theological Seminary, 1992.

Davis, James A. *Wisdom and Spirit: An Investigation of 1 Corinthians 1.18–3.20 against the Background of Jewish Sapiential Traditions in the Greco-Roman Period.* Lanham, MD: University Press of America, 1984.

Deissmann, G. Adolf. *Die Neutestamentliche formel "In Christo Jesu."* Marburg: N. G. Elwert, 1892.

———. *The Religion of Jesus and the Faith of Paul.* Translated by William E. Wilson. New York: George H. Doran, 1923.

Dennison, William D. "Indicative and Imperative: The Basic Structure of Pauline Ethics." *Calvin Theological Journal* 14 (1979) 55–78.

deSilva, David Arthur. *Honor, Patronage, Kinship and Purity: Unlocking New Testament Culture.* Downers Grove, IL: InterVarsity, 2000.

Dodd, Charles H. *The Interpretation of the Fourth Gospel.* Cambridge: Cambridge University Press, 1958.

Dodds, E. R. *Pagan and Christian in an Age of Anxiety.* Cambridge: Cambridge University Press, 1965.

Doty, William G. *Letters in Primitive Christianity.* Philadelphia: Fortress, 1977.

Dunn, James D. G. *Christology in the Making: An Inquiry into the Origins of the Doctrine of the Incarnation.* 2nd ed. London: SCM, 1989.

———. *Jesus, Paul, and the Law: Studies in Mark and Galatians.* Louisville: Westminster/John Knox, 1990.

———, editor. *Paul and the Mosaic Law.* Grand Rapids: Eerdmans, 2001.

———. *Romans 1–8.* Word Biblical Commentary 38A. Dallas: Word, 1988.

———. *Romans 9–16.* Word Biblical Commentary 38B. Dallas: Word, 1988.

———. *The Theology of Paul the Apostle.* Grand Rapids: Eerdmans, 1998.

Dunning, H. Ray. *Grace, Faith, and Holiness.* Kansas City: Beacon Hill, 1988.

Eisenman, Robert. *Maccabees, Zadokites, Christians and Qumran.* SPB 34. Leiden: Brill, 1983.

Elior, R. "Mysticism, Magic, and Angelology: The Perception of Angels in Hekhalot Literature." *Jewish Studies Quarterly* 1 (1993–94) 3–53.

Ellis, Edward Earle. *Paul's Use of the Old Testament.* Grand Rapids: Baker, 1957.

Epp, Eldon Jay, and George W. MacRae, editors. *The New Testament and Its Modern Interpreters.* Philadelphia: Fortress, 1989.

Fee, Gordon D. *The First Epistle to the Corinthians.* New International Commentary on the New Testament 7. Grand Rapids: Eerdmans, 1987.

———. *God's Empowering Presence: The Holy Spirit in the Letters of Paul.* Peabody, MA: Hendrickson, 1994.

———. *Paul, the Spirit, and the People of God.* Peabody: Hendrickson, 1996.

Ferguson, Everett. *Backgrounds of Early Christianity.* Grand Rapids: Eerdmans, 1993.

Filoramo, Giovanni. *A History of Gnosticism.* Translated by Anthony Alcock. Cambridge, MA: Blackwell, 1990.

Finegan, Jack. *Myth and Mystery: An Introduction to the Pagan Religions of the Biblical World.* Grand Rapids: Baker, 1989.

Forbes, Christopher. "Comparison, Self-Praise and Irony: Paul's Boasting and the Conventions of Hellenistic Rhetoric." *New Testament Studies* 32 (1986) 1–30.

Freed, Edwin D. *The Apostle Paul, Christian Jew: Faithfulness and Law.* Lanham, MD: University Press of America, 1994.

Furnish, Victor Paul. *Theology and Ethics in Paul*. Nashville: Abingdon, 1968.
———. *II Corinthians*. Anchor Bible 32A. Garden City, NY: Doubleday, 1984.
Gaventa, Beverly R. *From Darkness to Light. Aspects of Conversion in the New Testament*. Philadelphia: Fortress, 1986.
Gerger, P., editor. *The Other Side of God: A Polarity in World Religions*. Garden City, NY: Doubleday, 1981.
Goodenough, Erwin Ramsdell. *By Light, Light: The Mystic Gospel of Hellenistic Judaism*. New Haven, CT: Yale University Press, 1935.
Grant, Frederick C. *Roman Hellenism and the New Testament*. New York: Scribner's, 1962.
Greathouse, William. *The Epistle to the Romans*. Kansas City: Beacon Hill, 1968.
———. *Wholeness in Christ: Toward a Biblical Theology of Holiness*. Kansas City: Beacon Hill, 1998.
Grieb, A. Katherine. "People of God, Body of Christ, Koinonia of Spirit." *Anglican Theological Review* 87:2 (2005) 225–52.
Gruenwald, Ithamar. *Apocalyptic and Merkavah Mysticism*. Leiden: Brill, 1980.
Gunther, John J. *St. Paul's Opponents and Their Background: A Study of Apocalyptic and Jewish Sectarian Teachings*. Novum Testamentum Supplement 35. Leiden: Brill, 1973.
Hagner, Donald A., and Murray J. Harris, editors. *Pauline Studies: Essays Presented to F. F. Bruce*. Grand Rapids: Eerdmans, 1980.
Hamilton, Neill Q. *The Holy Spirit and Eschatology in Paul*. Scottish Journal of Theology Occasional Papers 6. Edinburgh; London: Oliver and Boyd, 1957.
Hamerton-Kelly, Robert B. "Sacred Violence and 'Works of Law': 'Is Christ Then an Agent of Sin?' (Galatians 2:17)." *Catholic Biblical Quarterly* 52:1 (January 1990) 55–75.
Hawthorne, Gerald F., editor. *Current Issues in Biblical and Patristic Interpretation*. Grand Rapids: Eerdmans, 1975.
Hays, Richard B. *Echoes of Scripture in the Letters of Paul*. New Haven, CT: Yale University Press, 1989.
Hellholm, David, editor. *Apocalypticism in the Mediterranean World and the Near East*. Tübingen: Mohr (Siebeck), 1983.
Hengel, Martin. *Crucifixion in the Ancient World and the Folly of the Message of the Cross*. Philadelphia: Fortress, 1977.
Hengel, Martin, and Ulrich Heckel, editors. *Paulus und das antike Judentum*. Tübingen: Mohr, 1991.
Hill, C. E. "Paul's Understanding of Christ's Kingdom in 1 Corinthians 15:20–28." *Novum Testamentum* 4 (1988) 297–320.
Himmelfarb, Martha. "Heavenly Ascent and the Relationship of the Apocalypses and the *Hekhalot* Literature." *Hebrew Union College Annual* 59 (1988) 73–80.
Hooker, Morna D. *From Adam to Christ: Essays on Paul*. Cambridge: Cambridge University Press, 1990.
Horgan, Maurya P. *Pesharim: Qumran Interpretations of Biblical Books*. Washington, DC: Catholic Biblical Association of America, 1979.
Hunt, Allen Rhea. *The Inspired Body: Paul, the Corinthians, and Divine Inspiration*. Macon, GA: Mercer University Press, 1996.
Inge, William Ralph. *Mysticism in Religion*. London: Rider, 1969.

James, William. *The Varieties of Religious Experience*. Cambridge, MA: Harvard University Press, 1985.
Jewett, Robert. *A Chronology of Paul's Life*. Philadelphia: Fortress, 1979.
———. *Paul's Anthropological Terms*. Arbeiten zur Geschichte des antiken Judentums und des Urchristentums 10. Leiden: Brill, 1971.
Jonas, Hans. *The Gnostic Religion: The Message of the Alien God and the Beginnings of Christianity*. Boston: Beacon, 1991.
Kanagaraj, Jey J. *"Mysticism" in the Gospel of John: An Inquiry into Its Background*. Sheffield: Sheffield Academic, 1998.
Käsemann, Ernst. "The Beginning of Christian Theology." *Journal for Theology and the Church* 6 (1969) 17–46.
———. *Commentary on Romans*. Translated and edited by William Bromiley. Grand Rapids: Eerdmans, 1980.
———. *New Testament Questions of Today*. Translated by W. J. Montague. Philadelphia: Fortress, 1969.
Katz, Stephen, editor. *Mysticism and Philosophical Analysis*. New York: Oxford University Press, 1978.
Kee, Howard Clark. *Christian Origins in Sociological Perspective: Methods and Resources*. Philadelphia: Westminster, 1980.
Kennedy, George A. *New Testament Criticism Through Rhetorical Criticism*. Chapel Hill: University of North Carolina Press, 1984.
Kevan, Ernest Frederick. *The Evangelical Doctrine of Law*. London: Tyndale, 1956.
Kim, Seyoon. *Paul and the New Perspective: Second Thoughts on the Origin of Paul's Gospel*. Grand Rapids: Eerdmans, 2001.
Kittel, Gerhard, editor. *Theological Dictionary of the New Testament*. 10 vols. Grand Rapids: Eerdmans, 1964–74.
Küng, Hans. *The Church*. Translated by Ray and Rosaleen Ockenden. Garden City, NY: Image, 1967.
Ladd, George Eldon. *A Theology of the New Testament*. Grand Rapids: Eerdmans, 1974.
Lapide, P. *Paulus—zwischen Damaskus und Qumran: Fehldeutungen und Übersetzungsfehler*. Gütersloh: Mohn, 1993.
Lincoln, Andrew T. *Ephesians*. Word Biblical Commentary 42. Dallas: Word, 1990.
———. *Paradise Now and Not Yet: Studies in the Role of the Heavenly Dimension in Paul's Thought with Special Reference to His Eschatology*. Cambridge: Cambridge University Press, 1981.
———. "Paul the Visionary: The Setting and Significance of the Rapture to Paradise in II Corinthians 12:1–10." *New Testament Studies* 25 (1979) 204–20.
Lindstrom, Harald. *Wesley and Sanctification*. Wilmore: Francis Asbury, reprinted 1980.
Longenecker, Richard N. *Galatians*. Word Biblical Commentary 41. Dallas: Word, 1990.
———. *Paul, Apostle of Liberty*. New York: Harper & Row, 1964.
Louth, Andrew. *The Origins of the Christian Mystical Tradition: From Plato to Denys*. Oxford: Clarendon, 1981.
Luedemann, Gerd. *Paul Apostle to the Gentiles: Studies in Chronology*. Philadelphia: Fortress, 1984.
Lull, David J. "'The Law Was Our Pedagogue': A Study in Galatians 3:19–25." *Journal of Biblical Literature* 105 (1986) 483–93.

Lyons, George. *Pauline Autobiography: Toward a New Understanding.* Society of Biblical Literature Dissertation Series 73. Atlanta: Society of Biblical Literature, 1985.

Lyttelton, Margaret, and Werner Forman. *The Romans: Their Gods and Their Beliefs.* London: Orbis, 1984.

Mack, Burton L. *Rhetoric and the New Testament.* Minneapolis: Fortress, 1990.

Malherbe, Abraham J. *Moral Exhortation: A Greco-Roman Sourcebook.* Philadelphia: Westminster, 1986.

Malina, Bruce. *The New Testament World: Insights from Cultural Anthropology.* Atlanta: John Knox, 1993.

Marcus, Joel, and Marion Soards, editors. *Apocalyptic and the New Testament: Essays in Honor of J. L. Martyn.* Journal for the Study of the New Testament Supplement Series 24. Sheffield: Sheffield Academic, 1989.

Martin, Brice L. *Christ and the Law in Paul.* Leiden: Brill, 1989.

Martin, Ralph P. *2 Corinthians.* Word Biblical Commentary 40. Waco, TX: Word, 1986.

———. *A Hymn of Christ: Philippians 2:5–11 in Recent Interpretation and in the Setting of Early Christian Worship.* Downers Grove, IL: InverVarsity, 1997.

McGinn, Bernard. *The Foundations of Mysticism.* London: SCM, 1992.

McRay, John. *Archeology and the New Testament.* Grand Rapids: Baker, 1991.

———. *Paul: His Life and Teaching.* Grand Rapids: Baker, 2007.

Meeks, Wayne A. *The First Urban Christians.* New Haven, CT: Yale University Press, 1983.

———. *The Origin of Christian Morality: The First Two Centuries.* New Haven, CT: Yale University Press, 1993.

Moo, Douglas. *The Epistle to the Romans.* New International Commentary of the New Testament 6. Grand Rapids: Eerdmans, 1996.

———. "Paul and the Law in the Last Ten Years." *Scottish Journal of Theology* 40 (1987) 287–307.

More, Paul E. *Christian Mysticism: A Critique.* London: SPCK, 1932.

Morray-Jones, Christopher R. A. "Paradise Revisited (2 Cor 12:1–12): The Jewish Mystical Background of Paul's Apostolate. Part 1: The Jewish Sources." *Harvard Theological Review* 86 (1993) 177–217.

Morris, Leon. *The Epistle to the Romans.* Grand Rapids: Eerdmans, 1988.

Mounce, William. *Pastoral Epistles.* Word Biblical Commentary 46. Nashville: Thomas Nelson, 2000.

Munck, Johannes. *Paul and the Salvation of Mankind.* Translated by Frank Clarke. Richmond: John Knox, 1959.

Murphy-O'Connor, Jerome, editor. *Paul and Qumran.* Chicago: Priory, 1968.

Neugebauer, Fritz. *In Christus, Untersuchung zum paulinischen Glaubens-verstandnis.* Göttingen: Vandenhoek and Ruprecht, 1961.

———. "Das paulinische 'in Christo.'" *New Testament Studies* 4 (1958) 124–38.

Newsom, Carol Ann. *Songs of the Sabbath Sacrifice: A Critical Edition.* Harvard Semitic Studies 27. Atlanta: Scholars, 1985.

Nielson, John B. *In Christ: The Significance of the Phrase "In Christ" in the Writings of St. Paul.* Kansas City: Beacon Hill, 1960.

Nilsson, Martin P. *A History of Greek Religion.* Translated by F. J. Fielden. Westport, CT: Greenwood, 1980.

Oden, Thomas. *John Wesley's Scriptural Christianity.* Grand Rapids: Zondervan, 1994.

Otto, Rudolph. *The Idea of the Holy: An Inquiry into the Non-Rational Factor in the Idea of the Divine and Its Relation to the Rational.* Translated by John W. Harvey. New York: Oxford University Press, 1958.
Parry, R. St. John. *The Epistle of Paul the Apostle to the Romans.* Cambridge: Cambridge University Press, 1921.
Patterson, O. *Slavery and Social Death: A Comparative Study.* Cambridge, MA: Harvard University Press, 1982.
Pearson, Birger A. *Gnosticism, Judaism, and Egyptian Christianity.* Minneapolis: Fortress, 1990.
Philip, J., editor. *The Bible in Modern Scholarship.* Edited by J. Philip Hyatt. Nashville: Abingdon, 1965.
Pierce, C. A. *Conscience in the New Testament.* London: SCM, 1955.
Price, Robert M. "Punished in Paradise." *Journal for the Study of the New Testament* 7 (1980) 33–40.
Proudfoot, Wayne. *Religious Experience.* Berkeley: University of California Press, 1985.
Purkiser, W. T., et al. *God, Man, and Salvation: A Biblical Theology.* Kansas City: Beacon Hill, 1977.
Rad, Gerhard von. *Theologie des Alten Testaments.* Vol. 2. Munich: Kaiser, 1966.
Ridderbos, Herman N. *The Epistle of Paul to the Churches of Galatia.* Translated by H. Zylstra. New International Commentary of the New Testament. Grand Rapids: Eerdmans, 1953.
———. *Paul: An Outline of His Theology.* Translated by John Richard de Witt. Grand Rapids: Eerdmans, 1975.
Ringgren, Helmer. *Faith of Qumran: Theology of the Dead Sea Scrolls.* Translated by Emilie T. Sander. New York: Crossroad, 1995.
Rudolf, Kurt. *Gnosis: The Nature and History of Gnosticism.* Edinburgh: T. & T. Clark, 1983.
Sanders, E. P. *Paul and Palestinian Judaism.* Philadelphia: Fortress, 1977.
———. *Paul, the Law, and the Jewish People.* Philadelphia: Fortress, 1983.
Sandmel, Samuel. *Philo of Alexandria: An Introduction.* Oxford: Oxford University Press, 1979.
Sandnes, Karl Olav. *Paul, One of the Prophets?: A Contribution to the Apostle's Self-Understanding.* Wissenschaftliche Untersuchungen zum Neuen Testament 2/43. Tubingen: Mohr Siebeck, 1991.
Schnelle, Udo. *Apostle Paul: His Life and Theology.* Translated by M. Eugene Boring. Grand Rapids: Baker Academic, 2005.
Scholem, Gershom G. *Jewish Gnosticism, Merkabah Mysticism, and Talmudic Tradition.* New York: Jewish Theological Seminary of America, 1960.
———. *Major Trends in Jewish Mysticism.* 3rd ed. London: Thames & Hudson, 1955.
———. *On the Kabbalah and Its Symbolism.* Translated by Ralph Manheim. New York: Schocken, 1969.
Schreiner, Thomas R. "The Abolition and Fulfillment of the Law in Paul." *Journal for the Study of the New Testament* 35 (1989) 47–74.
Schütz, John. *Paul and the Anatomy of Apostolic Authority.* Society for New Testament Studies Monograph Series 23. Cambridge: Cambridge University Press, 1975.
Schweitzer, Albert. *The Mysticism of Paul the Apostle.* Translated by William Montgomery. New York: Henry Holt, 1931.
Scott, Walter, editor. *Hermetica.* 2 vols. Oxford: Clarendon, 1924, 1925.

Segal, Alan F. "Paul and Ecstasy." In *Society of Biblical Literature 1986 Seminar Papers*, edited by Kent Harold Richards. Society of Biblical Literature Seminar Papers Series 25. Atlanta: Scholars, 1986.

———. *Paul the Convert: The Apostolate and Apostasy of Saul the Pharisee*. New Haven, CT: Yale University Press, 1990.

Sherwin-White, A. N. *Roman Society and Roman Law in the New Testament*. Oxford: Clarendon, 1963.

Smit, Joop F.M. "'Do Not Be Idolaters': Paul's Rhetoric in First Corinthians 10:1–22." *Novum Testamentum* 39 (1997) 40–53.

Smith, Morton. "Ascent to the Heavens and the Beginning of Christianity." *Eranos Yearbook* 50 (1981) 403–30.

Snaith, Norman H. *Distinctive Ideas of the Old Testament*. New York: Schocken, 1964.

Snodgrass, Klyne. "Spheres of Influence: A Possible Solution to the Problem of Paul and the Law." *Journal for the Study of the New Testament* 32 (1988) 93–113.

Stace, Walter T. *Mysticism and Philosophy*. Philadelphia: Lippincott, 1960.

———. *The Teachings of the Mystics*. New York: New American Library, 1960.

Stambaugh, John E., and David L. Balch. *The New Testament in Its Social Environment*. Philadelphia: Westminster, 1986.

Stendahl, Krister. *Paul among Jews and Gentiles, and other Essays*. Philadelphia: Fortress, 1976.

———, editor. *The Scrolls and the New Testament*. New York: Crossroad, 1992.

Stewart, James S. *A Man in Christ: The Vital Elements of St. Paul's Religion*. New York: Harper, 1935.

Stowers, Stanley K. *The Diatribe and Paul's Letter to the Romans*. Chico, CA: Scholars, 1981.

Strugnell, John. "The Angelic Liturgy at Qumran—4Q Serek Šîrôt 'Ôlat Haššabbāt." In *Congress Volume: Oxford 1959*, edited by G. W. Anderson et al., 318–45. Supplements to Vetus Testamentum 7. Leiden: Brill, 1960.

Tabor, James D. *Things Unutterable: Paul's Ascent to Paradise in Its Greco-Roman, Judaic, and Early Christian Contexts*. Lanham, MD: University Press of America, 1986.

Tannehill, Robert C. *Dying and Rising with Christ: A Study in Pauline Theology*. Beiheft zur Zeitschrift für die neutestamentliche Wissenschaft und die Kunde der älteren Kirche 32. Berlin: Töpelmann, 1967.

Thomas à Kempis. *The Imitation of Christ*. Translated by Leo Sherley-Price. New York: Penguin, 1952.

Underhill, Evelyn. *Mysticism: A Study in the Nature and Development of Man's Spiritual Consciousness*. Cleveland and New York: World, 1965.

Vanhoye, Albert, editor. *L'Apôtre Paul: Personnalité, style et conception du ministère*. Bibliotheca Ephemeridum Theologicarum Lovaniensium 73. Leuven: University Press, 1986.

Wallace, Daniel B. *Greek Grammar Beyond the Basics*. Grand Rapids: Zondervan, 1996.

Wanamaker, Charles A. *The Epistles to the Thessalonians*. New International Greek Testament Commentary 13. Grand Rapids: Eerdmans, 1990.

Wedderburn, Alexander J. M. "Some Observations on Paul's Use of the Phrase 'In Christ' and 'With Christ.'" *Journal for the Study of the New Testament* 25 (1985) 83–97.

Wengst, Klaus. *Pax Romana and the Peace of Jesus Christ*. Translated by John Bowden. Philadelphia: Fortress, 1987.

Wesley, John. *Explanatory Notes upon the New Testament.* Vol 2. London: Thomas Cordeux, 1813.

———. *The Works of the Rev. John Wesley.* Edited by Thomas Jackson. Vol. 5. London: Wesleyan Methodist Book Room, 1872.

Westerholm, Stephen. *Perspectives Old and New on Paul: The "Lutheran" Paul and His Critics.* Grand Rapids: Eerdmans, 2004.

Wikenhauser, Alfred. *Pauline Mysticism: Christ in the Mystical Teaching of St. Paul* Translated by Joseph Cunningham. New York: Herder, 1960.

Wiley, H. Orton. *Christian Theology.* Vol. 3. Kansas City: Nazarene, 1943.

Willis, Wendell. *Idol Meat in Corinth: The Pauline Argument in 1 Corinthians 8 and 10.* Society of Biblical Literature Dissertation Series 68. Chico, CA: Scholars, 1985.

Wink, Walter. *Naming the Powers: The Language of Power in the New Testament.* Philadelphia: Augsburg/Fortress, 1983.

Winston, David. *Logos and Mystical Theology in Philo of Alexandria.* Cincinnati: Hebrew Union, 1985.

Woods, Richard, editor. *Understanding Mysticism.* Garden City, NY: Image, 1980.

Wright, N. T. *Paul: Fresh Perspectives.* London: SPCK, 2005.

www.ingramcontent.com/pod-product-compliance
Lightning Source LLC
Chambersburg PA
CBHW070322230426
43663CB00011B/2192